Passing Rhythm

Passing Rhythms

Liverpool FC and the Transformation of Football

**Edited by
John Williams, Stephen Hopkins and
Cathy Long**

Oxford • New York

First published in 2001 by
Berg
Editorial offices:
150 Cowley Road, Oxford, OX4 1JJ, UK
838 Broadway, Third Floor, New York, NY 10003-4812, USA

Berg is an imprint of Oxford International Publishers Ltd.

Library of Congress Cataloging-in-Publication Data
A catalogue record for this book is available from the Library of Congress.

British Library Cataloguing-in-Publication Data
A catalogue record for this book is available from the British Library.

ISBN 1 85973 397 2 (Cloth)
     1 85973 303 4 (Paper)

Typeset by JS Typesetting, Wellingborough, Northants.
Printed in the United Kingdom by Biddles Ltd, Guildford and King's Lynn.

For our families and all Liverpool supporters in the
Flat Iron pub, Liverpool 4.

Contents

Contents

Notes on Contributors

Dr Raymond Boyle is Head of the Film and Media Studies Department and a member of the Stirling Media Research Institute based at the University of Stirling. He has published on sport and the media and is co author (with Richard Haynes) of *Power Play: Sport, the Media and Popular Culture* (2000). He sits on the editorial board of *Media, Culture and Society.*

Liz Crolley teaches in the Department of Languages at Manchester Metropolitan University and she has written widely on football. She is a review editor for *Soccer and Society* and is the co-author, with Vic Duke, of *Football, Nationality and the State* (1996) She is also the co-author of *Imagined Identities? Football in the European Press* (2001).

Dave Hill is a writer and researcher who has a special interest in issues of 'race' and masculinity. There are plans to publish a new version of *Out of His Skin*, Dave's seminal book on John Barnes and racism in football, which was first published in 1989. He is also the author of *England's Glory* (1996), a book about the 1966 World Cup Finals, and he has published widely on sport, and on relationships and the family, especially in the *Guardian* and the *Evening Standard*. His latest project is a book on masculinity and sex.

Stephen Hopkins teaches in the Politics Department at the University of Leicester and is an associate member of the Sir Norman Chester Centre for Football Research. He is a Liverpool season ticket holder and his main research interest is in the politics of Northern Ireland

Cathy Long works for the FA Premier League and the Football League on supporter panels research. She also co-ordinated and reported on activities at the Fans' Embassies for the Football Supporters' Association during Euro 2000 in Belgium and Holland. She is currently working on a project on football families and is an active researcher on the music scene in Liverpool. She is a Kop season ticket holder.

Colin Moneypenny is a Liverpool supporter, FSA member, and was the Liverpool City Council Committee Clerk to the Hillsborough Working Party.

Rick Parry is an accountant by trade, but as the first Chief Executive of the FA Premier League he is also one of the architects of the 'new' football in England. A life-long Liverpool supporter, and with a goalkeeping son coming through the junior ranks at the club, Parry took over as Chief Executive at Liverpool in 1996 and he now has the task of piloting the club into the new commercial sporting future.

Andrew Ward is a freelance writer who has written a number of books on the history of football. He is the co-author (with Rogan Taylor) of *Kicking and Screaming: an Oral History of Football in England (*1995). He is currently the Royal Literary Fund Writing Fellow at the University of Aberystwyth.

John Williams is the Director of the Sir Norman Chester Centre for Football Research at the University of Leicester, and he has published widely on football fan cultures and the structure and future of the game, including *Is it All Over: Can Football Survive the Premier League?* (1999). He is currently writing *Into the Red*, a book based on Liverpool FC and the 2000/2001 League season in England.

Introduction

John Williams, Stephen Hopkins and *Cathy Long*

Writing about football

This book is about football in the city of Liverpool, but it is mainly about the history and place of one football club in that city, Liverpool FC. The other major football club in Liverpool, Everton FC, has a key role to play in the very beginning of our account of the origins of professional football on Merseyside, but it soon fades from obvious view. In fact, of course, Everton, though not often mentioned explicitly in what follows, never fully disappears from our vista at all. 'The Blues' are forever helping, dialectically, to shape their Liverpool football counterpart in their vital co-struggles for Merseyside – and latterly national – footballing hegemony. The nature and meaning of this domestic struggle between near neighbours, born of the same seed, also changes as the respective identities of these clubs shift over time.

Today, for example, in an era of football 'brands' and global marketing, when 'What is increasingly being produced are not material objects but signs' (Lash and Urry, 1994: 14), footballing antagonisms and rivalries in the city are as likely to revolve around *symbolic* – as well as commercial and spatial notions of Liverpool FC as a 'national' or 'global' club, with Everton as a more 'local' or 'regional' concern – as they are around more historic and domestically-rooted religious, kinship or territorial distinctions around Merseyside football (Williams, 2000). The meanings and values specifically attached to Everton Football Club deserve their own extended investigations, of course, not least because of the club's extraordinary history, but also because of more recent struggles around the ownership and control of this famous North West football club. But this is the subject of another book: it is not our task here.

Local histories, fan remembrances, life biographies and statistical accounts are pretty much all available now on most top football clubs in England. They are part of the astounding growth of recent interest in football as a cultural product: football is certainly one of the key media sports 'texts' which are at the leading edge of the recent 'culturalization' of economics (Rowe, 1999: 70). The market for books and other media texts about football and its fans seems to be an ever-expanding one. Indeed, as this book was being written, a number of popular other books about Liverpool FC and the recent managers and players of the club, emerged

(Keith, 1999; Kelly, 1999; Souness, 1999; Barnes, 1999; Molby, 1999; Hansen, 1999). This is a signal, of course, both of the century's end and the enduring national popularity of Liverpool FC, but also of the extent to which the really great days of the Liverpool club are now increasingly seen as a matter of historical fact, to be celebrated and reviewed as new anniversaries come and go. Most recently at a home match in December 1999, the club and its fans celebrated the 40th anniversary of the arrival in Liverpool of the architect of the modern Anfield approach, the still-idolized and iconic Scottish manager of the club in the 1960s and early 1970s, Bill Shankly.

Recent contributions from football supporters and writers who, using personalized accounts, have excavated the recent history of their own clubs, all tell us something about the character and traditions of those clubs and of their fans. Nick Hornby (1992), famously, has trawled through Arsenal's recent past and has offered hope for all young male suburban football fans who are wracked with questions about place, identity and especially, perhaps, concerns about the role of *gender* in shaping their football allegiances. Colin Schindler's (1998) account of Manchester City's (and Lancashire County Cricket Club's) place in the North West sporting landscape mainly in the 1950s and 1960s tells us much more about ethnicities and family/sport relationships drawn from a very different era, even if such accounts are tinged with more than a little distorting nostalgia. Nick Varley's (1999) review of the post-Hillsborough English football landscape is quite different, set as it is against memories of his active support among sometimes truculent Leeds United fans in the 'hooligan' era of the 1970s and 1980s. This is also a very different north of England from that 'lived experience' of 'northernness' and football support on Merseyside during the same period. Jim White's (1994) recent treatise on 'following' Manchester United in the mid-1990s is shaped, substantially, by the suffocating dominance of United by Liverpool in the 1970s and 1980s, hence the book's rhetorical title: *Are You Watching Liverpool?* Finally – although there are many more books we could mention in the same vein – Alan Edge's (1999) funny and heartfelt description of the 'pseudo-religious' aspects of supporting Liverpool Football Club, mainly in the 1950s and 1960s, is definitely one for those fans who are weaned on the familial traditions of generations of local club support in 'two-club' football-obsessed northern cities. Edge, at times, like Schindler, talks fondly and sadly here of a world which now seems almost completely lost.

The scope of the work reported on above is entertaining and impressive, and we can learn something about the 'meaning' and the particular culture of football clubs and their supporters from nearly all of these popular sources. But these are also partial and deeply personal accounts. None of these popular books does what we try to do here, namely to consider the deeper significance of the relationship between professional football and other local cultural practices in a major footballing city in England. We would also argue that few, if any, *academic* accounts of football supporters or football culture do the same thing as we are trying here, either. Indeed, a common approach to football fans and 'spectator cultures' in Britain and elsewhere in recent years has been to look only at its *contemporary*, rather than its *processual* manifestations over time, and to *equate* such cultures either simply with 'hooligans' or else with those largely male 'activist' supporters who are involved in fanzine culture or supporter organizations (see Giulianotti, 1999, Ch. 3 for an example). The vast bulk of 'ordinary' fans effectively disappear from these accounts (see also King, 1998). We favour a rather wider approach here, and we try to examine fan traditions and cultures from a number of perspectives which, when taken collectively together, we would argue, rather more successfully locate football, both historically and culturally, in the life of one of the great trading cities of the North West of England.

Our main propositions are these: first, that football has become a central part of the taken-for-granted 'social practices' that characterize the social formation in the city of Liverpool and help – along with highly distinctive patterns of politics, work and consumption, relations of religion, gender and ethnicity and socio-economic and spatial distributions – to provide the city with a specific 'structure of feeling', to use the 'frustratingly underdeveloped' (Taylor et al., 1996) notion originated by Raymond Williams (1965). Williams's concerns with the 'ordinary', 'lived' cultures of specific social formations and the intangible 'elements of impulse, restraint and tone', as well as the 'specifically affective elements of consciousness and relationships', which shape such formations at the local and regional level (Williams, 1977: 132; Taylor et al., 1996: 5), fits well with our own preferred approach to the analysis of the contemporary 'place' of football in the city of Liverpool at the turn of the twenty-first century.

Secondly, we contend that Liverpool FC's relative fall from national football dominance in the 1980s, and its more recent struggles to revive the club's fortunes, can tell us much which is significant in furthering our understanding of the *wider* transformations of English football in the 1990s. Here, we are interested in the new occupational practices in the sport, the rise of a new doctrine of 'profession-alism' in English football, the links between footballing and general well-being and post-Fordist prosperity in host areas, the tensions involved in opening up the game to continental influences, and the new commercial and cultural imperatives involved in the TV-dominated global version of the game's recent development.

The way top football in England has been transformed culturally, but perhaps especially *economically*, over the past decade is a theme which runs though many of the contributions to this book. Top football clubs in England, such as Liverpool, these days are no simple sporting concerns: they are also now sites for multi-various forms of consumption and they have important global symbolic, as well as economic, resonances. Television is at the heart of these changes. In the 1970s and 1980s, when Liverpool was *the* dominant force in the British game, club income was made up very substantially of revenues taken directly through the turnstiles. In 1998/99 matchday income made up only 37 per cent of cash inflows into FA Premier League clubs, with TV revenues now accounting for some 30 per cent of total income. This TV figure will rise again following a new television deal established between the FA Premier League and various media partners from 2001 which will more than double income from these sources for top clubs (Deloitte and Touche, 2000: 44). Liverpool FC also recently announced that its own new media partner, the Granada leisure group, will seek to exploit the club's 'brand' value around the world by selling initially delayed coverage of the club's activities and matches over the internet.

But almost matching these new revenue streams have been ever increasing demands from top players and their agents. Although Liverpool FC was reported to be in the top ten richest clubs in the world in 1998 (Deloitte and Touche, 1999), and had net assets of £46.1 million in 1998/99 (the fifth highest in England and compared to Manchester United's £107.9 million), *wages* at Liverpool FC in 1998/ 99 took up an astonishing 80 per cent of club turnover. Football analysts, Deloitte and Touche (2000: 20), eschewing just for a moment their generally positive support for 'free market' developments in the sport, warned sternly that wages of over two-thirds of football club turnovers were unlikely to be sustainable in the long run.

Already it must be clear that this is no simple *homage*, of course, to Liverpool FC or to the people of the city; far from it. The history – especially the recent history – of football at Anfield is, it must be said, run through with extraordinary and unmatched playing success in England: it includes eighteen League titles and four European Cups. It seems barely plausible, even through the long lens of history, to argue, as the *Independent* (16 December, 1999) did recently, that *Arsenal* (eleven League titles; no European Cups), not Liverpool, was the most successful English football club of the twentieth century. But, notwithstanding this extraordinary record on the pitch, the recent history of football in Liverpool is also intertwined with real tragedy, as well as with established local patterns of both inclusion and exclusion.

The City and the Club: some History

In many ways, the city of Liverpool is a vibrant, creative and highly inventive urban base. In its music and in its sport, especially, the people of the city reveal and celebrate themselves and their heroes in ways that belie the negative images often peddled elsewhere about the 'failings' of its culture and of its people. Liverpool has historical claims on the basis of its role as a dynamic and cosmo-politan seaport, and to evoke in its people both a 'natural' tendency towards democratization and also a fierce independence (Lane, 1997: 7; 59–98). The people of the city are especially prominent today, nationally, in popular cultural and performance domains – sport, music, comedy, drama – although this strong sense of a wider public perception of 'Liverpool-ness', as read mainly through sport and popular culture, especially, is probably a relatively recent tradition, dating back only to the late 1950s.

Many of the people in the city also jealously defend its openly 'emotional', Celtic 'separateness' and 'opposition' to conventional English formations (Walter, 1991), and they also guard its reputation from what sometimes seems to the people who live in Liverpool like sustained public attack from outside – about 'militant' politics, about crime, family life, poverty and conflictual industrial relations. It is in this sense that some people who live and work in Liverpool hold the view – perhaps mistakenly and obsessively so – that: 'Liverpool is the only city in Britain (apart from London) upon which other Britons have definitive opinions', and who believe Liverpool 'is seen as a city of problems where the people themselves are reckoned to be part of the problem' (Lane, 1997: xiii).

Liverpool certainly does have deep-seated – perhaps intractable – post-industrial problems of insecurity and underemployment, of crime, deprivation and racism, and a political culture which many of the people in the city still find macho, opaque or unwelcoming (Parkinson, 1985). In such circumstances, to talk glibly here about top football clubs on Merseyside simply 'reflecting' or somehow 'representing' the aspirations of their local 'communities' in the year 2000 is both to simplify the long history of local social and economic problems in Liverpool and the structure of local identities which this troubled history has helped to solidify. In addition, it fails to recognize the new ways in which top football clubs, such as Liverpool FC, now must locate themselves *internationally* in the new 'global' age of the sport (Williams, 1999) in terms of their responses to new, more affluent, supporter markets that stretch way beyond both regional and national boundaries. It also understates the *independent* creativity and resourcefulness of Liverpool FC supporters themselves, as the club they passionately support tries to recapture the footballing successes which were writ large for an earlier generation of followers of the club.

The city of Liverpool has been in long-term economic decline probably since the period immediately before the First World War. The central dependence for local employment on the unskilled and uncertain occupations of the docks and its ancillary industries has meant that the commercial fortunes of Liverpool have ebbed and flowed with those of its international sea trade. In 1914, the Port of Liverpool accounted for 31 per cent of the UK's visible imports and exports. By 1938 the Liverpool share had already fallen to 21 per cent (Lane, 1997: 14). Only from the global depression of the 1930s did the relative lack of a local industrial base in the city and its overdependence on the port become of critical concern to local politicians. Even in the late 1940s, unemployment in Liverpool rose to two-and-a-half times the national average and it has been some way above the national average ever since, catastrophically so in the 1980s (Parkinson, 1985: 11).

Until the mid-1960s, Liverpool's share of national sea trade remained reasonably constant, but the movement, from this period onwards, of manufacturing industry, population – Liverpool suffered particularly here – and the growth of cheaper, overseas competitors accelerated Liverpool's fall from a position of world significance to one in which the city's new service industries of heritage and tourism are the only real reminder today of the city's once dominant sea-trading traditions. Between 1966 and 1994 Liverpool's share of all ship arrivals in the UK was halved and east coast UK ports had effectively eclipsed those on the west (*ibid.*: 23). In the wake of wider economic depression under the neo-liberal political onslaught of Thatcherism in the 1980s, unemployment – especially youth and long-term unemployment – reached quite staggering proportions in some parts of Liverpool (see Williams, 1986).

In specifically footballing terms, the decline of Liverpool FC from a position of world strength has been more recent and rather less emphatic, though the connections of this football failing to the wider economic decline of the city should not be underplayed. However, the successes of the major local football clubs on Merseyside in the 1980s were at least a minor bulwark for local people when set against the realities of startling economic meltdown. Back in 1901 and 1906, when the port of Liverpool was still a world trading power, Liverpool FC won its first League Championships. More League titles followed in 1922 and 1923, and one more immediately after the Second World War, in 1947. In 1954, the club was relegated to the obscurity of the Second Division, before being revived by the arrival of Bill Shankly in December 1959. Shankly's teams won League Championships in 1964, 1966 and 1973 and two FA Cups, in 1965 and 1974. Then, under Bob Paisley, Joe Fagan and Kenny Dalglish, from 1976 to 1990 Liverpool won an astonishing ten League titles in fifteen seasons, finishing second in all other seasons except 1980/81 (when they were fifth). During this period, too, the club were also FA Cup winners twice (1986 and 1989) and European Club Champions four times (1977, 1978, 1981, 1984), as well as dominating the domestic League Cup competition.

In the 1990s, by way of contrast, Liverpool won but two trophies – the FA Cup in 1992 and the more lowly Coca-Cola Cup in 1995. We chart in this book the decline of Liverpool FC from its real dominance of the 1970s and 1980s to the relative struggles of the 1990s. In this context we are mindful of King's (1998: 207) important contention that the reversal of fortunes between Liverpool FC and the now dominant and publicly owned Manchester United also correlates symbolically with the contrasting economic developments of the two cities. Although there are clearly other forces at work here, there seems little doubt that, 'in an image-saturated age, where brand-sign value is paramount' (Rowe, 1999: 72) the fame and success of Manchester United *has*, indeed, contributed to the wider resurgence of the city of Manchester in the post-Fordist world economy. We look here at the beginnings of recent attempts in Liverpool to harness the commercial and symbolic power of the two main Merseyside football clubs in attempts to get them to contribute more strategically to the wider economic restructuring of the city.

New Directions

We also map in this book recent indications of a relative resurgence of the fortunes of the Liverpool club both on and off the field. In this last respect, according to club 'insiders', a home defeat against modest Leicester City in April 1999 proved to be a watershed of sorts ('Loss to Leicester opened the door to Granada', *Sunday Telegraph*, 18 July 1999). After the game, the club's directors were reported to have gathered to consider the future of the club. The questions raised here were definitive: did Liverpool FC want to end up on a par with middle-sized, mid-table domestic football rivals? Or did the club want to compete effectively, once more, with the 'new' giants of the world game, such as Real Madrid, SS Lazio and Manchester United? A new future for the club had already been set in motion by the appointment months earlier of City analysts Schroeders to look at the prospects for a commercial buy-in at Liverpool FC, a club still effectively owned and controlled by the local Moores family, owners of the Liverpool-based conglomerate, Littlewoods.

The eventual result of these deliberations was the purchase by the North West-based Granada group in 1999 of a 9.9 per cent share in the Liverpool club, worth £22 million. The club was reported to be especially interested in using Granada's merchandising expertise in order to promote the Liverpool FC 'brand', via Granada's network of hotel (Trusthouse Forte) and restaurant (Little Chefs) interests *(Guardian*, 14 July 1999). In return, Granada would run a future Liverpool FC TV station and be given lucrative internet rights in order to market more effectively the club's considerable global appeal. Liverpool FC, a relatively benign local 'family' fiefdom pretty much since its earliest days as a professional club, and one which had made a virtue of its very *lack* of 'distracting' external commercial partners, even in an age of public flotations and diverse forms of club ownership, was now, itself, beginning to look to a very different – a rather more corporate and 'global' – future. Part of this new future may involve a new 70,000 capacity stadium, built on nearby Stanley Park, to replace the hemmed-in and commercially limited space currently occupied by the club's historic Anfield Road base. Liverpool FC had, in fact, spent £7.3 million redeveloping Anfield in 1998/99 alone (Deloitte and Touche, 2000: 80). According to Liverpool fanzines at least, at the start of the

2000/2001 season the club was in grave danger of overstretching its ambitions on proposed ground redevelopment when the important matter of *team* rebuilding was still far from complete.

Even in a city ravaged by economic depression and the restructuring of the global economy, two locally controlled businesses with a combined turnover of not much over £70 million (1998/99 season, Deloitte and Touche, 2000) may not sound like an important major focus for regional economic regeneration. But, in an era of 'cultural citizens' (Rowe, 1999: 69) sports texts also have very high 'sign value' in the new global economies of 'signs and space' (Lash and Urry, 1994: 14–15). In the mid-1990s there were small signals that the city might, ham-fistedly, be trying to put this fact to work: Robbie Fowler and Ian Rush appeared on Merseyside Development Corporation ads to 'remind' potential employers that the Merseyside area had 'other' kinds of strikers too. Global sports businesses these days also mean selling 'signs' globally, while trying to produce some jobs *locally*. In July 1999 a survey of the economic benefits of football in the city of Liverpool carried out by the Football Research Unit at the University of Liverpool (Johnstone et al., 1999) estimated that in the region of 3,000 full-time jobs in the wider Merseyside economy are dependent on the football industry. The report also argued that 1,400 part-time jobs are produced by the clubs on matchdays and that for every 100 jobs in the retail sector around the two football grounds, five are dependent on matchdays. For every £1 spent by the two clubs combined, 31p remains within the local Liverpool economy. Around 78 per cent of interviewees in service sectors (pubs, bars, sports shops, restaurants) noted a 'significant increase' in takings when Liverpool FC play at home and estimate the increase in takings to be 10–25 per cent. A smaller proportion of businesses (37 per cent) noted the same increase for Everton home games, again reflecting the national and inter-national draw of Liverpool FC *versus* the more local appeal of Everton. Although it is unclear how exactly the figure is arrived at, the report estimates that 750,000 visitors come to the city of Liverpool for what the authors call 'football-related' reasons (*ibid.*: 26).

Echoing our own observations about the lack of 'embeddedness' of the two football clubs in Liverpool in local political and cultural networks and in the local economy – in part a consequence of these successful clubs being controlled by strong political and economic Conservatives in a city dogged in the 1960s and 1970s by lack of political leadership and a failing economy, and in the early 1980s by economic ruin and a radical form of 'centralised municipalism' (Parkinson, 1985: 18–20) – the report argues for more collaboration between 'stakeholders' in the city. Stakeholders here are taken to include the clubs, supporters, the City Council, the Mersey Partnership and local businesses. Some local *accountability* was on the agenda here, promised, too, in a limited way *nationally* in 2000 by the establishment of an Independent Football Commission to check on relations between top English clubs and their fans, via new *Customer Charters* (see FA Premier League, 2000: 39–41). A possible starting point for a new relationship on Merseyside is outlined by the Liverpool study. (Johnston et al., 1999: 27):

- A collaborative network of shareholders is needed to ensure that the local football industry adds to the competitive advantage of the entire locality and is used to avoid a competitive cycle of decline within the whole economy
- The two Premiership clubs need to be (and be seen to be) an embedded and highly valued part of the local Merseyside economy
- There is a need to develop a collaborative approach to enticing more football-related tourism into the city centre, i.e. to develop an integrated tourism and football industry strategy (Johnston et al, 1999: 27)

These suggestions may seem both obvious and important but also highly *relevant* recommendations for the City of Liverpool and its people, though how they might play in the new 'global' economies of top football, where television income and returns from the internet from a *global* market seem likely to be the major new income generators at clubs such as Liverpool FC, is unclear. The report concludes, unsurprisingly:

> There is no blueprint to the future of the football industry on Merseyside. There is no co-ordination, or plan, about how this sector might be developed for the benefit of the two clubs, the local economy and the Merseyside community. There needs to be a first step in realising the potential of the football industry on Merseyside. (Johnston et al., 1999: 27)

An important part of this general shift of emphasis at Liverpool FC in the late 1990s, and a signal for wider shifts in the English game towards the end of the century, was its appointment for the first time in 1998 of a *foreign* football manager, the French technocrat, Gérard Houllier. Houllier's arrival in Liverpool, and that of other foreign football coaches in England, is a sign not only of the sorts of accelerated 'global flows' – of capital, players, spectators and coaches – predicted by post-Fordist global economic developments in sport (King, 1998: 206), but it also signals the relative shedding by English football of its historic and icy isolationism, which has been such an established feature of the game's relations with foreign rivals, at least since the establishment – without the reluctant English – of the world governing body FIFA in 1904 (Wagg, 1984; Tomlinson, 1991). In the 1990s, the flood of foreign players into the English game has provided more ammunition for the historic tensions which have always existed here between the needs and aspirations of top clubs and the fortune of the England national team (Williams, 1999). These concerns reached something of a climax in 2000 when

England failed to qualify for the knock-out stage of the European Championships – a competition won by a French side containing a core of FA Premier League-based stars. Surprisingly for some, one of the *England*'s keenest and least critical supporters in Holland and Belgium was Anglophile Liverpool manager, the Frenchman Houllier.

Notwithstanding these first signs of a new, more commercialized and more internationalized direction for the structure of the club, and one shaped in part by financial partners drawn from *outside* the city of Liverpool, there are still important ways, of course, in which Liverpool Football Club still 'stands' for, still symbolizes, the hopes for 'something better' among the 'Red' half of the city. This remains the case, too, even if some local followers of the club are now excluded from attending football by price, or by the new climate around the sport which seems, to many, increasingly to prioritize commerce and order over the playing side of the game, and over the local passions which have traditionally – and sometimes dangerously – been roused in support of *both* of the established Liverpool football clubs. We return to some of these important issues later in the chapters which follow.

Finally, we also want to look seriously in this book at something which is little covered in discursive academic books about football. Indeed it is not much covered either, in any analytical way, in popular football books or by more than a small number of broadsheet football journalists. That is, we want not just to look seriously at the cultural effects of the game and at its economic and social importance – though these *are* central issues we want to cover – but also to say something here about the way the sport is both managed and *played* in England, and especially in Liverpool. Talking here of both organization and aesthetics, and also about the specific management strategies and capabilities – and limitations – at Liverpool FC over time, we hope this exploration may stimulate further social science work in this much neglected area, which is otherwise likely to be left to the much narrower focus provided, for example, by physical educationalists and the sometimes crude positivism of sports scientists.

Introducing the Chapters

We begin at the beginning. Chapter One examines the historical origins of Liverpool Football Club, its intimate early relationship with Everton, and the unusual development of non-sectarian football clubs in a city that remained marked by religious and sectarian undertones, even into the post-Second World War period. **John Williams** explores the evolution of football in the city of Liverpool from the 1890s through until the late 1950s, within the wider context of Liverpool's economic and social profile in these years. He tries to account for how and why football became such a central feature of the cultural landscape of the city in an era before the maximum wage and national celebrity cultures. Clearly, the basis is laid here for the bedrock of the distinctive supporter cultures at Liverpool FC which emerged more clearly and much more publicly in the 1960s and 1970s.

In Chapter Two, **Raymond Boyle** investigates aspects of the complex inter-relationship between football and religion as experienced in two 'Celtic' British cities, Liverpool and Glasgow. Understanding the connections, as well as the contrasts, that clearly exist between the two cities, Boyle uses material from interviews with supporters to gain genuine insight into the 'religiosity' of many aspects of social life in the increasingly secular, multicultural city societies of contemporary Liverpool and Glasgow.

Andrew Ward (with **John Williams**), in Chapter Three provides a rich and unusual reading of the character of *Bill Shankly*, Liverpool manager from 1959–1974 and the founding father of the 'modern' Liverpool club. John Williams, first, provides some important general context here, making it clear exactly how Shankly both adhered to aspects of 'scientific' management first established in English football back in the 1930s, but also differed markedly in his approach to player preparation and motivation at Liverpool in the 'modern' era of the post-maximum wage 1960s. Using largely original sources, Andrew Ward's warm and evocative analysis of the combination of factors that helped Shankly to his unique place in the affections of Liverpudlians, then demonstrates the way in which Shankly matched, and to some degree manufactured, the Liverpudlian spirit of the time.

Stephen Hopkins addresses in Chapter Four the *playing* styles adopted by Liverpool teams under the managerial dynasty set in place by Shankly, and maintained by Bob Paisley, Joe Fagan and Kenny Dalglish until the end of the 1980s. Playing techniques or styles, and their aesthetic appreciation, have not figured very highly in the recent huge growth of football literature, but this chapter seeks to explore the fundamental character and social and cultural roots of 'the Liverpool way', with its emphasis upon passing and movement. The importance of the collective ethos of teamwork, the nature of Liverpool's experiences in European competition, and the lessons learned from contact with other footballing cultures exploring similar principles form part of this unique analysis of an era of yet-unmatched dominance by Liverpool FC.

In Chapter Five, **John Williams** concentrates upon the question of *supporter traditions* and styles at Liverpool, and the changing nature of this support since the early 1960s. By focusing attention upon the nexus of football, music and youth culture, but also looking at more *generalized* supporter traditions at the club, Williams highlights continuities and discontinuities in fans' perceptions, and external judgements with regard to the 'character' or 'identity' of Liverpool's supporters. An engaged – yet critical – analysis, this chapter discusses in detail responses in the city and outside to the aftermath of Heysel and Hillsborough. A final section uncovers the contemporary fan and fanzine cultures associated with

Liverpool, and places them in the wider context of ongoing, rapid change in the national and international game.

Dave Hill, in Chapter Six, revisits and extends some of the territory covered in his 1989 book *Out of his Skin*, which analysed John Barnes' reception in Liverpool as the first black player to be signed by the club, in 1987. The impact of Barnes's arrival on the 'submerged' racial issues on Merseyside and in English football at large is taken further here as this chapter explores the nature of the contrast between the situation then and the rather different situation now. Hill recognizes that important elements of the issue of race and racism have been exposed to critical enquiry during the last decade, and that black players have written themselves into Liverpool's history in a way that looked a long way off as little as fifteen years ago. He nevertheless argues strongly that the 'bigger story' of Liverpool the city, Liverpool the club and their relationships with people who don't fit the description 'white' still requires careful and considered scrutiny.

In Chapter Seven, **John Williams** analyses the development of the Liverpool club in terms of management and administration in the crucial period between the mid-1980s and 1998. Williams shows how the club both accumulated and then lost strategic advantages on its competitors during this period and argues, paradoxically, that the unparalleled success of Liverpool in the two decades when the club was the dominant force in English football actually hindered some of the necessary processes of adjustment to the rapidly changing new football world, and the global realities of the football industry at the turn of a new century. The ambivalences of discourses associated with 'tradition' or 'modernization' are interrogated fully, with the departure of Roy Evans in 1998 (after more than 30 years with the club) and the arrival of Gerard Houllier viewed as seminal, yet complex, events in the ongoing negotiation of this transitional era.

In Chapter Eight, **Stephen Hopkins** and **John Williams** address the new 'Europeanization' of Liverpool FC – and of the English game – following the arrival of new manager Gérard Houllier. The authors guide the reader through the debates about the quality and future of English football in an era when foreign managers and players begin to dominate key aspects of the English game. The editors' extensive interview with Liverpool manager Gérard Houllier provides a fascinating account of his long-standing attachment to Liverpool as a city (Houllier spent a year teaching and writing a Masters' thesis on poverty in Liverpool in 1969) and his depth of understanding and feeling for the people (as fans and as citizens), something that is unusual for a top club manager in England. Still, this is no misty-eyed account, for Houllier is also critical of aspects of the club's recent administration. He reveals his philosophy and plans for Liverpool FC, both in terms of the short-term team-rebuilding, and also the necessary longer-term restructuring of the club. As well as the enthusiasm of Houllier for the game in general, what shines through this interview is his deep-seated admiration for what was achieved by Liverpool FC, and the style in which their football has, traditionally, been played.

In Chapter Nine, **Liz Crolley** and **Cathy Long** examine the issue of *gender* and football in Liverpool, paying special attention to the role of female players, as spectators and as general football enthusiasts in the city. The authors do this, in part, by talking to past and present female Liverpool fans. They also try, critically, to 'unpack' the notion that the game in England has been 'feminized' recently, and they offer challenging contentions about the 'masculine' standing terraces of Liverpool's Spion Kop experienced by female fans as a generally safe and inviting space, rather than the dangerous terrain identified in official reports. Finally, the authors explore the extent to which recent changes in football in Liverpool and elsewhere in England are actually supported or welcomed by most female fans.

Rick Parry has now seen the development of 'new' football in England both from his pivotal position as Chief Executive of the fledgling FA Premier League, and later as the Chief Executive of Liverpool FC, as the club faces an uncertain and changing future. In Chapter Ten, Parry provides excellent insights into the sorts of choices which faced the FA Premier League in the early 1990s, and he also offers the League's rationale for striking lucrative but controversial partnerships with satellite broadcasters in the early 1990s. He then surveys the powerful European football arena and locates the Liverpool club in terms of policy issues and debates about the likely future direction for the sport and its clubs in Europe and the world in the twenty-first century.

Finally, **Colin Moneypenny** is a Liverpool supporter, prominent member of the Football Supporters Association (FSA) in Liverpool, and Hillsborough survivor who offers a moving comment on the continuing struggle for 'Justice' for the Hillsborough bereaved. He is strongly critical of administrators and officials in their handling of both Hillsborough and Heysel, but he also notes how the awful events at Sheffield presaged a rather less intense, less aggressive, period for rivalries between opposing supporter groups in England. His assessment properly leaves our final thoughts with the families of the 96 who lost their lives on 15 April 1989 and those of the 39, mainly Italian, fans who perished in another tragedy involving Liverpool, at the Heysel Stadium on May 29 1985.

References

Barnes, J. (1999) *John Barnes: the Autobiography*, London: Headline.

Deloitte and Touche (1999) Annual Review of Football Finance, Manchester: Deloitte and Touche Sport.

Deloitte and Touche (2000) Annual Review of Football Finance, Manchester: Deloitte and Touche Sport.

Edge, A. (1999) *Faith of our Fathers: Football as a Religion*, Edinburgh: Mainstream.

FA Premier League (2000) FA Premier League Handbook, Season 2000/2001.

Giulianotti, R. (1999) *Football: a Sociology of the Global Game*, Cambridge: Polity.

Hansen, A. (1999) *A Matter of Opinion*, London: Partridge.

Hornby, N. (1992) *Fever Pitch*, London: Victor Gollancz.

Johnstone, S., Southern, A., and Taylor, R. (1999) *The Economic Benefits of Football in the City of Liverpool*, Football Research Unit, University of Liverpool.

Keith, J. (1999) *Bob Paisley: Manager of the Millennium*, London; Robson.

Kelly, S. (1999) *The Boot Room Boys*, London: Collins Willow.

King, A. (1998) *The End of the Terraces*, London: Leicester University Press.

Lane, T. (1997) *Liverpool: City of the Sea*, Liverpool: Liverpool University Press.

Lash, S. and Urry, J. (1994) *Economies of Signs and Space*, London: Routledge.

Molby, J. (1999) *Jan the Man: From Anfield to Vetch Field*, London: Victor Gollancz.

Parkinson, M. (1985) *Liverpool on the Brink*, Hermitage, Berks: Policy Journals.

Rowe, D. (1999) *Sport, Culture and the Media*, Milton Keynes: Open University Press.

Schindler, C. (1998) *Manchester United Ruined My Life*, London: Headline

Souness, G. (1999) *Souness: the Management Years*, André Deutsch.

Taylor, I., Evans, K. and Fraser, P. (1996) *A Tale of Two Cities: Global Change, Local Feeling and Everyday Life in the North of England*, London: Routledge.

Tomlinson, A. (1991) 'North and south: the rivalry of the Football League and the Football Association', in J. Williams and S. Wagg (eds) *British Football and Social Change*, Leicester: Leicester University Press.

Varley, N. (1999) *Parklife*, London: Viking.

Wagg, S. (1984) *The Football World*, Brighton: Harvester.

Walter, T. (1991) 'The mourning after Hillsborough', *Sociological Review*, **39**(3): 599–626.

White, J. (1994) *Are You Watching Liverpool?* London: Heinemann.

Williams, J. (1986) *Football and Football Hooliganism in Liverpool*, Leicester: Sir Norman Chester Centre for Football Research, University of Leicester.

—— (1999) *Is It All Over: Can Football Survive the Premier League?*, Reading: South Street Press.

—— (2000) 'Pool's apart', *When Saturday Comes*, September, No. 16.

Williams, R. (1965) *The Long Revolution*, Harmondsworth: Penguin.

—— (1977) *Marxism and Literature*, Harmondsworth: Penguin.

Out of the Blue and into the Red: The Early Liverpool Years
John Williams

The Origins of the Liverpool Clubs and Tales of Early Fandom

Students of the two main Liverpool football clubs know full well that Liverpool FC's origins actually lie inside Everton Football Club. When the Sunday school of St Domingo's was sited on Breckfield Road North in May 1870 and the adjacent Methodist chapel was formally consecrated in July 1871 it was to be the beginning of not one but two great north-west professional football clubs. In fact, despite its later centrality, football came rather late to Liverpool, with the Liverpool and District Football Association itself not appearing until 1882 and with the earlier Lancashire League being dominated by clubs from the eastern Lancashire cotton towns. Historian Tony Mason has speculated that the unique industrial structure of Merseyside, centring on sea trade rather than on manufacturing and producing a large semi-skilled and non-unionized casual workforce, may have played a part in inhibiting football's early growth in the city. He also points out, however, that the large number of clerks who made their living out of administering the trading industries in the city was probably central to the eventual rapid growth of the sport on Merseyside (Mason, 1985: 1). The late arrival of the Saturday half-day holiday for Liverpool's casual workers especially inhibited the growth of football playing on Merseyside. The local press in Birmingham recorded 811 football matches in the 'second city' in 1879/80. In Liverpool the local press noted only two (Russell, 1997: 13.)

The nineteenth-century muscular Christians who proselytized sport for moral health and Godliness in the working-class areas of Liverpool began their work on the urban poor, perhaps not surprisingly, with the gentleman colonizers' sport of cricket and with the popular American-imported baseball (still played in Liverpool). But working-class and lower-middle-class young men in the Anfield area soon demanded more physically robust team games for the winter months. Despite the early local popularity of the handling game, rugby, it was initially cricket and then street football which was favoured here and, under the auspices of the church's patrician Reverend Chambers, a football club, St Domingo's, was established in

1878 growing out of the summer's cricketing activities around the church. One year later, and with football clubs sprouting up elsewhere in the city – numbers grew from 2 in 1878 to 151 by 1886 – St Domingo's became Everton Football Club, locating their headquarters in a pub in Everton village, the Queen's Head. Everton played its first game – which it won – against nearby St. Peter's on 23 December 1879.

By 1880 Everton were already playing in the Lancashire League, using public land for home matches on Stanley Park. However, as 'football fever' took hold in working-class areas throughout England in the 1880s, and as football crowds grew in the North West, a league ruling in 1882 required that the new club find an enclosed ground for its home fixtures. At a club meeting hosted in his own Sandon Hotel in Anfield by John Houlding, an Irishman, a football follower and errand-boy-made-good as a self-made brewer and notable local Conservative politician, it was decided to rent a roped-off pitch off Priory Road, Anfield, for this purpose. But soon, following complaints about noise from the site, the club was once again without a home. With a brewer friend of Houlding's, John Orrell, called in to help, another venue was provided by Orrell for rent, at Anfield Road, where Everton first played on 28 September 1884, beating Earlstown, 5–0.

In the years which followed, the new club prospered and, like other successful football clubs of the day, terraces and small stands were erected at the new ground at Anfield Road to accommodate paying crowds which were now sometimes numbered in their thousands and were supporting professional players from 1885. However, the uncertain nature of club fixtures which resulted in many post-ponements and blank match days – and, thus some disappointed customers – eventually encouraged the small businessmen who ran twelve larger football clubs in Lancashire and the Midlands to ape the match arrangements of the established English County Cricket Championship. On 17 April 1888, at the Royal Hotel in Manchester, they agreed to establish a regular fixture list under the auspices of the new, national, Football League. One Alex Nisbet represented Everton at the inaugural League meeting, though more established neighbours Bootle FC were riled at being overlooked by the new organization, claiming, with some reason, to have a better ground and larger crowds than Everton (Inglis, 1988: 9–10).

With a regular list of fixtures and with dockworkers winning the right to half-day Saturdays in 1890, crowds continued to grow at Anfield Road. The national status of the Anfield ground was also rising, as evidenced by its hosting of an England v Ireland international match in 1889. The longevity of the place links of professional English football clubs is that even by 1991, some two years after the Hillsborough disaster, some 58 Football League clubs were still at the stadium sites they first occupied between 1889 and 1910 (Inglis, 1991: 10). In contrast to the often strong local opposition among planners and residents to the siting of new stadia today, so powerful and popular was the new professional football industry, and so prestigious to a local municipality was the siting of a new football ground, that clubs were able to monopolize some of the prime open land which might otherwise have remained or become private property. As Simon Inglis points out:

> A football ground was in many ways as much part of a burgeoning corporation as a public library, town hall and law courts, and was certainly used by more people. Furthermore, a football ground was often the only place in a town outsiders would visit. (Inglis, 1991: 12)

The civic pride invested in early professional English football clubs and their stadia was cemented, in the main, by highly localized forms of funding and control and by local sponsorship. This was certainly true in Liverpool. But a rift was also growing between the powerful Houlding and his colleagues at Everton. Houlding not only owned part of the land at Anfield Road but he also acted as the agent for the landlord for the rest. As the Everton club's profitability grew, Houlding decided to increase the Anfield Road rent, from £100 to £250. By 1891 Houlding had also formed a new limited company with a view to buying the Anfield ground and nearby land also owned by John Orrell, allegedly at a considerable potential profit to himself. Everton members were disgruntled. On 15 September 1891 the *Liverpool Football Echo* reported that an Everton member had told a shareholders meeting that: 'it seemed to him that they could expect nothing but the policy of Shylock from Mr. Houlding. He was determined to have his pound of flesh, or intimidate the club into acceptance of his scheme'.

When the Everton club's 279 members rejected the new rent proposals, in October 1891 Houlding served notice for his own club to leave land he now partly owned. In February 1892, Everton were set to quit Anfield, as four club shareholders agreed to contribute £1,000 each towards the £8,000 cost of a new ground at nearby Goodison Park, on the north side of Stanley Park. On 12 March 1892 a meeting of Everton members overwhelmingly voted Houlding out of office, and the move across the park was cemented. After Everton had departed Anfield, Houlding claimed that it was the 'teetotal fanaticism' of Everton's Methodist members which had forced him into his actions and which had produced the rancorous split. The *Liverpool Review* (19 March 1892) emphasized that the schism at Everton was 'purely a business one'. Greed and ambition certainly played their part, but to his credit Houlding also resisted the temptation to then sell his Anfield Road site for housing development and, instead, he set about 're-inventing' Everton FC – once more, at Anfield.

The New Liverpool FC

Houlding wanted to keep the name Everton for his 'new' football club, but the FA ruled in 1892 that the name should stay with the majority group. Although a rugby union club called Liverpool Football Club already existed in the city, on 15 March 1892 Houlding responded to the FA ruling by forming his own football club, rather grandly called the Liverpool Football Club and Athletic Grounds Company Limited, to play in the now empty Anfield Road venue. He charged the new club just £100 in rent and immediately donated £500 to its coffers. The club's application in the same year to join the Football League was rejected, however, on the grounds that 'they did not comply to regulations'. Everton's opposition to their upstart neighbour's bid for League membership was presumed to be the crucial factor in Liverpool's rejection (Inglis, 1988: 25).

Forced to join the Lancashire League instead of the more prestigious Football League, Liverpool's first fixture – a friendly against Rotherham Town at Anfield on 1 September 1892 – suffered badly from the fact that Everton also played its first Goodison fixture on the same day. The already established club hosted over 10,000 fans, while newly formed Liverpool could muster only a handful of spectators and could not even cover the Yorkshire club's financial guarantee. Early Liverpool matches in the Lancashire League – like the first, a local 'derby', at home to Higher Walton – attracted only 200 fans. But enthusiasm for the club soon spread; when, on 10 September 1892, Liverpool defeated Stockton to go top of the local league, Anfield crowds were already reported to have swelled to over 3,000 (Kelly, 1991: 7). Liverpool won the Lancashire League title and the Liverpool District Cup in 1892/93: both trophies were stolen, costing the club £130 in replacements (Rippon, 1980: 5).

Crowds of this size, however, were still 'lost' in Anfield. The Anfield Road ground in the 1890s could already accommodate up to 20,000 spectators, 4,000 of them on an exposed bank of wooden terraces at the Anfield Road end of the ground. At the Oakfield Road end a smaller stand stood in front of open fields, an area which would eventually house the new standing Kop. Fans who watched from here remember this part of the ground with the sorts of fears which were tragically realized much later in the English game. The original south end at Anfield was recalled by one early fan as 'A very old wooden stand with newspapers on the floor. I often used to wonder how it didn't catch fire, with people throwing their cigarettes down' (Liversedge, 1997: 22). On the west (Main Stand) side of the ground stood a modest pavilion and paddock, while the narrow Kemlyn Road stand was squeezed between the near touchline and the tight, terraced housing of the Kemlyn Road itself, behind (Inglis, 1996: 218).

By this time, an Irish rugby devotee who had been converted to football by his Everton involvement, 'Honest John' McKenna, a man who had controversially taken Houlding's part during the Anfield Road dispute, was becoming a key figure in the new Liverpool club. McKenna, from County Monaghan, was a grocer's boy who became a vaccinations officer in the West Derby district of the city. He lived modestly all his life in a terraced house near the Anfield ground. McKenna became famous in Liverpool football circles for his legendary player scouting trips to Scotland which resulted in the famous 'Seven Macs' Liverpool team of the 1890s – including one English 'Mac', goalkeeper McOwen. McKenna had recognized the tactical advantages of the co-operative cross-field passing popular in Scotland against the individual dribbling techniques still favoured in England. It was a lesson which would stand Liverpool in good stead throughout most of the following century.

Protestant or Catholic?

McKenna and Houlding, partners in the shaping of the new Liverpool club, were also both prominent local Freemasons and Conservatives and Houlding was also a well-known Orangeman with strong links to the Protestant-inclined Conservative Working Men's Associations. This fact, the existence of a large Irish Catholic community in Liverpool, and the strong – but not exclusive – early recruitment of Scottish Protestant players by Liverpool probably accounts, at least in part, for the popular mythologies which still persist today, about Everton's supposed Catholic heritage and Liverpool's alleged Protestant base. However, there seems no strong evidence for Everton's Catholic leanings nor for them recruiting fans strongly from 'Catholic' parts of the city. Also, both clubs had a tradition of contributing quite evenly to Catholic and Protestant 'good causes' in the city, and there is no pattern of player recruitment by the clubs which indicates any obvious sectarian divisions between them. As early as 1927 the teams from the city emerged on the field together for derby matches and, unlike the situation in Glasgow, for example, there are plenty of historical accounts from Liverpool of divided family loyalties and city-wide support for whichever of the local clubs was left playing in important cup ties or Cup Finals. There is evidence, in short, of a strong Liverpool footballing tradition around the clubs of both separation and togetherness, a tradition which does little to support notions of a divisive sectarianism between the clubs and their supporters (see Boyle, in Chapter Two). By the mid-1930s a social survey of Merseyside commented that: 'The intense religious antagonism which undoubtedly exists – and which from time to time breaks out into more than verbal strife – is also peculiar to Liverpool, but it should be added that this has declined in recent years' (Jones, 1934: 322).

Nevertheless, popular sentiments about the alleged religious leanings of the two clubs lingered well into the post-Second World War period, sentiments which remained important for some of the clubs' supporters in a city where education, for example, continued for many to be delivered along 'religious' lines. Indeed, strong 'religious' areal divisions in housing persisted in Liverpool until the city slum clearance programmes of the 1950s and 1960s, and employment practices on the docks and elsewhere in the city in the 1930s and 1940s could be shaped by religious background (Lane, 1997: 84–6). Longstanding football fans remember the two Liverpool football clubs still 'unofficially' recruiting youngsters from the Liverpool Boys' teams of the time largely along the lines of religious denomination well into the 1950s. This may have suited the clubs, of course, avoiding as it did unnecessary competition for local talent. The Protestant Irish roots of Liverpool FC are probably seen to strongest effect today in Belfast itself. The staunchly Protestant Shankill Road area in particular has been 'insularized' from the global push of 'Catholic' Manchester United, as well as from Everton; instead, Liverpool remains supreme as FA Premier League club of choice here. Everton, meanwhile, invested for a short spell in the 1990s in Home Farm, a Dublin football club, in an effort to revive the stream of Ireland player imports into Goodison Park, which was still strong in the 1950s.

However, the later example of Kenny Dalglish – a Rangers' supporting Protestant who went on to become a hero at both 'Catholic' Celtic and 'Protestant' Liverpool – is a good marker on the real mix of sentiments involved in football allegiances in the city of Liverpool today, perhaps especially as Liverpool FC has latterly become more of a 'national' and 'international' club in terms of its support. It has been argued that Liverpool FC's recent strong connections with Glasgow Celtic, in fact, go back to 1966 when supporters of the two clubs were reported to have joined forces for Liverpool's UEFA Cup Winner's Cup final against Borussia Dortmund in Glasgow in that year. This new alliance followed violent scenes involving Celtic fans at Anfield earlier in the tournament (Scraton, 1999: 21). These links, if they already existed, were certainly cemented, first by Liverpool playing at Celtic for Jock Stein's testimonial in 1986, and then by the support offered to Liverpool by the Celtic club and its fans following Hillsborough – including a match in Glasgow to raise funds for the Hillsborough victims.

Joining the Football League

In 1893, and unknown to other Liverpool FC officials who were quite happy to see the club find its feet slowly in the local leagues, it was John McKenna who applied on the club's behalf to join the newly expanded Second Division of the Football League. Under pressure from the emerging Liverpool FC, ambitious neighbours Bootle FC had fallen on hard times, and out of the Football League, allowing scope for Liverpool's opportunist application. When the club was duly elected, still reluctant club directors agreed that McKenna himself should travel to London to arrange the new fixture list. He did so along with representatives from Arsenal, Middlesbrough Ironopolis, Newcastle United and Rotherham United, all clubs elected into the League in the same year. By 1902 the gregarious and popular McKenna, a man of reputed even temperament who was known to speak with the humble and the elite on equal terms, was elected to the League

Management Committee, and in 1910 he became the third President of the Football League itself, a position he held until his death in 1936 when he was 81 years old. He stayed on the Liverpool board until 1922, only then fully devoting himself to his work with the Football League.

On 9 September 1893 Liverpool FC played its first home Football League fixture at Anfield, against Lincoln City, in front of a reported 5,000 fans. A 4–0 win signalled an amazingly successful first season drive for promotion – 26 wins out of 28 matches – via the end-of-season 'Test Match' system against the bottom three clubs in the First Division. With the club in the First Division in 1894/95, Anfield gates rose quickly, showing the obvious hunger among mainly working people for football in a city which was now already supporting two of the top sixteen football clubs in England. Frequently averaging over 10,000 spectators, Everton's were, comfortably, the highest attendances in English football until the late 1890s. Liverpool's attendances more than doubled between 1895/6 and 1896/7, from an average of just under 5,800 to just over 12,000. By the early 1900s Liverpool had pretty much already caught up their local rivals on this score, at the same time marking out the city of Liverpool as an authentic footballing 'hot bed' at the turn of the century, comparable to any site for the sport in England, even in the football-mad North. As Mason points out (1996: 46), 'Professional football ... was a Northern innovation at which Northerners were top dogs. Not only did they play it better than Southerners, they also watched it with more knowledge and intensity.'

On 13 October 1894 the city rivals met for the first time, at Goodison Park, in front of 44,000 fans, as well as the Lord Mayor and other local dignitaries. As early as the early 1880s, in fact, politicians had been keen to be present at football matches in the north, courting electoral interest from players and fans alike (Tischler, 1981: 138). Both teams, already embracing the new, 'modern' approach to match preparation, were using hotel retreats to prepare for major fixtures such as these. Everton's superior strength and experience produced a 3–0 home victory. Nearly 30,000 spectators also watched the return match at Anfield, a 2–2 draw, and early rivalry was predictably fierce. 'Local rivalry keeps the game alive', one contemporary remarked, 'It is never so much alive as when Liverpool and Everton meet. Then, the wonder is that instead of everybody being alive, everybody is not killed dead, as an Irishman would say' (Leatherdale, 1997: 132).

The step up to the top level had tested the Anfield club's resources and support, however. As relegation looked increasingly inevitable for Liverpool, one observer of the time reported that even under the astute stewardship of Secretary-Manager Tom Watson – recruited by McKenna from Sunderland in 1896, and reputedly 'the most popular man in all football' – at some Liverpool home matches, 'there were not enough spectators to go around the field' (Hodgson, 1978: 13). The Liverpool police might certainly have preferred larger football crowds in the city, having early on identified the sport as an important guard against disorder and drunkenness. The Chief Constable told the Royal Commission on the Liquor Licensing Laws in 1898 that before football Liverpool working men would simply move from pub to pub after work. Things had changed, as football seemed to have had a 'civilizing' and sobering effect on local men according to this senior officer (quoted in Mason, 1980: 176):

> I think that now when there is a match on the Everton or Liverpool grounds, a great number of working men, the instant they get paid, rush off home as quickly as they can, get a wash and a change, leave their wages with their wives, and are off to see the football, and I think that has led to a great decrease in drunkenness.

The First Championships and the New, 'People's' Kop

Despite these early relegation setbacks, with McKenna's backing and the recruitment of more quality players, these early 'yo-yo' years at Liverpool soon gave way, albeit briefly, to real success. In 1901 the club won its first Football League title, with a team built round the staunch, blond Scottish defender, Alec Raisbeck, and the English centre forward, Sam Raybould, dramatically clinching the Championship in the last match of the season at West Bromwich. On returning to Central Station in Liverpool at midnight on that mild Monday evening of 29 April 1901 the players were met by thousands of Liverpool fans and even a drum and fife band. The celebrations went on long into the night, and it mattered little to the supporters of the club that players in the victorious team were not raised in Liverpool; it was the territory of the *crowd*, not that of the players, which mattered. Players with no organic ties to the place of their clubs were given the task of bringing glory and social cohesion, shape and meaning to the lives of working men in the harsh industrial heartlands of northern England (Holt, 1989: 171). Not that the city of Liverpool was unfamiliar with transient populations. The Port of Liverpool, then close to the height of its powers, imported cotton for Manchester to spin and weave. Its core workforce was unskilled and casual and was substantially employed on the basis of the seasons, weather and tide. The city had a 'continuously transient population of seafarers to give it colour, variety and cosmopolitanism' (Lane, 1997: xvii). Socially and culturally the city was humming – and not only with its new-found footballing success. But new problems for what was now the leading football club in the city, Liverpool FC, were also just around the corner.

Liverpool FC, in a very short time, had become a relatively well supported and 'commercialized' and wealthy club for the period, and it little favoured the maximum players' wage of £4 introduced in April 1901 by a Football Association which was still troubled by what it saw as the pernicious effects of professionalism.

Key members of the first League Championship team at Anfield, for example, were reputed to be earning as much as £10 per man, as Liverpool FC recorded a profit for every season between 1900 and the curtailing of football by the First World War, in 1915. McKenna complained bitterly about those FA 'amateurs' being involved in the business decisions of professionals, a theme which would emerge many times later, of course, in disputes between the northern League clubs and the patrician and 'unworldly' southern-based FA (Tomlinson, 1991).

By 1904, when the FA eventually handed over to the Football League and its members complete control of professional clubs' financial affairs, objections to the maximum wage among the clubs had rather died. McKenna, himself, had changed his views in the light of the 'exorbitant demands of players' which made it difficult to see 'how free trade can be allowed' (*Athletic News*, 2 January 1910). Poorer clubs actually *liked* the imposed wage ceiling, of course; it offered welcome opportunities to keep down costs, provided strict regulation and control of players, and offered opportunities for the least well off to compete more equally with the northern city giants. Liverpool FC and other richer clubs were also hardly inconvenienced. They had simply got around the ruling by inventing additional 'jobs' for top players or simply by paying them 'under the counter'. Self-interest, and the militancy of the Player's Union, rather than any ideological opposition to laissez-faire policies, were what determined McKenna's attitude – and that of others like him (Tischler, 1981: 65). Everyone – except the Union and the players who were not paid illegally – was happy, and this also helped release funds for limited work on grounds. Around the same time, and once again with Liverpool back in the Second Division, a roof was built at the Anfield Road end of the Liverpool ground, perhaps in fond expectation that more goals might be scored at home games at this lower level (Kelly, 1991: 12).

Mason (1985: 5–6) has illustrated the extraordinary stability of the Liverpool FC Board from the early years of the new century right up until the Second World War, made up as it was for most of this period by brewery managers, local merchants, solicitors and, for a time, an undertaker and even a schoolteacher. These were by no means the wealthiest or most influential people in the town; they were, above all, comfortable and respectable local citizens who knew how to tend to local business and to 'community' interests. The early directors were also carefully selected by John Houlding in order to ensure a large measure of personal control over the club – especially given his problems at Everton (Tischler, 1981: 74). Brewers were especially prominent in hosting northern clubs, charging rent for ground use and selling their products at matches. Despite early talk in the city of making the club more popular and of, 'putting football in the hands of the people', it was clear that this did not include even ordinary shareholders – mainly clerks, managers and bookkeepers – never mind the modest sixpenny spectator. The members of the Liverpool board clearly meant, in this respect, themselves (Mason,

1985: 6). As Russell (1997: 71) has argued, in the early years of professional football, 'While the working-classes might have imposed themselves on the game, they exercised little real control over it.' Nothing much was to change in this respect over the next hundred years.

In 1905/06 Liverpool won the League Championship again, just one year after another promotion, and Everton won the FA Cup. Liverpool was the national centre of football excellence with an aggregate average attendance of 34,400 fans, higher than for any English city outside London. Tom (T.V.) Williams, later Liverpool chairman and the club's first life president, first heard singing in the Liverpool crowd during the promotion campaign of 1905 (Keith, 1999: 53). Many more people in Liverpool than actually attended matches also had an investment, emotional or otherwise, in the outcome of matches there; a survey in 1907 revealed that nearly 80,000 football pools coupons were collected in a single week in the city (Holt, 1989: 183). Some connection to football was, clearly, widespread in the Merseyside area. Some Liverpool fans also already travelled to away matches; around 1,000 Liverpudlians were reported to have made the trip for a vital match at Bolton in 1906. In the same year, the club's directors, encouraged by the gate returns from the second League Championship season, and perhaps anticipating more new support and better prospects for increasing gate receipts, entered into the second phase of major ground development at Anfield. For this, the celebrated Scottish Engineer, Archibald Leich, was called in. According to the proud *Liverpool Echo* (25 August 1906): 'The entire scheme is modelled on a new departure from what football grounds are generally supposed to be. The stands . . . are as safe as skill and good workmanship can make them.' The Anfield pitch was raised five feet and the ground was, for the first time, totally enclosed, reportedly by 'fancy brick walls' and with turnstiles on all four sides (Inglis, 1996: 218). At this time, too, Leich designed and built the barrel-roofed Main Stand, with its famous curved mock-Tudor gable, which survived until 1970. There were now 3,000 covered fans housed here on seats, with an enclosed standing paddock area below.

But even the new Main Stand was dwarfed by the huge cinder and wood-support banking which was rising out of the fields behind the old open terrace at the (Oakfield) Walton Breck Road end of the ground. Known originally, if rather inaccurately, as the Oakfield Road bank, the new standing area was not the first major bank of terracing at an English football ground, but with 132 treads from top to bottom it was quite probably the tallest. From the back of the open Kop supporters had a 'spectacular' view of Liverpool, 'all the way across Anfield and Stanley Park and down to Goodison' (Kelly, 1993: 15). According to Simon Inglis (1996: 219), Arsenal had already used the term 'Kop' to describe football terracing in north London. Perhaps local journalist, Ernest Edwards, of the *Liverpool Daily Post and Echo* had heard the term being used in London? In any case, Edwards is accredited with 'christening' Liverpool's great, dark bank 'Spion Kop', after a hill in Natal District upon which many young infantrymen from local regiments had perished in a losing battle in January 1900 in the still-strong-in-the-memory Boer War.

The imposing new standing Kop, with a capacity for some 28,000 fans, was clearly no staunchly home preserve at this time; in 1907 Blackburn Rovers supporters on the Kop were reported to have 'waved their colours to a set motion and sent forth a weird, unearthly cry', when the teams appeared for a League match; contrast this with the views of a local weekly paper, *Porcupine*, which argued in 1905 that 'We in Liverpool are more reserved or less enthusiastic than our brethren up country . . . Liverpudlians rarely wear their colours conspicuously, even when they travel abroad' (Mason, 1985: 16). Goal celebrations on the Kop at this time comprised mainly of ranks of male fans, in their flat caps and mufflers, joyously throwing their hats in the air and chancing on getting their own headgear returned. Local betting syndicates were also rife among Kopites, as they were at most other major football grounds of the time. Even opposing fans on the Kop were invited to be involved in informal home fans' 'sweeps' on the first scorer (Kelly, 1993:19). Betting coups might replace lost wages: attendance at football frequently drew workers from their jobs, much to the consternation of local employers. While an FA official in Liverpool noted that dock workers in the city in the winter months 'Rush home from work and hand over their wages before going to the match' (*Liverpool Football Echo*, 28 February 1909), one northern mill owner complained that working men in the north had adopted the motto: 'if your work interferes with football, give it up' (Quoted in Tischler, 1981: 127). Fans' support, however, was far from unconditional, and directors at top clubs at the beginning of the century already knew they had to strive, by fair means or sometimes foul, to produce a winning team in order to attract larger crowds.

Women fans were clearly something of a feature of the landscape at Anfield at this time, but some men saw little in the new Kop to further attract members of the fairer sex. In the *Liverpool Echo*, a local male fan complained, soon after its opening, about the narrowness of the Kop turnstiles, which meant that if the club directors thought that, 'any gentleman would ask a lady to squeeze through such an aperture, to the destruction of her dress, they are mistaken' (Inglis, 1996: 219). It is hard to imagine too many females in valued dresses braving the driving wind and rain and the various other trials on the new banking, though the Kop did harbour very young children, including young girls, even in its earliest days (see Liversedge, 1997: 22). The *playing* was tough, too, emphasizing the sort of 'entertainment' both male and female fans now expected. In April 1914, for example, a survey of the top 1,701 players in England and Scotland found that only 61 had survived the season without missing a match through injury. Poor medical and training facilities extended the amount of playing time footballers lost through 'accident or illness' (Tischler, 1981: 97).

In 1913/14 Liverpool reached the FA Cup Final, played at Crystal Palace, for the first time. It was an all-Northern affair, against Lancashire rivals Burnley, and the first to be played in the presence of the King. It was an occasion on which to parade, ritualistically, the distinctiveness of Northern cultures to the 'soft' South. But the Cup Final was also a growing *national* event, rich in the symbolism of community and country: 'What it sought to assert, in the face of division, was a civic and national unity of seamless communities' (Hill, 1996: 107). Northern fans were determined, however, to resist the sophistication – and exploitation – of London, a common feature of complaints about Wembley FA Cup Final trips later. Spectators for the 1914 Final, for example, had to pay a shilling (5p) admission to the pleasure grounds before gaining access, for an *additional* payment, to the football stadium. This was naturally frowned upon by the thrifty Lancastrians who had 'gone down' for the Cup (Hill, 1996: 104). Liverpool lost the Final. It would take another fifty years of hard work to secure a Cup Final victory.

The Inter-war Years

The formidable Tom Watson, Liverpool's first identifiable 'manager', died in 1915 and he was briefly followed into the manager's chair at Liverpool in 1920 by David Ashworth, an ex-referee, and then by Matt McQueen, an ex-Liverpool player who had first arrived at the club in 1892. Forced to retire by ill health, McQueen himself was eventually replaced by the club secretary, George Patterson, in 1928. As Stephen Wagg (1984) has shown, the role of early football managers was not to select or coach the team, but to deflect local accountability from directors in the face of increasing demands for success from club supporters. Managers only slowly developed any sort of public profile until, in the 1930s, they began to make the transition from glorified clerks to tacticians and horsetraders (Wagg, 1984: 57). Formal coaching was resisted by professional players in England right up to the 1960s, and early football 'managers' spent most of their time in suits and in the office, identifying upwards, with the club proprietors, rather than downwards with the players on the shop floor (Wagg, 1984: 48). Most managers – with the exception of early technocrats such as Herbert Chapman at Huddersfield Town and Tom Buckley at Wolves – would certainly not have signed players themselves or tried to instruct professionals on how to play. Manager Tom Watson, for example, famously remained in his office during the second half of Liverpool v Newcastle United at Anfield in 1909, thus missing a comeback by his side from 2–5 down to a remarkable 6–5 victory.

By 1921 the Kemlyn Road enclosures at Anfield were covered, but it was not until 1928 that local architect Joseph Watson Cabre was asked to place a roof on the Kop, with Anfield then claiming covering on all four sides, a capacity of 68,000 fans, and scope for 45,000 'reds' as shilling spectators under cover. The acoustics produced by the new roof offered encouragement to working-class standing supporters who wanted to generate more of a 'participatory' supporter culture at Anfield, and to get more 'involved' with their heroes on the pitch. It was also the beginning of spectator rituals that still survived at the club more than 70 years later. Though singing of club songs and popular tunes seems already to have been established at some other football clubs by the late 1920s (Russell, 1997: 100), it seems it was still largely absent at Liverpool. Harry Wilson, a Kopite from the late 1920s onwards, recalled the informal but clear 'class' divisions inside Anfield in this early period, and also the effect on the Liverpool crowd of the arrival of the new Kop roof (Kelly, 1993: 16):

> There was no singing in those days, I can tell you that. But there was lots of chanting. We used to chant the names of the players. When Harry Chambers, our centre forward, scored we'd all chant, 'Cham-bers, Cham-bers'. He was one of our favourites. And then there was Elisha Scott, the greatest goalkeeper of them all. We called him 'Lisha' He was idolised by the Kop. They would shout, 'Lisha, Lisha'. When the players came out on to the pitch they would run down to the Kop end, just as they do now, and Lisha would wave to us. He also used to give us a wave when he left the pitch. He was a great favourite . . . The opposition fans would be there as well [on the Kop] but there were never any problems . . . It was a very working-class crowd on the Kop, mainly dockers and the like. The 'toffs' were in the Paddock and the stands. We called them 'the mob' or the 'toffs'.

In the 1920s and for the whole of the inter-war period it was possible to walk all the way around inside Anfield, and some fans used to 'follow' their clubs at half time by changing ends, bringing plenty of visitors onto the Kop to join the locals (Taylor and Ward, 1993: 28). Links established with visiting supporters at home could even be used to set-up future away trips. The football camaraderie is very clear in accounts of football support at this time, but working men could also fall out at football. Football culture enshrined older forms of toughness and rudeness, a working-class code of 'masculinity' rather than a middle-class 'manliness', and one which strongly resisted the 'civilising process' of fair play and sportsmanship (Holt, 1989: 173). Life on the football terraces was not always sweetness and light, though the police were seldom called in to sort out disputes in the crowd. 'Fights didn't last that long', according to Kopite, Harold Atkinson. 'In fact, some of the Kopites used to sort it out themselves' (quoted in Taylor and Ward, 1993: 29).

In 1933 Liverpool signed the Rangers centre forward, Sam English. When the feisty English tangled soon afterwards with a rival defender in front of the Kop, a member of the home crowd enthusiastically came to his rescue. The incident is recalled by a Liverpool supporter, Billy O'Donnell (Taylor and Ward, 1993: 31):

I'm standing on the Kop one day with a little friend of mine who also idolised Gordon Hodgson. Well, this English got in a little bit of trouble with a full-back, who was a bit rough, a bit of a character, and they were wrestling with one another, and Gordon Hodgson got in between them. Well, my mate jumped up, 'I won't be long, Billy', he says. He jumps over the barrier and he gets mixed up in it. This [police] Inspector grabs him, and he lets fly at the Inspector. I never saw him for six months after that. 'I won't be long', he says. He got six months.

As can be seen from the example above, the working-class members of crowds at matches in this period were far from paragons of virtue. Nor were images of football crowds at the time overly idealized. In fact: 'The impressions of contemporary observers were all that football belonged to the working-class, whether this was described as the "rougher element", "working men" or even a "howling, booing mob"' (Fishwick, 1989: 56). Football spectators of the time were mainly working-class men of working age who were generally young enough to endure what was often a long walk to the ground and two hours standing in often poor conditions at the match for what was frequently a cold, wet and sometimes depressingly dull fortnightly ritual (*ibid.*: 64).

The size of crowds at Goodison Park and at Anfield, however, was reasonably stable throughout the inter-war period, though usually these were well below respective stadium capacities. In 1914/1915, as the First World War took hold, average crowds at Everton had fallen from 25,250 in 1913/14 to 18,530, and at Liverpool from 24,315 to 16,805. In the 'War season' of 1914/15, scandal briefly enveloped Anfield: four Liverpool and four Manchester United players were suspended by the FA *sine die* after allegations about match fixing following the Good Friday fixture between the two relegation-threatened clubs at Old Trafford. This impropriety seemed to have little effect on fan enthusiasm. Both Liverpool and Everton averaged almost 30,000 fans at home games in the season immediately after the War, in 1919/20, enjoying, as did other football clubs, the working-class hunger for leisure and sport in Britain after the carnage of battle, with minimum admission charges now raised from 9*d* to one shilling.

In both 1922 and 1923 the Elisha Scott-inspired Liverpool were League Champions again, with Anfield crowds for these seasons averaging 36,105 and just under 33,500, respectively. The defensive strength of the Liverpool team was widely admired. Although working-class fans enjoyed seeing skilful forwards outwit thumping full backs, it was more the capacity to work hard, to take punishment and to play the required role in a team performance which were the qualities northern football crowds looked for (Holt, 1989: 163). Merseyside fans keenly *played* football, too, in the inter-war period, on the city's parks and open fields. A survey of Liverpool in 1934 found that 15,000–20,000 adults played the game 'fairly regularly' in the city alone (Jones, 1934: 291).

Trams and bicycles were favoured forms of transport to Liverpool matches at the time; tram drivers often used to park their vehicles near kick-off time and watch the games, and those riding bikes contributed to the local informal economy around Anfield by paying for them to be minded in nearby gardens and yards (Kelly, 1993: 19–20). But droves of fans would also, maybe, grab a bag of chips and walk home after games, even to the South End of the city (Taylor and Ward, 1993: 28). Kids would be deposited by Kopites in the 'boys pen', which took up a section of the terraced area of the Kemlyn Road side of the ground in the 1930s, to be collected again after the match. For the rest of the decade, average crowds at Anfield stayed in the high 20,000s/low 30,000s, as the club struggled for consistency on the field. Average attendances in the First Division as a whole increased from just over 23,100 in 1913/14 to 30,700 in 1938/39.

Football attendances generally fell in the North, including Liverpool, in the recession years from the mid-1920s, but by the late-1930s crowds in the city were actually quite similar in size to those which had watched football in the city more than a decade before. Neither of the Liverpool clubs, however, averaged home gates of 40,000 or more in any season during this period – a figure consistently exceeded by the dominant Arsenal club in the Herbert Chapman years in the 1930s, for example. But, in 1920/21, aggregate crowds in the city of Liverpool averaged a period high of just over 72,600, and for the whole inter-war period, and despite crippling economic depression, aggregate football crowds in the city only once dipped below 50,000 fans, in 1932/33. The First Division average in this season was the lowest reported for the inter-war depression years, at 23,225. As a source of specifically *northern* comparison, crowds at Newcastle United dropped to an average of just 19,483 in 1935/36; aggregate combined crowds in Sheffield only ever exceeded 50,000 right at the end of the inter-war years; and aggregate average crowds in Manchester, combining 'gates' at City and United, fell to as low as 37,200 in the hard times of 1931/32.

Though faced with recession, as well as with the rising number of entertainment competitors in the 1930s – nationally, the number of cinemas grew from 3,300 in 1929 to almost 5,000 in 1938 (Fishwick, 1989: 51) – the city of Liverpool remained a football stronghold in the 1930s. Liverpool FC could not match the draw of some of the more glamorous London clubs of the time, especially the all-conquering Arsenal, which were in any case much better sheltered from the effects of national recession and also identified by the fans in the North as a symbol of southern economic advantage (Russell, 1999: 20). Nevertheless, the city of Liverpool was, arguably, *the* centre for northern football support in England in the inter-war period.

Football players of the time also remained culturally and economically *connected* to the people who supported them. Contrasts elsewhere were striking. In 1930 the American baseball star Babe Ruth visited Liverpool and met Everton's

Dixie Dean. Both men had recently scored a record 60 goals (Dean) /home runs (Ruth) in their respective sports. Dean was earning £8 per week and was astonished to learn that Ruth earned £300. Average weekly manufacturing earnings in Britain were £3 a week at the time. Despite these disparities and the growing size of football crowds, the effects of the national economic depression in England and the weak bargaining position of players kept most footballers 'contented'. A £9 maximum wage was agreed for players after 1945, with a bonus for a win (£2) and a draw (£1). By 1952 the maximum football wage had been raised to £15 and £12 in the off season. The *average* professional player, however, earned only around £8 compared to the £10 average industrial wage, a fact which encouraged player unrest and corruption and which led to many clubs making 'under the counter' payments (Szymanski and Kuypers, 1999: 93).

Cost clearly limited football attendances in the city in the 1930s, as it did elsewhere especially in the north and even when entry prices were relatively cheap. From the earliest days of the Championship sides at Anfield, for example, people who couldn't afford to attend matches would simply stand outside the ground and, on hearing a roar inside, would collectively ask 'Who scored?', to be quickly answered from within (Liversedge, 1997: 22). The perimeter gates at matches in the city would be opened at three-quarter time to allow for early departures and opportunities for those outside to watch the last 20 minutes of games. That the general enthusiasm for football in the city in the entire period up till the Second World War remained high cannot be doubted. When the Pilgrim Trust reported on unemployment in Liverpool in 1938 it noted that unemployed men who could not afford the shilling entrance fee still used to turn up on Saturday afternoon just to watch the crowds going to the match (Mason, 1985: 20).

The 'Golden Age'?

After the Second World War, football attendances in England soared to record levels. In 1946 Entertainment Duty, first levied in 1916, was reduced for theatre and sports, and the Chancellor specifically requested football clubs to reduce the minimum admission price from 1s. 6d. to 1s. 3d. Football was not alone in flourishing in Britain: in the post-war glow, 45 million fans watched greyhounds in 1947, three million went to cricket and 300,000 a week to speedway. Cinema attendances topped one billion (Szymanski and Kuypers, 1999: 43–4).

In 1946/47 Liverpool's fifth League Championship season drew average crowds of 45,732, bettered only by the 49,379 average at Newcastle United. Liverpool had signed star centre forward Albert Stubbins from Newcastle for a record fee of £12,500 just after the War. Stubbins, Jack Balmer, and a young Billy Liddell, tore up defences in 1946/47 under then Liverpool manager, George Kay. Kay, an Irishman and an ex-player, notably in the first Wembley Cup Final for West Ham

United in 1923, and renowned for his 'deep thinking' about the sport, had been appointed in 1936. He had shrewdly taken his team to the USA to build up on their frugal post-war diet for the successful campaign. He was also praised later by Stubbins and Bob Paisley for his willingness to offer organization on the field, but to allow good players the freedom to 'go out and play', something which was to become an established trait at the club under both Shankly and Paisley (Keith, 1999: 32). But a collective slump in Liverpool form, predictably, soon followed. Despite the fact – or maybe because of it – that the city of Liverpool in the early 1950s remained badly scarred and dishevelled from war damage and that the city itself was 'poverty stricken, having had nothing like its share of the post-war boom' (Channon, 1976: 21), up till Liverpool FC's eventual relegation in 1953/54, attendances at Anfield nevertheless remained consistently high. But they were generally rather lower than those enjoyed in North London, at Tottenham and Arsenal, where average gates now regularly topped 50,000, and also at rejuvenated Newcastle United, even minus their prized goalscorer, Stubbins.

Aggregate average football crowds in Liverpool came close to 90,000 for the first time, in 1948/49, when attendances in England also reached an all-time peak of 41.27 million admissions. In September 1948 the record football crowd for the city of Liverpool – 78,299 – was shoe-horned into Goodison Park to watch the 1–1 draw in the local 'derby' match. In the same year, the record Football League attendance of 83,260 watched bomb-damaged Manchester United entertain Arsenal at Maine Road. By February 1952, when Liverpool had its own record home gate of 61,905 for an FA Cup tie against Wolves at Anfield, minimum League admission prices had already been raised to 1s. 9d. They were raised again, in 1960, to 2s. 6d. Nationally, and perhaps unsurprisingly, English football attendances dropped in that one season, at the start of the 1960s, by 3.9 million. The post-war football 'boom' was deemed to be over, though many football clubs, Liverpool among them, were actually destined to enjoy their own best average attendance figures in the 1970s, rather than in the national 'peak' years for attendances of the 1940s and early 1950s.

In the 1940s and early 1950s football remained the ruling passion of working men without television and cars, whose world still revolved around the communal passions of the works, the pub and the match (Holt, 1989: 297). Rising living standards, growing levels of car and television ownership, and an increasingly 'privatized' and domestic focus for personal consumption are generally blamed for declining football attendances in England in the 1950s and 1960s (see, Dunning et al., 1988). TV sets especially, a rarity in 1950, could be found in 75 per cent of all households by 1961 (Russell, 1997: 135). The relative growing power of women to demand different from their men in weekend leisure time was almost certainly another feature of the changing place of attending football in the lives of more affluent working men (Walvin, 1994: 166). The working week also was gradually shortened to five days, so the early industrial link with football diminished. 'Football started to become the province of the die-hard fan rather than the recreation of the working man' (Szymanski and Kuypers, 1999: 46). These changes, plus the growing contrast between the privations of facilities at football grounds such as Anfield which had changed little since the 1930s under club directors who could see no reason to change what was offered, added to shifting leisure priorities.

The growing attractions of staying home on Saturdays, for DIY, gardening and other home entertainments – including more and more Saturday afternoon TV sport – began the long decline of mass active working-class support for local football clubs as a central and 'organic' feature of the way skilled working men, in particular, 'connected' to their towns and cities and defined themselves socially, culturally and geographically. Later, the impact of hooliganism would make more fast this initial social division in post-Second World War football crowds (Dunning et al., 1988). From 1953 to 1977 football attendances nationally fell by an average of 1.4 per cent per season, but admission prices rose 4.2 per cent per season, revealing a relative 'price inelasticity' of football. At the same time the wealth of the population increased and consumer expenditure grew by 2.4 per cent per year. Thus, increased consumer income enabled clubs to charge higher prices but it also created competition from alternative pastimes (Szymanski and Kuypers, 1999: 45).

On the Kop, and in the rest of Anfield, life was also slowly changing for spectators. The old 'boys pen', later quite brilliantly captured in all its terrifying glory by Alan Edge (1997: 64–66) had been moved some years before from the Kemlyn Road into the Kop and it was the first sign of the later, more informal, segregation by age which was to become such a defining feature of terrace life on the football 'ends' in Britain from the early 1960s. For 'big' matches in the early 1950s it was not unusual even for adults to climb into the boys pen on the Kop to escape the crush on the main terrace (Paul, 1998: 122).

Of course, lacking 'penning' arrangements or any reasonably sophisticated system of *counting* fans onto the Kop, and also with adults passing children over the turnstiles for free entry, it was impossible to gauge with any real accuracy, when and whether the terrace was actually 'full' at any time. The spectator tragedy which occurred at Burndon Park on 6 March 1946, in which 33 people died and 500 were injured when an exit gate was left open by a man leaving the ground, thus allowing thousands more spectators inside, was less likely to happen at Liverpool simply because of the sheer scale of the Kop terrace. But Anfield, in general terms, was no 'safer' than any other football ground of the time, and injuries caused by a swaying and excited crowd were a common feature of life on the Liverpool terraces in the post-war period. This became more of a problem from the early 1960s onwards, however, especially as core goal-end terrace support became exclusively younger, and ever more vociferous.

Floodlit football finally came to Anfield in 1957, a move which also stayed the mass absenteeism on the docks and in other local industries when midweek games had been staged in the city in daylight (Kelly, 1993: 25–6). The very rhythms of the sport in England were now beginning to change, especially as English clubs began to take their first, tentative, steps into Europe. On the administrative side of affairs, even following promotion to the top level in 1961/62, the Liverpool club remained pretty much in the Dark Ages, sometimes to literally tragic effect, though they were certainly not alone in this at the time. Jimmy McInnes, a club administrator, hanged himself in the turnstile area at the Kop end of the ground, soon after Shankly's arrival, allegedly because of pressures produced by lack of resources or the necessary staff or technology to deal with the new demands from spectators (Paul, 1998: 120–1).

Most fans at this time simply queued and paid their money at the gate; neither segregation of rival fans, nor fan safety seems a major concern of the time. But, singing among the crowd seems finally to have arrived at Anfield in the early 1950s in interesting circumstances, which also display aspects of the sharp humour of the people of the city, and their abject refusal to be co-opted by 'official' sources. Albert Stubbins, who played for Liverpool from just after the Second World War, remembers hearing 'witty' remarks from Kopites while playing in the early 1950s, and also, 'some singing, but it was usually drowned out by the vast noise' (Kelly, 1993: 22). A visit to Anfield by Wembley's own Arthur Kagan around the same period probably set the Kop off for some of the major singing 'performances' which still lay some time ahead.

Kagan was the man who was made famous in this period for his conducting of the community singing before Wembley FA Cup Finals, and he toured Football League grounds in the 1950s. At Anfield, before a match against Matthews' Blackpool, Kagan arrived, complete with a brass band, in order to 'conduct' the home end Liverpool club's supporters in what was still for these times some unusual pre-match singing. Things did not go as planned. As Kagan and his band went hard at one popular tune, the Kop, to its own collective amusement, and probably surprise, piped up with quite another song, wilfully refusing to follow the frustrated Kagan's lead (Kelly, 1993: 26–7). Others who have since tried, 'officially', to guide the Kop's singing, especially from the pitch, suffered similar fates. Nor were Liverpool supporters easily convinced later by new ways of presenting the sport – music, video screens, or electronic scoreboards, for example – in the 'entertainment-driven' era of the 1990s. If sport in the United States was a 'highly orchestrated production' (Schaff, 1995: 45), and some English football clubs had followed this lead, it found no welcoming space at Anfield among fans, administrators or staff. These events involving Kagan, however, were the early post-war signs of the exuberant, creative and irreverent singing cultures on the Kop, which were only to get fully into gear about a decade later.

The career end for the great 1950s hero of the Kop and of other Liverpool fans, Billy Liddell, a flying Scottish winger but a modest man and a devout Christian, probably symbolized the end of an era at Anfield – and in English football. Liddell played in every part of the team, except in goal, and every new Liverpool signing in the 1940s and 1950s was ritually photographed on arrival shaking the great man's hand for the benefit of the local press and fans. Liddell, like many other highly localized top football players of the 1950s, was retained firmly within the cultural confines of the everyday working-class world from which players of the time were mainly recruited.

From this, traditional/located base, players drew their style: of playing, bearing and appearance (Critcher, 1991: 74–5). The status of northern sporting hero of the sort inspired by Liddell's career and routine presentation of self would soon be replaced by the more extrinsic status of sporting celebrity, an attribution based on personality, not character (Holt, 1996; Giulianotti, 1999: 118). Constructions of sporting 'northernness' in Liverpool also had quite different cultural meanings and inflections, of course, from those attributed for example to the great industrial/ rural cotton towns of Lancashire, whose once dominant football clubs were about to fall into sharp decline. For one thing, to move east out of Liverpool, into Warrington, Wigan and St Helens, was to move almost immediately into deep rugby league country and into quite a different set of local sporting practices and traditions evoked by these tightly knit industrial villages.

Billy Liddell, and other top footballers of his day, neither suffered nor would have enjoyed the sort of massive public exposure which awaited most top sportsmen in the approaching television age for sport. He seldom appeared on TV and his image was only really available to local kids in Liverpool on cigarette cards and, to men, in articles in football magazines such as *Football Monthly*. Liddell was not, and could not be, a 'celebrity' in the sense in which we understand the term today, but he was still celebrated by youngsters and their parents in Liverpool, even if, as a young Alan Edge recalls, few youngsters of the time would actually have *recognized* Liddell if they had met him face-to-face (1999: 42).

All of this would soon change. As images of players became more recognizable, players would also become more socially and economically distant from many fans. Soon, few players would travel on the tram or bus anymore, or live among even affluent working-class supporters, as had been common in the 1950s and before. Instead, here we are on the brink of the emergence of lifestyles and identities for top footballers in England, after the end of the maximum wage in 1961, which would increasingly stress image management, commerce and consumption as central, defining features for the sport's new stars (Wagg, 1984: Walvin, 1986: 33–4).

Liddell, like Preston North End's Tom Finney, had also *worked* while he had been a professional player. Liddell was an accountant, Finney a part-time plumber.

Also, as Tom Finney's testimonial did at Preston North End in the same year, 1960, Liddell's retirement from Liverpool after 22 years at the club and a then record 536 appearances, signalled the emergence of a quite new set of social and economic relationships in English football, as well as the effective end of a long-established set of quite specific *supporter* traditions in the sport. Above all, it signalled the beginnings of the redefinition of football, in Stephen Wagg's words, 'as a television show' (Wagg, 1984: 133). Here, too, the technocratic vocabulary of 'the professional' and 'the job' would increasingly replace the traditional language of northern football of toughness and virility, thus producing a new code in the sport whose moral categories were altogether less distinct (ibid.: 151).

As Dave Russell (1997: 154–5) points out, the whole style of Tom Finney's testimonial event, with its speeches and traditional songs, belonged to a mode of civic culture and spectator behaviour at football that had emerged in the nineteenth century and was now coming to an end. In just a few years, both Liddell and Finney, loyal club servants and essentially gentle and 'ordinary' sons of their clubs and its followers, but men blessed with quite extraordinary gifts, would seem increasingly anachronistic figures as the effects of the lifting of the maximum wage and the new 'commercialism' in 1960s football kicked in. Football crowds were about to change, too, in the youth-dominated swinging 1960s – as we shall see later, dramatically so.

References

Channon, H. (1976) *Portrait of Liverpool*, London: Robert Hale.

Critcher, C. (1991) 'Putting on the style: aspects of recent English football', in J. Williams and S. Wagg (eds) *British Football and Social Change*, Leicester: University of Leicester Press.

Dunning, E., Murphy, P. and Williams, J. (1988) *The Roots of Football Hooliganism*, London: Routledge.

Edge, A. (1999) *Faith of our Fathers: Football as a Religion*, Edinburgh: Mainstream.

Fishwick, N. (1989) *English Football and Society, 1910–1950*, Manchester: Manchester University Press.

Giulianotti, R. (1999) *Football: a Sociology of the Global Game*, Cambridge: Polity.

Hill, J. (1996) 'Rite of spring: Cup Finals and community in the North of England', in J. Hill and J. Williams (eds) *Sport and Identity in the North of England*, Keele: University of Keele Press.

Hodgson, D. (1978) *The Liverpool Story*, London: Arthur Barker,

Holt, R. (1989) *Sport and the British*, Oxford: Oxford University Press.

—— (1996) 'Heroes of the North: sport and the shaping of regional identity', in J. Hill and J. Williams (eds) *Sport and Identity in the North of England*, Keele: Keele University Press.

Inglis, S. (1988) *League Football and the Men Who Made It*, London: Willow Books.

—— (1991) *The Football Grounds of Great Britain*, London: Collins Willow.

—— (1996) *Football Grounds of Britain*, London: Collins Willow.

Jones, D. C. (1934) *The Social Survey of Merseyside*, London: Liverpool University Press.

Keith, J. (1999) Bob Paisley: *Manager of the Millennium*, London: Robson.

Kelly, S. (1991) *You'll Never Walk Alone: the Official Illustrated History of Liverpool FC*, London: Queen Anne Press.

—— (1993) *The Kop: the End of an Era*, London: Mandarin.

Lane, T. (1997) *Liverpool: City of the Sea*, Liverpool: Liverpool University Press.

Leatherdale, C. (ed.) (1997) *The Book of Football*, Westcliff-on-Sea: Desert Island Books.

Liversedge, S. (1997) *Liverpool, We Love You!*, Stroud: Soccer Books.

Mason, T. (1980) *Association Football and English Society, 1863–1915*, Brighton: Harvester Press.

—— (1985) 'The Blues and the Reds: A history of the Liverpool and Everton Football Clubs', *History Society of Lancashire and Cheshire*, University of Liverpool, mimeo.

—— (1996) 'Football, sport of the North?', in J. Hill and J. Williams (eds) *Sport and Identity in the North of England*, Keele: University of Keele Press.

Paul, D. (1998) *Anfield Voices*, Stroud: Tempus.

Rippon, A. (1980) *The Story of Liverpool FC*, Ashbourne: Moorland Publishing.

Russell, D. (1997) *Football and the English*, Preston: Carnegie.

—— (1999) 'Associating with England: social identity in England', in G. Armstrong and R. Giulianotti (eds) *Football Cultures and Identities*, London: Macmillan.

Schaff, P. (1995) *Sports Marketing: Not Just a Game Anymore*, New York: Prometheus Books.

Scraton, P. (1999) *Hillsborough: the Truth*, Edinburgh and London: Mainstream.

Szymanski, S. and Kuypers, T. (1999) *Winners and Losers: the Business Strategy of Football*, London: Viking.

Taylor, R. and Ward, A., with Williams, J. (1993) *Three Sides of the Mersey: an Oral History of Everton, Liverpool and Tranmere Rovers*, London: Robson.

Tischler, S. (1981) *Football and Businessmen*, New York and London, Holmes and Meier.

Tomlinson, A. (1991) 'North and South: the rivalry of the Football League and the Football Association', in J. Williams and S. Wagg (eds) *British Football and Social Change*, Leicester: University of Leicester Press.

Wagg, S. (1984) *The Football World*, Brighton: Harvester.

Walvin, J. (1986) *Football and the Decline of Britain*, London: Allen Lane

—— (1994) *The People's Game: the History of Football Revisited*, Edinburgh and London: Mainstream

Williams, J. (1994) 'English football stadia after Hillsborough' in J. Bale and O. Moen (eds) *The Stadium and the City*, Keele: Keele University Press.

—— (1999) *Is It All Over: Can Football Survive the FA Premier League?* Reading: South Street Press.

–2–

Football and Religion: Merseyside and Glasgow
Raymond Boyle

Indeed, to state that sport is a modern, secular form of religion is something of a cliché. (Bale, 1994: 134).

Like Liverpudlians, Glaswegians pride themselves on their corporate sense of humour, their love of an eccentric, their ability to laugh loudly in the darkness. (Moir, 1995).

The Scouse lads on Hertford Road think England will beat Scotland, but apart from that, feel a closer affinity to Glasgow than London. 'You know in Glasgow, they are pretty much like us, like', yells one. 'There's only two things that matter, football and getting bevvied' (Lappin, 1996).

Introduction

Football fandom has often been described as displaying many of the symbolic and ritualistic aspects of religious belief. Liverpool fan Alan Edge (1999) went as far as to subtitle his book about his love affair with the club simply *Football as a Religion*. For other supporters, following a football club can also be part of a wider social network which may involve specific religious affiliations, such as those Celtic fans who might view their Catholic identity as being integral with their support of that club.

Football, almost inevitably, dramatizes the religious conflicts and inequalities that exist around the world where the game is played (Giulianotti, 1999: 17). Religious or ethnic tensions can sometimes 'settle' on the sport or else, more usually, football clubs are historically and culturally tied to religious or sectional affiliations.

This is especially the case in the British context, of course, in the city of Glasgow, although even here there is considerable debate today about the extent to which sectarianism fundamentally underpins the affiliation to, and rivalry between, the two major Glasgow clubs. Liverpool is often compared to Glasgow, partly because of the working-class occupational and religious traditions in the two cities, partly because of the strong Irish influence in the history and cultures of the two locales, but also because of the particular passion for football in both Liverpool and Glasgow. So in this chapter, and although it is fashionable in some circles to describe modern-day football as a new 'religion', my aim is *not* to examine in any depth the ways in which the game *itself* might be compared in its rituals and traditions to the religious devotions of other faiths. I have much more limited ambitions here. Instead, I want first to try to say something about the differences in this respect between the character of football support in these two great northern British cities, Liverpool and Glasgow. Secondly, I want to spend a little time looking at the 'religious' connotations of the Hillsborough disaster as it was experienced by fans in the city of Liverpool, and also the specific role of 'Celtic expressiveness' in both the style and the depth of the mourning which followed in the city. Finally, I want to return to a modern-day comparison of football and religion in the two places, and to say a little about the importance of new 'cross-religious' links, as it were, which have been established recently between Liverpool FC and Celtic FC and between the supporters of these two football clubs.

This chapter draws, then, on interviews with supporters and examines the role that religious identities have had in shaping the fan culture which surrounds football in Liverpool and Glasgow. By contrasting the two cities – both ostensibly very similar in character – we can see the way that even in an increasingly secular society aspects of religiosity have helped mould the character of both the cities and the footballing culture which each helps to sustain.[1]

And if You Know Your History...

Both Liverpool and Glasgow are cities unique in Britain, long associated in popular consciousness with football, a strident working-class culture, urban deprivation and particularly in the case of the latter city sectarian violence. In addition they have strong connections with Ireland, both being subject to a massive wave of Irish immigrants in the nineteenth century. All immigrants help to shape the character of the cities in which they settle; the mainly Catholic Irish in Britain were no different, bringing aspects of their cultural and religious beliefs to a largely hostile indigenous population.

The development and origins of football and football clubs throughout England and Scotland are closely associated with various Church organizations. Initially the Christian Churches viewed football as a way of channelling the energy of the new urban working-class. Sport was accepted as a healthy pursuit which could

---

1. This chapter draws upon work and interviews with supporters (whose names have been changed) in both cities undertaken as part of research for R. Boyle, (1996) *Football and Cultural Identity in Glasgow and Liverpool*, unpublished PhD, University of Stirling: Stirling.

install both moral and spiritual values into this potentially volatile section of the population and keep them away from other less respectable forms of popular culture. However, such was the popularity of the sport of football, and the financial rewards available within the professional game, that by the 1870/80s it had become an organized and institutionalized mass spectator sport on both sides of the border.

Although coming to the game later than other cities, by the end of the nineteenth century Liverpool was widely regarded as the footballing centre of England. The origins of Liverpool and Everton can be traced to the formation in 1878 of St Domingo's. The club changed its name in order to attract a wider cross-section of players and called itself Everton after the local district of the city. The driving force behind the club was a one-time Lord Mayor of the city, local businessman and Tory politician, John Houlding, as discussed in Chapter One (see pp. 17–20).

In 1892 after falling out with his fellow club members on the Everton Board, who promptly relocated with the team to Goodison Park, Houlding now had a ground at Anfield, but no football team. He recruited individual players from Scotland (nicknamed the Scottish Professors), put together a team drawn from players many of whom were in fact Irish Glaswegians, and formed Liverpool Football Club. Ironically then it was an Orangeman who effectively founded the two biggest clubs in the city of Liverpool, and the steady flow of Scottish footballing talent (which would include Shankly, St John and Dalglish among others) to Anfield had been established.

There is little doubt that the origins of the clubs in the city are important in understanding how neither club became closely identified with a specific religious community in the city. While the question of how extensively these two clubs became associated with particular ethnic or religious groupings can be contentious, it appears that it was only in Glasgow that football took on sectarian overtones. In Liverpool there are some suggestions that popular folk memory recalls the 1920/30s as a time when Everton was seen by some as the Catholic club on Merseyside but there is little evidence to back this up.

What was crucial however was that neither club imposed a religious ban on who could or could not play for them, and as a result, the Merseyside rivalry was unlike that which existed in Glasgow between Celtic and Rangers, with the latter operating at various times in their history a Protestant-only signing policy, clearly marking the club as anti-Catholic. Indeed the recent autobiography by former Rangers player and Manchester United manager Sir Alex Ferguson (1999) makes clear that this anti-Catholic signing policy was still evident in the late 1970s.

In Liverpool there was a period during the 1950s when Everton (partly due to the large number of Irishmen they had playing for them at the time) did in the eyes of some fans become identified as the team supported by Catholics. However, neither Everton nor Liverpool operated sectarian player signing policies and with the origins of the clubs being such, any religious identification was at best transient (see Chapter One, pp. 19–20).

Football and Sectarianism

While there are great footballing rivalries throughout the world, most are based on regional/national differences (Barcelona/Real Madrid) or particular intra-city rivalry (Inter Milan/Milan). In Glasgow it is the identification with specific religious and ethnic groups that makes the derby games between Rangers and Celtic different.

Bradley (1994: 432) has argued that: 'Many Catholics in Scotland have an identity in relation to both Ireland and Scotland which varies in intensity and emphasis depending on circumstance and environment.' He suggests that the close interplay between a religious identity (Catholic) and a cultural identity (Irish) mark out this group as being a distinct ethnic community in Scotland. It could be argued that this ethnicity finds one arena of public expression in its support of Celtic F.C. In this sense the linkage between football support, religion and identity differs from the situation in Liverpool. Here there is no clear religious or ethnic identity attached to any specific club in that city despite the existence of a strong city-wide identity heavily influenced by nineteenth-century Irish immigration.

Support for a football club, with its emphasis on collective symbolic displays of loyalty and ritual, lends itself to being a very public marker of identity among groups. Bale (1991) has argued that many football supporters view their football stadium as a 'sacred space', which carries with it quasi-religious connotations of communal experience, a point which is developed below.

That sectarianism has shaped the culture of Scottish society is not disputed by social commentators (although there is a marked dearth of material on the subject). However there is disagreement as to the extent of this influence, and its presence in contemporary Scottish society. The sectarian culture which predominated in nineteenth-century Liverpool and which remained well into the twentieth century from the 1970s onward ceased to be a major force in the city. However in Scotland, and in particular in the west of the country, the debates about the continued influence of sectarianism in contemporary society retain a public profile which simply does not exist anywhere else in the UK outside of Northern Ireland.[2]

---

2. Witness the public furore surrounding the speech entitled 'Scotland's Shame', given by the composer James MacMillan at the 1999 Edinburgh festival in which he argued that anti-Catholic prejudice was still rife in Scottish society. He was attacked by a number of commentators as having overstated a problem, which they suggested did not exist, while others commended him for speaking out.

This clear religious affiliation with Catholicism among Celtic supporters is in marked contrast to the situation in Liverpool, a point noted by supporters of Liverpool:

Dave: I mean you do have Everton or Liverpool families, but it's also common to find supporters of both clubs under one roof, you don't expect to find that in Glasgow.

Helen: I was never aware that there were separate Catholic schools like there are in Glasgow.

Pete: I think there was a big sectarian divide in Liverpool from the generation before, my parents told me about it, similar to Glasgow. But it seemed to fade away in the 1960s, you had separate Catholic schools in the city, but it was never a big thing. There is still a Protestant/Catholic divide in the city, but not like Glasgow, and it's never, as far as I am able to see, affected the football. So you can't say one was a Catholic team or one was a Protestant team.

Mike: I get young people in my taxi cab and they don't know who the Catholic team was. Some of the older people do, but a lot of the younger ones don't. A lot of it's to do with success, and following success and wanting to be associated with success, you've had success at Liverpool for almost 25 years.

Helen: Everton, who were supposed to be Catholic, had a lot of support from North Wales, which doesn't tie in because that part of the country isn't Catholic.

Among contemporary supporters in Liverpool sectarianism was not viewed as being an issue, whereas race and racism were deemed important in modern Liverpool (see Chapter Six).

Pete: Yeah it's strange really, I think that race is the bigger problem than religion in Liverpool. Because let's face it the founder member of both clubs was an Orangeman. Among younger fans there was a broad consensus that attaching a religious dimension to football support was in fact a problem, or a potential problem.

Liverpool, Religion and Football

The focus of this section is on the aftermath of the Hillsborough disaster of 1989. What is of particular interest is the extent to which religion, religious ritual and football all played a key role in shaping the manner in which Liverpool mourned the supporters who died at the FA Cup semi-final match. Moreover, it offers a striking insight into the central position that ritual occupies in the life and culture of the city of Liverpool.

This sense of ritual is directly informed by the city's past (the influx of Irish immigrants in the nineteenth century) and its more recent economic and political isolation within contemporary Britain. It also presents a contrasting view of the position of religion and religious ritual in public life to that which exists in Glasgow. As we see below, far from viewing the link between religion and football as a problem, as is sometimes the case in Glasgow, in post-Hillsborough Liverpool it became a positive force. In part it allowed a sense of collective identity to find expression in the form of public rituals. This enabled the city to engage in a process of collective mourning. In many ways how the city of Liverpool coped with this tragedy offers an insight into the extent to which religiosity and football are intertwined in that city.

Walter (1991) has argued that the mourning which took place in Liverpool after Hillsborough offers a rebuttal to the conventional wisdom that people in late twentieth-century Britain were unable to deal as publicly with death and bereavement as they had in times past. He argues:

> Though there are major class, ethnic, gender and regional variations, British people have in the twentieth century become less expressive about their grief in public; lengthy periods of mourning that were expected in Victorian days collapsed in the 1914–18 war, and by mid-century people expected to get back to normal as soon as possible (Walter, 1991: 606).

The outpouring of public grief in the city of Liverpool in the days and weeks that followed Hillsborough were, it could be argued, unique to that city and are explained in part by the influence of the traditions and rituals of its Irish-Catholic-descendant working-class, and both the centrality that football occupies in the city's sense of identity and the marginal position of the city in the political and cultural life of English society.

One of the dominant characteristics of the mourning which took place in the city was that it was public, much of it spontaneously organized and centred around both traditional places of mourning (the Catholic and Anglican Cathedrals) and Anfield, the home of Liverpool F.C. It was here on the morning after the disaster that fans gathered to pay their respects to those who had died and to seek solace among supporters going through similar pain.

> *Jane:* I woke up on Sunday the 16th, didn't really sleep. And I just had to go down to Anfield. I really thought that there would maybe be a few people there, but that was all. I'm not really religious but it seemed right to go to the Shankly Gates at Anfield. When I got there was hundreds of people, all with the same idea. The club opened the gates and we walked around the ground and laid flowers at the Kop end of the ground, and cried openly in public among friends.

The football ground became what Taylor (1989) called part of 'a mass popular religious rite'. The ground became a shrine, with the Kop end of the ground bedecked with flowers, scarves and other football memorabilia. Over a million people would file past the Kop over the next two weeks (many queuing for up to six hours just to get in). Bale notes: 'Mourners filed slowly past as they would at a cemetery. The stadium, not a church, was selected for this rite, making it a sure site for topophilic sentiments' (Bale, 1991: 132).

While there are quasi-religious overtones to much football supporting, the ritual of regular attendance at games, collective chanting and singing and a particular devotion to a club and its ground, it was never more pronounced than in Liverpool in the days and weeks after Hillsborough. Ian Taylor notes:

> The reconstruction of the ground as a shrine is a natural extension of existing relationships of the club to the fan: football grounds across the country have always had an almost religious hold on football fans and, indeed, on the families and kin on whom these, mainly male, fans have imposed their weekend and midweek-evening obsessions (Taylor, 1991: 5).

In addition, the spontaneous nature of the public collective outpouring of grief was commented upon not only by those directly involved. For example, a photographer, Steve Shakeshaft, sent by his newspaper to cover the story, arrived at Anfield only to find:

> I felt I was imposing. I had to take photographs, and yet I didn't want to. I felt as if I was exploiting the situation [. . .] A Salvation Army band followed us into the ground, and they grouped around in a circle inside the penalty area and then began playing 'Abide With Me'. It was so spontaneous. We were all in tears. Suddenly, I had a different perspective on the Kop and all those who stand on it. It had become a shrine, their shrine (Kelly, 1993: 182).

In general the coverage of the Hillsborough disaster in the national media, and the press in particular, generated a great deal of resentment among many people in the city. The portrayal of Liverpool fans as drunken louts, who looted the dead and abused the police as they attempted to offer assistance, was not only carried in the many national newspapers, but reproduced in papers throughout Europe. The *Sun* in particular suffered a drop in its Merseyside circulation of up to 150,000 as a result of its untrue stories, although it was not the only paper to upset people in the city. The *Daily Mirror* was the first to be criticized for its use of explicit colour photographs of fans being crushed to death against the fences at the Hillsborough stadium.

Tony Walter offers this explanation of much of the hostile reaction among other parts of England to the public communal outpouring of grief after Hillsborough. It is worth quoting at length because it raises a number of central themes in this chapter:

> In white UK culture, there are (apart from class differences) two cultures: an English reserve and a Celtic expressiveness. These are seen dramatically in the different feel of Manchester versus Liverpool, or even Edinburgh versus Glasgow. Celtic expressiveness offends English reserve (though it may be enjoyed by the English on holiday in Southern Ireland). To the English, Celts are dangerously unpredictable, and a crowd of Celts even more so – hence the stereotype of Liverpudlian football supporters as always liable to get into trouble, despite their generally good humour and unusually good police relations. Hence perhaps also the stereotype of the Liverpool worker as likely to take unofficial strike action at the drop of a hat (Walter, 1991: 607/8).

He argues that the expressive nature of the public mourning was in part a reflection of this Celtic cultural influence on the city of Liverpool, in turn fuelled by the sense of 'non-Englishness' felt by many in the city.

The contrast, however, with Manchester (itself a city with a large community of Catholic/Irish descent) seems misplaced. Differences between these two cities (both economic rivals in the north-west of England) are best understood by their differing patterns of economic development, decline and regeneration, rather than being purely cultural (although there is at times a link between the two).

There is no doubt, however, that the enormous influx of Irish into Liverpool has left a residual stamp on the character of the city, and its own self-identity. Samuel notes:

> The Irish brought with them into the country a complex of popular devotional practices, whose warmth and externality were often contrasted with the more reserved tradition of worship which prevailed among the English (Samuel, 1989: 101).

However accurate Walter's analysis, and its generalizations leave it open to criticism, there is no doubt that this view reflects the self-image held by many in the city as to its relationship with the rest of England. This perception of difference is reinforced by the position and character of the city in various aspects of popular culture, of which the tradition of supporting football is one of the most high-profile.

It should be noted that not all reaction was hostile to the city. Many football fans shared in the grief felt by the city. Over a million people passed through Anfield to pay their respects, well over double the population of the entire city. Significantly, the first match to be played by the club was at the invitation of Celtic F.C. and took place in Glasgow before an emotional crowd of over 60,000, with all proceeds going to the Hillsborough Disaster Fund.

The ties between the clubs for many supporters revolved around Kenny Dalglish, the former Celtic player and then Liverpool manager. But the ties between the clubs pre-date this and clearly have much to do with the mutual respect and friendship that developed in the 1960s between the two managers who laid the foundations of the modern clubs, Bill Shankly and Jock Stein. During a match in 1973 Celtic made a presentation to Shankly at Celtic Park. Shankly noted that:

> It was a magnificent gesture by Celtic to even consider making a presentation to me and as for the Celtic fans, their reception gave me an even greater thrill if that was possible. Any nervousness about being introduced onto the pitch disappeared as he 'heard the crowd and felt so much at home, it was like standing in the middle of the Kop at Anfield' (*The Celtic View*, 8 August 1973).

The adoption by Celtic fans of the Liverpool anthem 'You'll Never Walk Alone' also stems from this period and the communal singing of this at the post-Hillsborough match was commented upon by Ken Gaunt of the *Liverpool Echo*.

> Liverpool players came out in ones and twos to a great reception in the warm-up, but that was nothing compared to the thunderous roar of applause as the teams came out to the haunting strains of 'You'll Never Walk Alone'. Thousands of green Celtic scarves suddenly took the salute in one of the most remarkable messages of friendship I can ever remember at a football ground (*Liverpool Echo*, 1 May 1989).

There is little doubt that the relationship between both clubs and sets of fans became significantly closer after this particular match.

The role of official religion

In addition to the spontaneous organization of communal mourning there were also the formal religious rituals. The Catholic Cathedral in the city attracted twice its capacity to a Requiem Mass on the Sunday after Hillsborough. Memorial services were held in many local churches and in the Anglican Cathedral on the 29th of the month. However, something else occurred in Liverpool that emphasized the blurring of the religious lines of division that were once evident in the city and that still inform much of the public life of Glasgow. This involved the coming together of the Anglican and Catholic Churches in the city. Their leaders, Bishop David Sheppard and Archbishop Derek Worlock, spoke out together, defending the city against attack and ridicule from outside. In addition, they also argued for solutions to its economic and social problems, while all the time projecting a more positive image of the city to the outside world.

Walter (1991: 621) notes that perhaps more so than any other city in the UK 'Durkheimian religion – in which religious or neo-religious totems represent the entire community – operates in Liverpool.' He argues that this situation has become more acute with the collapse of traditional local politics which began to occur in the 1980s. While it has to be asked to what extent the large black community in the city feel represented by either the predominantly white Catholic or Anglican clergy, it is true to say that this coming together of the Churches, speaking on behalf of the city, does not occur in Glasgow.

While in that city in particular the Catholic Church frequently speaks out on a range of social and political issues relating to the Scottish situation (Cardinal Winning in particular), it makes no pretence that it is doing anything other than defending the interests of the Catholic community and certainly not speaking for the city as a whole.

The overwhelming post-Hillsborough sense in Liverpool was of a city pulling together to grieve for its own: Protestants and Catholics attending services together, with the unique sight of professional football players and fans helping and supporting each other at services and funerals. It represented a unique moment in the history of the city, and, it could be argued, produced a city-wide solidarity the like of which is rarely seen in contemporary urban Britain.

Nancy: It was a truly weird time to live in the city. They say that Liverpool is small and that everyone knows everyone's business. But at that time it felt like a small village. Actually at times it was suffocating, and I know a lot of people needed to get away for a while.

Pete: Yeah I mean you don't want to get sentimental about it, but there was a sense of togetherness, I don't know if it's the Irish thing or what, but I can't see that public grief being displayed elsewhere in England.

Dave: It sounds clichéd but everyone did feel a sense of loss and grief. It engulfed the city. I couldn't have coped without the public rituals. I mean there was the private grief as well, but the thought that you could see people and they were feeling the way you were was very important. I'm not religious, but that sense that you are not alone is very important. It was like an extended family in the city, it sounds daft to say it, but that was how it felt. I mean football means more than it should to this city and for that to happen at a match, well . . .

Walter sums up the aftermath of Hillsborough as:

A city retaining an unusual blend of Celtic and working-class mourning patterns, which it enacted in highly dramatic form due to the unique circumstances surrounding Hillsborough, was on view to the whole nation. Middle-class people throughout the country saw on Merseyside a model for the handling of grief to which they aspired, yet lacked the communal identity to achieve (Walter, 1991: 623).

The most recent comparison which saw public mourning on this scale was that which followed the death of Diana Princess of Wales and which was centred in

London. However, rather than being generated by a sense of traditional community, this appeared in part to represent a specific media-connected community. It is also significant that by the second anniversary of her death the public displays of remembrance predicted by the media had failed to materialize.

It could also be argued that in part the survival of that communal model (or aspects of it) in Liverpool is in part a result of the economic and political isolation felt by the city, particularly in the 1980s and into the 1990s. This isolation involved a turning inward for community strength and an outward articulation of that identity through its high-profile and, until recently, highly successful football teams. What, then, does this tell us about the relationship between football and religion in the cities of Liverpool and Glasgow?

Religion and Football: a Sense of Belonging

What clearly emerges from this chapter is the fact that religion and displays of religiosity occupy different social roles in both cities. In Glasgow, religious labelling (and this usually is limited to being either Catholic or Protestant despite the multitude of faiths evident in contemporary Glasgow) is still an important boundary-marker of difference between social groups in certain circumstances. In other words, in specific situations, affiliation to either Celtic or Rangers football club or whether the name of the school you attended began with a Saint's name marks you as either Catholic or Protestant (and of course this can often be innaccurate).

Being earmarked as a Catholic also carries with it connotations of Irishness and support for things Irish and this in turn can be held by some as an indication of that person's lack of loyalty to all things supposedly Scottish. To a few the fact that a person is Catholic means that they can never be truly Scottish.

Of course much of this operates at the level of generalization. All Rangers fans for example do not hold bigoted attitudes towards Catholics, and all Celtic supporters do not necessarily feel that they are Irish. However, to play down the role of religious labelling in the west of Scotland is to be guilty not only of denying its influence (both historical and contemporary) but also of presenting Scottish culture as some sort of homogeneous entity not subject to the internal contradictions and tensions that all national cultures experience. More importantly, it denies the importance of confronting issues of division and, in this instance, specifically the issue of sectarianism. As Scotland embarks on a new political era, with its own Parliament, recognizing that a problem exists remains an important first step towards finding a solution.

This point was made by novelist Andrew O'Hagan in a polemical article entitled 'Scotland's Fine Mess'. He commented on his experience of an Orange Walk in the town of Alloa during the summer of 1994:

The first of 130 buses roared into West End Park [. . .] The Bannockburn True Blues adjusted their gear. They began to flute and drum and march out of the park [. . .] There was wildness in every direction: you felt anything could go off. I felt very Catholic, very open to assault. [. . .] England, for all that's said, is not really a target of everyday Scottish venom. We save most of that up for ourselves; we spend it recklessly on each other (*Guardian Weekend*, 23 June 1994).

Interestingly, the issue of a Catholic/Protestant divide does not exist to any great extent in modern Liverpool. If religious discrimination is viewed as a problem in Glasgow then it is not seen as such in Liverpool.[3] Historically, sectarianism had an important influence on the political and economic development of the city, yet with the city's economic and political decline, internal city divisions have, to a large extent, been replaced by a more common citywide identity. Perhaps the major internal issue to threaten this cosy city image is that of race and racism. The invisibility of the city's black community from dominant images of the city is as striking as it is worrying.

Again, it is worth emphasizing that while much of the discussion in this chapter has been on the issue of religion, it is true to say that the population of both cities is overwhelmingly secular in nature. However, this does not negate the importance of religious labelling or aspects of religiosity in the culture and identity of both cities. Glasgow is not the warring sectarian battleplace of some media representations, yet vestiges of sectarianism do exist and are not confined to the working-class population of the city. Witness the resignation in 1999 of Rangers Vice-Chairman Donald Findlay QC, following his capture on video singing sectarian songs as Rangers players celebrated winning the domestic treble. Some commentators suggest that the 'Old Firm' rivalry simply continues 'because the fans enjoy it so much. They are not about to give up their ancient traditions just because they no longer believe in God' (Kuper, 1994: 218). To what extent this rivalry could be sustained without it having any connection with the contemporary social and economic reality of life in Glasgow is hard to believe. However complex this connection may have become over the years, for many this rivalry is fuelled by more than mere rhetoric.

In Glasgow, the position of a separate state-funded Catholic system of education is vital in sustaining a specific identity among the Catholic population of the west of Scotland. In addition, the Catholic Church takes an active part in the public issues of the day affecting its laity in this part of Scotland (Boyle and Lynch, 1998). By contrast, the situation in Liverpool sees both the Anglican and the

---

3. The signature tune from the 1960s television series *Z Cars* was played by Everton before matches. It was apparently played once before a match at Celtic Park during this period. One fan recalls the Celtic supporters 'went bananas and started shouting for it to stop. The reason? They thought it was an Orange tune and, when you think about it, I suppose there is a similarity' (Quinn, 1994: 179).

Catholic Churches occupying central positions as representatives and spokespeople for the city in a way that neither the Catholic Church nor the Church of Scotland does in Glasgow. Ironically, in terms of profile, the situation in Liverpool is more akin to the position of Church spokespeople in Northern Ireland, where media time is often given to Church leaders calling for consensus between the separate communities which they claim to represent.

In Liverpool, as the reaction to Hillsborough demonstrated, quasi-religious links between football and organized religion take on a heightened cultural significance in this particular city, partly due to its historical character and its contemporary position within English culture.

There are links between football and aspects of religiosity in Glasgow and Liverpool. The continued interest and popularity of football in these cities, while a testimony in part to the resilience of working-class culture in the cities, is also an indicator of the importance of ritual and spectacle in urban life. What you find in both cities is an interweaving of public and private culture, of religion and sport, the configuration of which is informed by the specific characteristics of the cities. In common they play a central role in the identity of many people in both these cities, yet in many ways, as shown above, they manifest themselves differently and tell us how, for all their similarities, Glasgow and Liverpool are very different cities.

Yet this is not to downplay the more secular links which help bind clubs such as Liverpool and Celtic together. Post-Hillsborough, alliances between supporters of the clubs have been strengthened, both by the epic UEFA Cup matches of 1997 and more recently by the arrival at Celtic in 1999 of the two Liverpool legends, Kenny Dalglish as Head of Football Operations and John Barnes as Head Coach. Ironically this is at a time when the former Rangers manager Walter Smith is in charge at Everton. In many ways, the 'traditional religious' allegiances between the cities is being superseded by new more secular patterns of loyalty and interest.

While Glasgow and Liverpool have both been shaped by the influx of nineteenth-century Irish immigrants, it is clear that this process has been different in each city. Differing political and economic environments have conspired to give each city a distinctive character. One characteristic shared by both is the important position that football occupies in their cultural lives. It seems reasonable to assume that, despite any impact that political and economic change may have on both cities, football will remain symbolically important in Glasgow and Liverpool, both reflecting and giving shape to a range of identities.

Acknowledgements

I would like to thank all the fans who spoke with me, and the editors for their helpful comments on an earlier draft.

References

Bale, J. (1991) 'Playing at Home: British football and a sense of place', in J. Williams and S. Wagg (eds) *British Football and Social Change: getting into Europe*, Leicester: Leicester University Press.
—— (1994) *Landscapes of Modern Sport*, Leicester: Leicester University Press.
Boyle, R. and Lynch, P. (eds) (1998) *Out of the Ghetto? The Catholic Community in Modern Scotland*, Edinburgh: John Donald.
Bradley, J. (1994) 'Ethnicity: the Irish in Scotland – football, politics and identity', *Innovation*, 7(4).
Edge, A. (1999) *Faith of Our Fathers: Football as a Religion*, Edinburgh and London: Mainstream.
Ferguson, A. (with Hugh McIlvanney) (1999) *Managing My Life: My Autobiography*, London: Hodder & Stoughton.
Giulianotti, R. (1999) *Football: a Sociology of the Global Game*, Cambridge: Polity.
Kelly, S. (1993) *The Kop: the End of an Era*, London: Mandarin.
Kuper, S. (1994) *Football Against the Enemy*, London: Orion.
Lappin, T. (1996) 'Engerlaaand Engerland', *Scotsman*, 15 June.
Moir, J. (1995) 'A man of two halves', *Observer Life Magazine*, 17 September.
O'Hagan, A. (1994) 'Scotland's Fine Mess', *Guardian Weekend*, 23 June.
Quinn, J. (1994) *Jungle Tales: Celtic Memories of an Epic Stand*, Edinburgh: Mainstream.
Samuel, R. (1989) 'An Irish religion', in R. Samuel (ed.) *Patriotism: The Making and Unmaking of British National Identity*, London: Routledge.
Taylor, I. (1989) 'Hillsborough, 15 April 1989: Some Personal Contemplations', *New Left Review*, No. 177.
—— (1991) 'English football in the 1990s: taking Hillsborough seriously', in J. Williams and S. Wagg (eds) *British Football and Social Change*, London: Routledge.
Taylor, R., Ward, A. with Williams, J. (1993) *Three Sides of the Mersey: An Oral History of Everton, Liverpool and Tranmere Rovers*, London: Robson.
Walter, T. (1991) 'The mourning after Hillsborough', *Sociological Review*, **39**(3): 599–626.

Bill Shankly and Liverpool
Andrew Ward with John Williams

Introduction

What we want to try to do in the first part of this chapter is to look at the circumstances of Bill Shankly's arrival in Liverpool in 1959 and to try to locate him and the Liverpool coaching staff of the time within the context of wider shifts in the post-war English game and debates about the domestic 'governance' of the sport, at least with respect to the issues of football management and coaching. John Williams tries to set the scene in this respect, by arguing that the Shankly era at Liverpool both recalls earlier developments in coaching and football club administration in Britain and also stands some way at odds with aspects of emerging new orthodoxies in England in the 1960s and 1970s about how football should be both played and coached.

Then, Andrew Ward in the second, longer, part of this chapter tries to evoke something of the particular *flavour* of the man, and of the Shankly years on Merseyside, and also of his relationship with supporters and players in Liverpool. How does Shankly both engage with and contribute to the particular 'structures of feeling' in the club and the city in the 1960s? Ward displays this in a highly original way by presenting a number of *vignettes* which highlight important aspects of Shankly's character and his approach to relationships in the sport. Much of this material is from original, unpublished, sources and is used in this inventive and unusual way especially to try to highlight the special features of Shankly's relationship to football, to Liverpool Football Club and to the city of Liverpool itself. Let us begin, then, by briefly trying to locate Shankly and his influence more broadly within the British game.

The Shankly Era Begins

Promotion for Liverpool FC from the Second Division under the young Bill Shankly in 1961/62 ushered in the beginning of a new era for the football club, a time when Liverpool FC would pursue European football adventures for the first time and the club would remain, for very different reasons, resolutely centre stage in public debates about football and its possible futures. In the early 1960s, Liverpool FC was becoming an international focus because of the synergy between music and football in the city and the cultural inventiveness of its fans; in the 1970s the spotlight fell on Liverpool because of the excellence and dominance of the club's extraordinary football team and management; in the 1980s it was more footballing excellence, but also an altogether harsher glare on the character of the city following the fatal hooliganism at Heysel and the crowd disaster at Hillsborough; by the 1990s the focus was on the prospects for reviving the club's football status in a new, global era, but also on the new economics of the sport as the club struggled to adapt to the new era of the game's development, eventually investing in a new business structure, a talented foreign coach and a roster of imported foreign players (see Chapters Eight and Ten).

The so-called 'December earthquake' when Bill Shankly arrived at the club in the winter of 1959 (Hodgson, 1978) almost blew itself out before the footballing transformation at the club could even begin. Shankly had explosive early confront-ations with the club's conservative directors, who were accused by the ambitious and abrasive Scot of complacency and of being, 'scared, like gamblers on a losing streak who were afraid to bet any more' (Hodgson, 1978: 78). Shankly persuaded the Liverpool board to 'modernize' the poorly developed Melwood training ground in 1960, and he aimed at transferring out twenty-four players in just over a year after his arrival in December 1959, bringing in key young replacements, especially from his native Scotland. Even as a young manager of a Second Division club in the late 1950s it was clear that Shankly's ideas were from a very different era from that represented by the departing Phil Taylor, who had served the club as player, coach and manager since 1936. The *Liverpool Echo* reported on 14 December 1959 that:

> Shankly is a disciple of the game as played by the Continentals. The man out of possession, he believes, is just as important as the man with the ball at his feet. Continental football is not the lazy man's way of playing soccer. Shankly will aim at incisive forward moves by which Continentals streak through a defence when it is 'closed up' by British standards. He will make his players learn to kill a ball and move it all in the same action ... he will make them practice complete mastery of the ball.

Shankly was determined to introduce 'modern' methods of training and preparation with his new club; as early as February 1960, for example, Liverpool players flew to Plymouth for a League meeting with Argyle, something which was highly unusual for the time, especially for a club in the Second Division of the League. Shankly also described the crumbling and disjointed Anfield ground of the time as an 'eyesore'. He was right. There had been no serious structural work on the stadium since 1928, and in 1963 a new 'daringly modern' (Inglis, 1996: 220) cantilevered stand for 6,700 fans was built to replace the shambolic barrel-roofed Kemlyn Road stand. As if to salute this expensive and impressive new structure, following promotion from the Second Division Shankly's young team carried off the League title in 1964 and, for the first time in the club's history, the FA Cup in 1965. With the Cup Final profits the Anfield Road end of the ground was also re-roofed, as Anfield was slowly transformed to meet the new demands of a European football age.

On the coaching side at Anfield, Shankly had inherited what were to become a number of key figures in the successful period which followed. They included later manager, the low-key but knowledgeable Joe Fagan, and chief coach Reuben Bennett, a severe physical education disciplinarian who used to wail at the 'softness' of players and tell his injured men to rub the offending area with a wire brush or even a kipper (Kelly, 1999: 59). Ex-Liverpool players Ronnie Moran and Roy Evans would join the back room later, but the most important of all the coaching staff was Bob Paisley, a long-serving Liverpool player himself, who had been offered the job of reserve team trainer by club director and later chairman and president T.V. Williams in 1954. Paisley took over at Liverpool from Albert Shelley, the archetypal white-coated British football club trainer, who by this time was limited to sweeping out the changing rooms and swapping banter with the hardened professionals. Paisley, a north-easterner from a mining background, already had a 'native' interest in fitness and the body which he attributed to his father's prodigious strength in the mines and a northern working man's industrial/rural deep interest in the performance of pigeons and his beloved racehorses. Paisley often compared players to racehorses, noting their common 'edginess', and also the ways in which both football players and thoroughbreds responded to *different* sorts of training, dependent upon their temperament. Even when he became club manager Paisley was probably most at home in the local bookmaker's studying form (Keith, 1999: 12; see also Chapter Four). He shared many of the pragmatic, 'communitarian' values and football enthusiasms of Shankly's own Scottish industrial heritage, which produced a crop of great British football managers from Shankly, Matt Busby and Jock Stein through to Alex Ferguson (Giulianotti, 1999: 128; McIlvanney, 1995).

Paisley had taken a correspondence course in physiotherapy, but Williams had also secured an open letter from local friend John Moores, founder of the Littlewoods group, requesting that Paisley be allowed in local hospitals to study medical methods and operations. For years the training staff and players at the club trusted to Paisley's intuitive insights into injury, but he was also aware of the paucity of specialist knowledge in the sport about treatment of injuries. He was one of the few trainers in the Football League in the 1950s to have any formal medical qualification (Kelly, 1999: 33). Paisley was also tactically astute, more so than Shankly. Their combination of strong, inspiring leader and shrewd 'medical' and tactical second-in-command dominated the English game for the following 25 years. Incredibly, in a total of 784 matches in charge at Liverpool, each missed only one match on the bench – Paisley due to illness, Shankly to scout elsewhere.

Shankly's predecessor at Liverpool, Phil Taylor, had resigned in 1959 after failing to take the club out of the Second Division and had also suffered humiliating defeat at the hands of non-league Worcester City in the FA Cup. Taylor had retired from playing at the same time as had Paisley and became club coach to Don Welsh in 1954. Welsh was sacked two years later, the first Liverpool manager to suffer this fate and followed since only by Graeme Souness. Tellingly, however, Bill Shankly had been interviewed for the job when Welsh had been appointed and was told, ominously, that the directors reserved the right to change the team (Wagg, 1984: 157). This time Shankly insisted he take charge at Liverpool with complete control over team matters, signalling the arrival of the 'modern' manager at Anfield, more than 30 years after the emergence in the 1920s of the first modern football technocrat, Herbert Chapman, at Huddersfield Town, and later the dominant force at 1930s Arsenal.

Chapman, like Shankly, believed in the unchallengable centrality of the manager's expertise – the board could deal with tickets and economics – and in 'organized' systems of play, which focused on the *team* not the individual. He was also concerned, again like Shankly, not just with the *playing* skills of his professionals, but with their general attitudes and lifestyles: 'How does he behave? What sort of life does he lead? Unless the answers are satisfactory, I do not pursue the matter further' (quoted in Wagg, 1984: 49). He understood the importance of delegation to a trusted staff and also the crucial matter of player fitness. He appointed Tom Whittaker as trainer and in the latter's resort to modern science in the treatment room threatened to revolutionize the whole approach in the game to physical fitness (Young, 1968: 175). At Anfield, Paisley and Bennett kept meticulous records on the fitness and preparation of players and strived for improved medical expertise.

Unlike his starch, be-suited contemporaries, Chapman, like Shankly, was also a players' manager who argued that one must get close to players, share their difficulties, understand their problems: though, if truth be told, at Liverpool Bob Paisley was more a players' *pal* than was Shankly. Finally, Chapman, again like Shankly, was an innovator who had a genius for psychological ploys and public relations and club promotion. Chapman experimented with a white football and numbering on players shirts, and introduced a 45-minute clock at Highbury. He had the press in thrall. Shankly sought more a special relationship with *fans,* but he was also a marvellously untutored proselytizer for the club on TV and with the press. Managers at Liverpool who followed him had quite a different approach to such matters as the press became more voracious – and vicious – and television much more intrusive and demanding in the TV age of football.

Shankly and his staff at Liverpool shared much, then, with the early revolutionary Chapman approach, but like most coaches and managers in England they were also much more reluctant to embrace aspects of the newly emerging postwar coaching orthodoxies. Wagg (1984: 74–100) describes well the struggle in the English game between the traditional 'muddy boots' approach of the English ex-professionals-turned-managers and the 'chalky fingers' philosophies of the new generation of qualified football technocrats, sponsored by the Football Association and led by the first England manager, an ex-school-master, Walter Winterbottom. Later, Charles Hughes, the Technical Director at the Football Association championed so-called 'scientific' approaches to coaching and playing which stripped the sport down to the conclusions of data analysis which purported to show that 90 per cent of goals scored came from moves of five passes or fewer. This peculiar form of 'industrial deskilling' (Giulianotti, 1999: 133), which effectively championed the long ball game in England, was followed more recently, in the 1990s, by new calls for a more 'scientific' approach to football coaching here. One dimension of this, recalling aspects of the obsessive scientific Taylorism of Charles Hughes, is the endless match analysis, conducted for the FA, designed to try to quantify the key features of some optimum international playing style. As this sort of rank positivism continues, the England team at the outset of the twenty-first century continues to fail, miserably, in the face of much more flexible opponents. Key deficits here seem to be in the processes of preparation, mental agility and strength, and in the crucial areas of creative decision-making and technically proficient and imaginative play.

Hostility among football professionals and managers back in the 1950s and 1960s to the new 'football theorists' – the 'outsiders', the blazered 'amateurs' at the FA who had never played the game, so what could they know? – was rooted both in a strongly defensive professional ideology and in an assertion that by invoking a more 'scientific' approach to coaching, especially, the theorists were in danger of making a 'simple' game unnecessarily complicated. In the 1960s, the old League player's ethos of native skill and masculine toughness had to be reconciled with a new orthodoxy based on formal knowledge and detail to strategy (Wagg, 1984: 100). At Liverpool, following Shankly's arrival, the struggle was soon on. Early in his reign, Shankly, Paisley, Fagan, Reuben Bennett and Ronnie Moran attended an FA coaching course at Lilleshall, reporting to their hosts on Saturday evening. Paisley was unimpressed and Shankly hated the formal 'theorizing' and wanted to leave immediately. He lasted until Tuesday, and never returned. Moran and Fagan, however, enjoyed meeting other coaches and went back for five or six years. According to rotund Liverpool 'keeper, Tommy Lawrence, Shankly 'didn't like Lilleshall, he didn't like boards with diagrams on them or somebody talking posh about football, that wasn't Bill' (quoted in Kelly, 1999: 77; see also Chapter Four). Until the arrival at the club more than 30 years later of Gérard Houllier, formal approaches to 'scientific' coaching were largely decried at Liverpool in favour of tried and trusted schemes of preparation honed under Shankly and Paisley and passed on via custom and practice to those who followed.

Why was all this 'book learning' necessary, it was argued at Anfield, when regularly playing in *Europe* also meant that coaches at the club were open to, and could adapt, innovations from abroad? After an unusual and comprehensive defeat, home and away, by Red Star Belgrade in 1973, for example, the Liverpool coaching staff concluded that the old 'stopper' English centre backs were now outmoded and they successfully converted more mobile midfielders – Hughes, Thompson – to these defensive positions (Keith, 1999: 119). Experience and flexibility, rather than theory and what were deemed to be fixed practices, were extolled as the central virtues at Anfield.

This surprise European defeat by Red Star occurred, in fact, during what was to prove to be Shankly's last season at Liverpool. Despite a crushing FA Cup Final win against Newcastle United and with a team crammed with new young talent including Ray Clemence, Phil Thompson, and the player who was to become the standard bearer for the new football commercialism, Kevin Keegan (Wagg, 1984: 144), Shankly resigned. Although he routinely told his staff he was 'packing in' the game, this was a stunning moment. Perhaps he sensed another, more consumer-driven period of the game's development lay ahead, where *players* would hold more of the whip-hand, and where television would increasingly dominate? Football had certainly changed enormously since his early days as a manager. Perhaps he fretted at his lack of serious European success? Perhaps, as some have argued, his decision was a spasm, quickly regretted? Whatever the reason, here was the end of the beginning of a period of club dominance in the English game which would surpass even Chapman's remarkable record at Huddersfield and Arsenal back in the 1920s and 1930s. Bill Shankly, often at odds with the new coaching gurus at the FA, had been a central figure in establishing the modern 'Liverpool way'.

Nine points of Shankly

In this section Andrew Ward selects nine features that helped to mould Bill Shankly into the unique managerial talent that oversaw Liverpool Football Club from his arrival in December 1959 to July 1974 when he suddenly retired. Some of these features are common to many football-club managers. It is the combination that produced the legendary influence which has been the subject of a stream of recent books about Shankly the man and his Liverpool legacy (Thompson 1993; Bowler 1996; Kelly, 1996; Bale, 1996; Darby, 1998; Keith 1998).

Bill Shankly moved to Liverpool in December 1959 after a decade of managing at Carlisle United, Grimsby Town, Workington Town and Huddersfield Town. He joined a club that was consistently missing promotion to the old First Division by one or two places. Helped by an injection of money for the signings of two fellow Scots, Ian St John and Ron Yeats, Shankly turned the club around inside three years. The Second Division Championship (1961/62) was followed by three League Championships (1963/64, 1965/66 and 1972/73), two FA Cup Final victories (1965 and 1974) and the club's first European trophy, the UEFA Cup (1973).

Through Shankly, and the mythologies which were generated by his presence, we can understand what *kind* of organization Liverpool Football Club became in the 1960s and early 1970s. Also, through these key features, we can sense how Shankly matched, and to some degree manufactured, the Liverpudlian spirit of the time. The relationship between Shankly and the bulk of Liverpool fans was largely compatible. Both sides were tough and cocky with plenty of swagger. Together they were a bit lippy and a little crazy, and they made each other laugh. As Kelly (1996) explains in the introduction to his recent Shankly biography, the people of Liverpool and Shankly *shared* the same fighting spirit, humour and obsession with football.

The Obsession

One cold April night, in the early 1950s, a party of football-club managers travelled by train together from London to Aldershot. They had met in London to help prepare the Football League AGM agenda, and now they were on their way to play a charity football match – Bob Jackson's All Star XI against Aldershot, then of Division Three (South). Snow was falling, toes were freezing, and there seemed little chance of the game being played. As the train approached Aldershot a third of the ground was visible, shrouded in snow, and the majority view was confirmed. The game would be postponed.

The group walked from Aldershot railway station and entered the ground. Johnny Carey, then manager of Blackburn Rovers, was the first to see that the referee was conducting a pitch inspection. The referee was skating around and falling over, and the pitch was obviously unfit. Carey relayed the news to the others.

The young Workington Town manager, Bill Shankly, was down the terraces and over the perimeter wall in a trice. A few well-balanced strides on the icy surface and he was coercing the referee: 'It's fit tah play, Sah, it's fit tah play.' And so they played.[1]

1. Told to Andrew Ward by his father, Tim Ward, who also played for Bob Jackson's All Star team of managers.

All managers love football and live football but Bill Shankly's obsession for the game went further than most of his peer group. Similarly, most managers construct football analogies from everyday situations but Shankly was a master at it. If a player said 'Good morning, Boss', he would reply 'Aye, a good morning for football'. He would start training with a simple homily – 'It's great to be alive, boys, all you need is a round ball and the green grass' – and take it from there.[2] A rainy day was 'a good day for skidding the ball'.[3]

His obsession sometimes bordered on craziness or rudeness because he didn't waste time on preamble like 'How's the family?' or 'How are you?' It was straight to the football (Taylor and Ward, 1993: 95/6). Denis Law, who played under Shankly at Huddersfield Town in the late 1950s, has described Shankly as a football fanatic who never talked about anything else but football. Law accepted 'football talk' at a match, but after the game Shankly drove Law crazy.[4]

Neville Smith, author of *The Golden Vision*, a play set around Everton football fanaticism in the 1960s, tells of how he once met Bill Shankly on a Liverpool–London train in the late 1960s. It was over the Christmas holiday period and the League fixtures were being staggered for the first time. Liverpool had no game that day but there were a couple of matches in London so Shankly was going to watch one of them. It wasn't because he was watching a player. 'It's a game,' was Shankly's explanation. While everybody else was at home with families, Shankly was going to one of the few games available.[5] The obsession legend bubbled over when Shankly claimed to have celebrated his wife's birthday by taking her to a reserve-team match.

Shankly's obsession had always been there, but it must have been aggravated by frustrated ambition. As a Preston North End player he won three medals – FA Cup runners-up (1937), FA Cup winners (1938) and Wartime Cup winners (1941) – but defeat to Arsenal in 1938 had cost his club the Cup and League double and the Second World War had stopped him from adding to his five Scotland caps. Shankly later said that his best playing years were from age 28 to 33, and that those years had coincided with the war (1941 to 1946) (Keith, 1998: 75).

---

2. Interview with Brian Hall for *One Hundred Years of Merseyside Football*, a 32-part radio series broadcast by Radio City (Sound of Merseyside). The majority of interviews were conducted by Rogan Taylor and the scripts written by Andrew Ward. Footnotes here refer to material not used in the radio series or the subsequent book (Taylor and Ward 1993).

3. Interview with Tommy Smith for a six-part BBC-2 television series called *Kicking and Screaming*. The series was produced by Jean-Claude Bragard and the consultant was Rogan Taylor. Footnotes here refer to material not used in the series or the subsequent book (Taylor and Ward 1995).

4. Interview with Denis Law for *One Hundred Years of Merseyside Football*.

5. Interview with Neville Smith for *One Hundred Years of Merseyside Football*.

As a professional player and a manager, Shankly went from 1941 to 1962 without winning a trophy. That's a long time in football. Similarly, Liverpool Football Club went from 1947 to 1962 without winning anything of note. The frustration of their fans matched Shankly's.

Also, when Bill Shankly reached fifty, he wasn't even the most successful manager in his own family. That honour belonged to his brother Bob, who took Dundee to the Scottish League Championship in 1962 and to a European Cup semi-final a year later. It is often said that younger brothers, striving to catch up, are more likely to have football ambitions, and Shankly was the youngest of five brothers.

Similarly, again, Liverpool fans could be bridled, in a familial way, by Everton fans. The most persistent taunt was that Liverpool had never won the FA Cup. When Shankly's team finally did win the Cup, in 1965, it led to amazing scenes of 'red' celebrations. A few days after the Final, Liverpool entertained Inter Milan in a European Cup semi-final. Some fans set off to Anfield at nine in the morning to make sure of seeing the 7.30 pm game. At eleven o'clock in the morning Anfield was surrounded. The gates were opened soon afterwards and thousands were in that ground from noon to nearly half past ten at night (Taylor and Ward, 1993: 120). Thousands wanted to see the Cup. Thousands were as obsessive as Shankly. Without realizing it, Bill Shankly and Liverpool fans had been moving in parallel since the Second World War.

Scottish Socialism

There were no charter flights from Speke Airport, Liverpool, to Reykjavik, Iceland in 1964. When Liverpool made their European Cup debut, after winning the League under Shankly in 1963–64, it meant a coach ride from Liverpool to Scotland and a flight from Prestwick in Ayrshire. Having played West Ham in the Charity Shield on the Saturday, the team left on the Sunday. As the coach neared its destination, Shankly had an idea:

> *'We've got a couple of hours to spare,' he said. 'Let's go to Butlin's at Ayr.'*
> *The coach-driver pulled in at the gates of Butlin's Holiday Camp.*
> *'Who are you?' asked the man on the gate.*
> *'Bill Shankly, Liverpool Football Club, we're going to Reykjavik in Iceland.'*
> *'I think you've taken the wrang road.'*[6]

The idea of taking a European Cup team to a Butlin's Holiday Camp might seem ludicrous nowadays, but it says a lot for Shankly's roots that this seemed a

---

6. This story is taken from a number of sources, notably Keith (1998: 140), Kelly (1996: 161) and Taylor and Ward (1993: 134).

wonderful idea at the time. He was brought up in Glenbuck, a coal-mining village 30 miles inland from Ayr, and he had learned his basic values from the coal-mining community – you work hard and you work for each other. Every day was a day to be appreciated but if you wanted something special you went to Ayr.

Part of Liverpool's success in the 1960s and 1970s was built around the socialist ethic of collective effort with equal wages and no prima donnas. Liverpool supporters warmed to this all-red 'political correctness'. There was no room for anyone thinking he was above anyone else.

Bowler (1996: 8–9) links Shankly's lifelong socialism to his Glenbuck up-bringing, in particular his work in the mines and the formative influence of the General Strike (when Shankly was twelve): 'His political ideas grew from that time, leaving him a lifelong socialist who played like a socialist and managed like a socialist. Everything about Shankly was geared to fostering a community, a powerful team spirit that acknowledged the fact that no individual component was more important than the greater good.'

The work ethic also showed in training. A succession of players signed from other First Division clubs – Geoff Strong (Arsenal), Phil Chisnall (Manchester United) and Tony Hateley (Chelsea) – expressed surprise at how much harder the training was at Liverpool (Keith, 1998: 41). Shankly drew a distinction between exercise (less than needed in a match) and training (more than needed in a match). The epitome of this was the 'sweat-box' or 'shooting-box'. Players worked in pairs in a square box surrounded by four shooting boards. One player would shoot and the other player would have to hit the rebound in his stride. It was like a four-way squash game and was very hard work (Bowler, 1996: 160).

Shankly never lost his sense of how hard life could be. When he moved to Liverpool he lived in the same three-bedroom semi-detached house from 1960 to his death in 1981. The link between his origins and his socialism is best shown when Shankly hosted a Radio City chat show with Prime Minister Harold Wilson in November 1975. A transcription of the occasion shows their informed discussion of the Ayrshire coalfield and the values instilled from such communities (Keith, 1998: 184–210).

And, of course, Glenbuck was a football community. A village of fewer than a thousand people, it had produced top-class professional players such as Sandy Brown and John Crosbie at the turn of the century, and Shankly's two uncles on his mother's side – Bob and Billy Blyth. Glenbuck's footballers never lost their quintessential *Scottishness*. As Shankly told Welshman John Toshack after signing him from Cardiff City in 1970, 'Never lose your accent' (Keith, 1998: 175). This attitude suited Liverpool fans. They had always welcomed Scottish players, right from the 1890s when the club fielded predominantly Scottish teams (see Chapter One). In the 1950s the only playing star was the much-loved and devout Christian, Billy Liddell. He had hailed from a Scottish coal-mining community. Just like Bill Shankly.

Simple Strategy

*Throw-in to Liverpool in the mid-1960s. In their own half. On the right-hand side.
Quickly taken. Waist high to Chris Lawler, the full-back, about six yards away.
Lawler stoops and heads the ball back to the thrower. Liverpool in possession. In
their own half. Coming forward.*

This rehearsed throw-in, repeated hundreds of times without losing possession,
was about as complex as Bill Shankly's tactical innovation ever became. His basic
philosophy, derived from his Socialist origins, was very simple: You pass the ball
to another red shirt and then take up another available position.

> Pass, move, receive the ball.
> Pass, move, receive the ball.

You keep moving into good positions and give your team-mate alternatives. You
play to each other's strengths and your team keeps possession of the ball. And if
you're losing you don't change the system. You keep going till the end.

Bill Shankly was not a man for ostentatious display or fancy talk. He was
certainly not a man for jargonized team-talks. He despised expressions such as
'penetrative through-ball' and 'overlapping full-back' (Taylor and Ward, 1993:
97). He would have agreed with Joe Mercer that the way to learn how to play
football was by practising with a ball and playing against better and better players
(James, 1993: 16). His approach contrasted strongly with that of the Don Revie/
Syd Owen player dossiers in use at Leeds United in the late 1960s and early 1970s.

Shankly and Bob Paisley were probably more inventive in training than on the
playing pitch. For instance, they introduced shaped blocks of wood which changed
the direction of shots when placed in front of goal; they gave specialist practice to
the goalkeepers; and they paid close attention to other defensive tactics.[7] Shankly
moved midfielder, Tommy Smith, alongside Ron Yeats as a central defender, telling
Smith that he would be 'Yeatsy's' right leg. Less successful was the signing of the
tall but technically weak Tony Hateley which caused a switch in attacking tactics.
Because Hateley was a brilliant header of the ball but poor in build-up play,
Liverpool briefly switched unsuccessfully to a high-ball game. Hateley was
replaced by John Toshack, who not only was excellent with his head but had a
better touch with his feet.

Tommy Smith recalls the 1966 Charity Shield match, when Shankly decided
that Liverpool would try something different. 'Let's try a free-kick', Shankly said.
'Let's try somebody running over the ball and then maybe passing it sideways.

---

7. Interview with Tommy Smith for *Kicking and Screaming*.

Sort it out among yourselves.' When Liverpool got a free-kick at Manchester United's Stretford End, Tommy Smith jumped over the ball, Gordon Milne jumped over it and Willie Stevenson did likewise, leaving the ball on its own. 'Ah, forget it', said Shankly later.[8]

It sums up Shankly's whole approach to tactics. What mattered most was getting the *right players*.

Tough, Skilful Northern Players who had Served Apprenticeships

Playing against Tottenham in the Cup in the early 1970s, Tommy Smith injured a thigh muscle in his left leg. He knew that if he was seen to be injured Shankly would leave him out of the side. He was also aware, as was everybody at Liverpool, that Shankly did not like his players to strap their legs or put plasters on cuts because that was showing weakness to the opposition. In the treatment-room that week, Smith talked to trainer Joe Fagan.

'Maybe I can get away with this, Joe', said Smith. 'If you shave the top of me leg, I'll put a tight, sticky bandage on and we'll organize a pair of long shorts. I think I can get away with it.'
'Well, it's down to you', said Fagan. 'But let's not do it while Shanks is here.'
Smith got on the table, shaved the top of his leg, and was having his leg strapped when Shankly walked into the treatment-room.
'Oh Jesus', said Fagan.
Smith, lying flat, guessed who must have come in.
'What are you doing?' asked Shankly.
'Tommy's just putting a strap on the leg', said Fagan.
'You told me you were fit', Shankly said to Smith.
'I am, it's just a little safeguard.'
'Oh no, son. No strapping.'
'Well, I'm putting it on.'
'No, you're not.'
'I am.'
'No, you're not.'
'You can sod off, it's my leg.'
'Oh no, son, it's not your leg, it's Liverpool Football Club's leg, son.'
Shankly walked out.
Joe Fagan burst out laughing[9]

Shankly's players had to be tough. He didn't sign players who missed matches with injury. (Frank Worthington and Freddie Hill were only two of those turned

---

8. Interview with Tommy Smith for *Kicking and Screaming*.
9. Interview with Tommy Smith for *Kicking and Screaming*.

down on medical grounds.) There are legendary tales of Shankly reacting to injured players by ignoring them or making an amazing suggestion. One time while he was the manager at Carlisle United, during a five-a-side game, the unconscious Geoff Hill was carried from the field and laid on the dressing-room table, unattended, while the others finished the game (Bowler, 1996: 101). When Carlisle United goalkeeper Jim MacLaren injured a leg in the early 1950s, Shankly told him to walk *slowly*, so the opposition didn't notice that he was limping (Kelly, 1996: 54).

Shankly once told Neville Smith, 'I don't talk to players when they're injured. Good players don't get injured.'[10] The benchmark was set by Gerry Byrne, when he played through almost all the 120 minutes of the 1965 FA Cup Final with a broken collarbone. The Liverpool players of the 1960s and 1970s did their utmost not to miss matches. When Liverpool won the Second Division title in 1961/62 they used only seventeen players and three of those played only five games between them. The 1965–66 Championship team consisted of twelve players with two others sharing four games at the tail-end of the season. In 1972/73 the Championship was won by only fourteen players (plus Lane and Storton).

As a player at Carlisle United and Preston North End, Bill Shankly was enthusiastic, energetic, hard and fair. He was a small, wiry wing-half who always gave one hundred per cent and had a bit of skill. He covered an enormous amount of ground and seemed to tackle players from ten yards away. He urged on his colleagues with cries of 'Come on, yee, get in there!', even when they were trailing hopelessly with only a few minutes to play. He had no concept of an end-of-season match and all matches went to the final whistle.

As a manager, Shankly served an apprenticeship in the north of England. He spent over ten years in total at Carlisle United, Grimsby Town, Workington Town and Huddersfield Town, and this apprenticeship factor featured strongly in his quest for players. It is difficult to think of a Shankly equivalent in the modern game; someone who managed a series of lower-division 'outpost' clubs before being appointed to an unfamiliar club with great potential at the age of forty-six. It would have been a little like Asa Hartford or Joe Jordan being appointed manager of, say, Wolverhampton Wanderers in 1996 or 1997.

Shankly expected players to serve similar apprenticeships as himself and he identified most strongly with players from the working-class communities of Scotland, northern England and south Wales. He would never take a Londoner away from London, for example. When he did sign players from London clubs he knew that they had been raised elsewhere: in the north-east, like Geoff Strong (Arsenal) or the Midlands, as with Tony Hateley (Chelsea). Shankly looked for

---

10. Interview with Neville Smith for *One Hundred Years of Merseyside Football*.

players with 'good character' who had proved themselves in lower-level football. He told chief scout Geoff Twentyman to concentrate his efforts on the Third and Fourth Divisions (Kelly, 1996: 212). When he signed players such as Larry Lloyd (Bristol Rovers), Ray Clemence (Scunthorpe United), Peter Wall (Wrexham) and Alec Lindsay (Bury) he subjected them to additional apprenticeship spells in Liverpool Reserves.

Not all Shankly's lower-division signings became first-team regulars – there was also Stuart Mason (Wrexham), Frank Lane and Trevor Storton (Tranmere Rovers) and Alan Waddle (Halifax Town) – but the failures were not that expensive. And Kevin Keegan, signed from Scunthorpe United for a meagre £33,000, more than compensated for any losses. Shankly felt a special closeness to Keegan because Keegan's father was a coal miner. Similarly, Shankly took to Ian St John, who was still working in the steelworks when signed from Motherwell. Even the Liverpool club Secretary, Peter Robinson, appointed in 1965, had served his own football-administration apprenticeship in places such as Crewe and Scunthorpe.

Although Shankly, and contemporary First Division managers such as Harry Catterick (Everton) and Jimmy Hagan (West Brom), had served managerial apprenticeships, they differed significantly from managers such as Matt Busby (Manchester United) and Bill Nicholson (Tottenham Hotspur), who had hardly been out of the First Division as players or managers. Busby's signings came from clubs such as Arsenal (David Herd and Ian Ure), Celtic (Pat Crerand), Chelsea (Alex Stepney), West Ham (Noel Cantwell) and even Torino (Denis Law). Although Shankly spent large sums wisely on Ray Kennedy, Strong, Emlyn Hughes (Blackpool) and Peter Cormack (Nottingham Forest), such other big-money signings, as Phil Chisnall, Hateley, Jack Whitham (Sheffield Wednesday) and Alun Evans (Wolves), were not as successful as his lower-division coups.

As we have seen from his response to injured players, Shankly could also be abrasive, unsympathetic and aggressive. He was a boxing fan who loved gangster films. His favourite film-stars were the likes of Jimmy Cagney and Jack Pallance who excelled in tough-guy roles. Shankly would come into the players' dressing-room and throw photographs of people such as Bugsy Moran, Legs Diamond and Eliot Ness on the big, square dressing-room table: 'You think you've got a hard time coming up this afternoon? See about them. When these lads did anything wrong they'd get shot. You think you're a hard man, son? This is a hard man. He used a Magnum and he shot 55 people . . .'[11]

But Shankly's definition of courage extended far beyond the physical components.

11. A number of sources, including Taylor and Ward (1993: 99–100) and interview with Tommy Smith for *Kicking and Screaming*.

Courage is also the ability to get up when things are getting you down . . . to get up and fight back. Never to know defeat, let alone accept it. To have principles – be they of fitness or morality – and stick by them. To do what you feel you must do, not because it's the most popular thing to do but because it's the right thing to do.

Courage is skill, plus dedication, plus fitness, plus honesty, plus fearlessness. It is a big word, but it is one which should hang above your bed if you really want to be a footballer – and to be one that is a credit to the game and yourself (quoted in Bale, 1996: 128).

Shankly was keen to sign players of character and commitment, and he wanted his chief scout, Geoff Twentyman, to investigate every aspect of a player's life (Kelly, 1996: 211). Shankly wanted players who were dedicated to the game and passionate about it, not those who were likely to go out drinking excessively or those who might crack under pressure. But such players had to be skilful too. They had to be able to control the ball and pass it in the Liverpool way. Shankly once walked out of a game before kick-off because he saw in the warm-up that the fancied player couldn't control the ball and pass it.[12] He walked out of another game because he didn't like the way the player rolled over and feigned injury (Kelly, 1996: 211–12).

Shankly laid the foundations at Liverpool by choosing players who showed the personal responsibility of playing for the club (Keith, 1998: 175). The Liverpool way was to sign skilful, resilient players who could fit into the passing and movement game, players who would respond to tough training principles and serve an apprenticeship in playing the Liverpool way, players who could take responsibility for themselves and make decisions on the pitch for the good of the team.

A Way with Words

One day the great England centre-forward Tommy Lawton visited Anfield to see his contemporary Bill Shankly. Shankly called in the teenage groundstaff players and introduced them to Lawton, who scored 22 goals in 23 internationals and would probably have been England's all-time record goalscorer had the war not intervened.

'This is the greatest centre-forward who ever lived', said Shankly. 'He could head a ball harder than most of us could kick it. The only way to stop him was to stop the ball getting to him.' Shankly spent ten minutes extolling Lawton's strengths. 'Right, Tommy,' he said eventually. 'Now tell them who was the best wing-half you ever saw and why I was.'[13]

---

12. Interview with Larry Lloyd for *Kicking and Screaming*.

13. This is a story told by a number of people in football. Andrew Ward first heard it from his father.

Shankly had a way with words and a means of attracting an audience. As one of Shankly's close colleagues once said, 'He couldn't open his mouth without saying something.' Sometimes Shankly was serious and it came out funny. Sometimes it was carefully calculated:

> *If it had been a boxing match it would have been stopped at half-time.*
> *We beat them five-nil and they were lucky to get nil.*
> *The best team drew.*
> *He must be a good goalkeeper, he saved one of my shots last week.*
> *There are two teams in Liverpool – Liverpool and Liverpool Reserves.*
> *Aye, Tony Currie's probably a better player than Tommy Finney, but Tommy Finney's fifty-odd now.*

When Ron Yeats signed from Dundee United, Shankly was typically proud of his big centre-half and called him a Colossus. Liverpool beat Sunderland comfortably in the first home game and Yeats had been dominant. Yeats was just coming out of the bath when Shankly invited all the journalists into the changing-room. 'There's the big man there,' said Shankly. 'Go and walk round him' (Taylor and Ward, 1993: 96).

When Alan Ball was signed by Everton from Blackpool, Shankly phoned up the new signing to welcome him to the city. 'Congratulations, son,' said Shankly. 'You'll be playing near a great side' (Keith, 1998: 127–28). Sometimes it was difficult to tell whether the jokes originated with Shankly or not. In 1969–70, Everton won the League convincingly with their fabulous midfield trio of Kendall, Ball and Harvey. The story was that Shankly went to his barber for his fortnightly haircut. 'Anything off the top, Mr Shankly?' 'Aye, Everton.'

And when Neil Armstrong took his first step on the moon in 1969, news of his famous first words spread quickly around Anfield: 'It's just like Goodison Park – there's no atmosphere.' It was immaterial whether the jokes were started by Shankly or an anonymous fan. A symbiosis had formed between Shanks and Liverpool supporters.

Our Players are Better than Their Players

One Saturday in the early 1970s, Liverpool manager Bill Shankly took his usual position in the Anfield corridor where he could watch the Ipswich Town players arrive. After seeing what he needed to see, Shankly burst into the Liverpool dressing-room and delivered a typical oration that belittled the opposition:

'You'll have no problem today. I've just seen a centre-half whose glasses are like milkbottles. They're that thick, he's blind. I've just seen a little boy that plays midfield, his legs are like that, he won't be able to run . . .'

The Liverpool players had heard this sort of thing many times before, but they were still fired up by it. By ten to three – ten minutes to kick-off – they were ready to go out and beat Ipswich.

> *'Take your shirts off', said Shankly.*
> *'What, Boss?'*
> *'Take your shirts off.'*
> *They pulled off their shirts.*
> *'Throw em on the floor', said Shankly.*
> *They threw them on the floor.*
> *This was a new approach. The players hadn't heard this team-talk.*
> *'Now go and have a bath', said Shankly.*
> *'Wait a minute, Boss,' said one of the players. 'What's going on?'*
> *'Well, you lot go and have a bath, I'll throw these shirts out on the field and the shirts will beat Ipswich by themselves.'*

Shankly was famous for raising his own players' determination through comic, crazy team-talks like the one above (Taylor and Ward, 1995: 282–3). Players hung on Shankly's words and he rarely failed them. At the same time Shankly had a way of reducing the power of opponents: one had a heart as big as a caraway seed; another couldn't trap a bag of concrete; and a third, on a cold winter's day, would only want to play if he could wear a numbered overcoat.

Denis Law chuckles when he recalls the time when Huddersfield Town played Liverpool in the Second Division in 1959/60. Shankly was manager of Huddersfield at the time and his team-talk reduced Liverpool to the most awful team in the world. A few weeks later, when Shankly joined Liverpool, Law was told by Shankly that Liverpool were the greatest team in the Second Division and would soon be the greatest team in the world.[14]

Ian Callaghan remembers an occasion when Shankly prepared the team for a match against West Ham. Shankly played down the skills of Martin Peters and Geoff Hurst and described the great Bobby Moore as a robot. After the game he told Callaghan that they'd just beaten a great team, and Bobby Moore was one of the greatest players in the world.[15]

In *Crazy Horse*, Emlyn Hughes tells the story of his first ride in Shankly's car and how the Liverpool manager was stopped by the police. 'Do you realize who I've got in the car?' said Shankly. 'The future captain of England.' Hughes was nineteen at the time (Hughes, 1980).

Ron Yeats remembers how Shankly used to come and sit beside people and talk to them: 'Hey, you're playing against what-do-you-call-him today. You'll not

14. Interview with Denis Law for *One Hundred Years of Merseyside Football.*
15. Interview with Ian Callaghan for *One Hundred Years of Merseyside Football.*

give him a kick. Ask him, "Why are you on the same pitch as me?"' (Taylor and Ward, 1993: 100). In Friday team-talks, Shankly would demonstrate one or two things on a magnetic board and then use the setting to relax the players. It was common for him to sweep magnetic opponents off the board with the words 'They can't play anyway.' Similarly, when using Subbuteo players to symbolize the opposition, he would sometimes hold one back in his hand and then throw it flamboyantly across the room with a dismissive comment.

Shankly later attributed his memorable team-talks to what he learned during his early coal-mining days, when he saw how humour could help fellow workers relax before the task in hand. He recalled how one man in the pits told a story of how he single-handedly pushed a truck full of coal for a mile in the pit before realizing that it had come off the rails (quoted by Bale, 1996: 26 and Keith, 1998: 15).

This basic message – our players are great, their team are terrible – was perfect for Liverpool fans because it appealed to the natural Scouse cockiness and there were ready-made rivals in Everton (Keith, 1998: 124 and 149–50). But Shankly did not pursue this tactic relentlessly. Everton player Terry Darracott recalls how Shankly stopped him in the street a couple of days before his League debut and told him 'You'll do great, son.' Shankly could even raise the spirits of an Everton player.[16]

The Network of Friends (off the pitch)

Shankly told a story about his RAF boxing days during the Second World War. One evening in Manchester he was fighting an Army man in the finals of the Northern Command. In the dressing-room before the fight, Shankly took out some precious rubbing-oils that he had been given by Preston North End.

'How did you get them?' asked the man next to him.
'I can get them,' said Shankly. 'Do you want to use some of them?'
'Oh, yeah.'
'What are you in?' asked Shankly, watching the other boxer rub the oils in his body.
'The Army.'
'Who are you boxing?'
'A fellow called Shankly.'
'Have you got a towel I can borrow?'
'Yeah, use this one.'
Shankly took the towel and rubbed the oil off the other boxer.
'Hey, I'm fighting you, I'm not letting you have my oil.'[17]

16. Interview with Terry Darracott for *One Hundred Years of Merseyside Football*.

17. Told to Andrew Ward by his father, who encouraged Shankly to tell it on a number of return journeys from All Star charity matches in the 1950s.

Bill Shankly was everybody's friend until he got you into that arena. He was a great networker who was forever telephoning people in the game and making fair and supportive comments to them. He was very good at contacting people to congratulate them or commiserate with them. His network began with his family. His brother Bob managed Falkirk, Dundee, Hibernian and Stirling Albion and his other brothers had met a lot of footballers when playing for clubs as far afield as Barrow, Portsmouth, Blackpool and Southend. When Bill Shankly signed ex-Hibernian player Peter Cormack for £110,000 from Nottingham Forest before the 1972/73 season, he had heard all about Cormack from brother Bob.

Having managed clubs outside the First Division Shankly had a bigger natural network than the Busbys and Nicholsons of his era. Surprisingly, none of his biographers discuss the partnership with Fred Ford, who was trainer-coach at Carlisle United when Shankly was manager. Ford, who stayed in the game until his death in 1981, had as much intensity as Shankly (see Swann and Ward, 1996: 102–4); and he was in charge of Bristol Rovers when Larry Lloyd was transferred to Liverpool.

Shankly was probably not the first to joke that football was more important than life and death but he was probably the first to suggest it at a time when mass communication was able to run with it. Like the boxer Muhammad Ali, who learned his verbal bravado from wrestler Gorgeous George, Shankly had undoubtedly learned things mixing among Third Division (North) managers such as Fred Westgarth of Hartlepool United (see Alister and Ward, 1997: 53–6). Later, in August 1967, Shankly recruited Geoff Twentyman as Liverpool chief scout. Twentyman had played under Shankly at Carlisle United.

The most brilliant part of Shankly's network was his boot-room team, the loyalty of which helped sustain Liverpool through the 1980s. Kelly (1996: 118–25) discusses the origins of their dedication in deserved detail. Shankly inherited Bob Paisley, Joe Fagan and Reuben Bennett, but of course there were connections. Shankly had once wanted Fagan to sign for Grimsby Town, and Scotsman Bennett, a former Dundee trainer, was known through brother Bob.

If Shankly was the motivator, Bob Paisley was the real tactician. Paisley could sum up players quickly and assess their strengths and weaknesses. Paisley and Fagan could organize canny psychological tricks, such as ensuring that Tommy Smith was given the wrong pre-match meal at the Holiday Inn so that he was in a suitably bad mood for the match.[18]

Ron Moran, club captain when Shankly arrived at Liverpool, later joined the backroom staff as a coach. Shankly won over Moran when he sent him a letter with advanced notification of what he intended to do when he arrived at Liverpool.

18. Interview with Tommy Smith for *Kicking and Screaming*.

One of Shankly's virtues was his consideration. He never got above his station. He was never quite sure whether the dustbinman might have a better opinion. If you were passionate about football, then he would talk to you about the game. Bernard Bale recalls his first meeting with Shankly as a *Soccer Star* journalist. 'My time is football laddie', said Shankly. 'I'm busy with football, and you're busy with football – so let's talk about football and let the time worry about itself' (Bale, 1996: 127). Shankly's attitude to football was the same with everyone. Paul (1998: 94–104) and Darby (1998: 145–68) include stories from fans which show that it was easy to form a relationship with the man if you were a football fan.

Reaching the People

The Liverpool players were touring the city again in an open-top bus. Thousands of people lined the streets.

They were nearing the library when manager Bill Shankly suddenly turned to Brian Hall and said, 'Hey, son, who's that Chinaman with the sayings, you know, what's that man?'
Hall looked at Shankly as if his manager was mad.
'Chairman Mao?' asked Hall.
'That's him, son, that's him. That's the man. Aye.'
He's definitely cracking up, this fellow, thought Hall.
Then they reached St George's Hall and Shankly stood up in front of 300,000 people. Cheering burst out. Shankly held his arms aloft and the cheering stopped.
'Chairman Mao has never seen such a show of red strength as this', said Shankly. The cheering recommenced.
Perfect, thought Hall. Brilliant. The man's a genius.[19]

This was one of many times when Shankly talked to Liverpool fans and the people responded. Shankly orchestrated them. His arms could silence the largest of crowds. Then he addressed them in simple language with two clear messages – we have the greatest team in the world and you are the greatest fans. As Bowler (1996: 211) says, Shankly spoke without a safety-net. Simple expressions like 'you are the people' became sententious through their spontaneous delivery and sincerity. And Shankly was not beyond rescuing a fan's scarf and tying it round his own neck (Bowler, 1996: 151; Kelly, 1996: 23).

Shankly's effect on the people is best demonstrated by the supporters' reaction after the 5–1 European defeat to an outstanding Ajax team in Holland. Shankly

---

19. A number of sources, including Keith (1998: 133 and 146) and Taylor and Ward (1993: 101).

managed to convince 54,000 people that Liverpool could beat Ajax by six in the second leg. The ground was full for a game that was lost from the first minute (although Shankly still argued that had Peter Thompson's sixth-minute shot gone in rather than hitting the bar then they would have won the tie). As Bill Nicholson once remarked, Shankly never lost, not even in defeat (Keith, 1998: 154).

Shankly's messages appealed to the Liverpudlian confidence of the time. The Beatles were the most famous music group in the world, and in their slipstream came Gerry and the Pacemakers, Rory Storm and the Hurricanes, Billy J Kramer and the Dakotas, The Four Most, the Searchers and the Swinging Bluejeans. Cilla Black was a big pop star and local poets such as Roger McGeogh, Adrian Henri and Brian Patton were creating a national stir. Comedians Ken Dodd and Jimmy Tarbuck were household names, and the city produced a string of boxing champions from Alan Rudkin to John Conteh. Liverpool and Everton were winning trophies regularly and Roger Hunt, Ian Callaghan and Ray Wilson had played for England in the successful 1966 World Cup Finals. And, for several years in the late 1960s and mid-1970s, Harold Wilson ran Britain from the nearby Huyton constituency. All in all, the city had optimism, employment and good humour.

At Anfield the crowd had their say. They worshipped the team (*We're the Greatest in Europe and Shankly is Our King*), they commentated on the game (*Eee-aye-addyo, Rowdy's won the toss*) and they coached from the side-lines (*attack, attack, attack, attack, attack*). They introduced other aspects of Liverpool music culture: they adopted an old Cabaret song, 'You'll Never Walk Alone', which had been revived by Gerry and the Pacemakers; and they mass-sang the latest Beatles number, either for hours before the match or sometimes spontaneously during it.

In one incident in 1963 a player was concussed during a match. The trainer came on and helped the player to his feet, and then the player slumped forward across the trainer, who held his weight. The Liverpool fans burst into song: *He loves you, yeah, yeah, yeah.*[20]

Always a Player

When Liverpool players trained at Melwood, the gates were left open and fans gathered three or four deep around the touch-line.

One day in the early 1970s, a bigger crowd than usual watched a five-a-side match between the staff team and the young lads. Schoolchildren on holiday, sailors in port, workers on strike, they swelled the attendance to the level of an acceptable Fourth Division crowd.

20. Told to Andrew Ward by his father after the team he was managing, Derby County, had lost 5–0 at Anfield in January 1964.

Shankly, then nearly sixty, was on form that day, knocking his passes around, running the show.

'Eee, just think,' he said to a colleague, looking at the crowd. 'They're watching this for free.'[21]

Almost all managers bemoan the passing of their playing careers but few hang on to them as tenaciously as Bill Shankly did. In fact, Shankly never really let go of his playing days. In his 1960s, after retirement, he was still enjoying impromptu Sunday afternoon games with children. They would play for a couple of hours and then Shankly would go off and say, 'We had a great game, we won 19–17' (Taylor and Ward, 1993: 102–3).

Shankly's life had a theme of informal small-sided games. In his Scottish youth there were five-a-side competitions (Bowler, 1996: 36–7). During his managerial days he was five-a-side obsessed, with players at Grimsby recalling Scotland v England or Single v Married (Kelly, 1996: 75). When manager of Huddersfield Town he played on a local recreation ground (Kelly, 1996: 87–8) and then at Liverpool came intensive three-a-side games (Bale, 1996: 119) and the legendary five-a-sides at Melwood or in the Anfield car-park.

The car-park matches sometimes involved local dustbinmen on the days their round took them to the club. Shankly liked to arrange confidence-boosting games for his youngsters against the binmen, the latter considerably handicapped by their big boots and sacks tied round their heavy clothing. One day Shankly turned up just after the players had started a game. He was told that he couldn't play because the sides were equal. Shankly went away and came back five minutes later riding on a milk-float. The milkman complained that he'd never played football in his life. 'That's alright,' Shankly said, 'You can go in goal for them.'[22]

The Staff team was unbeaten for years, but only because the staff all had whistles. They took turns to blow for fouls and would add time on if they were losing. Joining in with the youngsters every day helped pass on the club's values. The staff watched players' reactions and studied their character. Shankly taught them good habits, which included little details such as practising one-twos when fetching the ball from behind the goal, just to get to know your players a little better.

Whereas Everton's Harry Catterick was a directors' manager who generally wore a suit to work, Bill Shankly kept his office near the changing-rooms, wore a tracksuit and was always looking for a game. He wanted to be close to the players and wanted to know all that was going on in their lives. 'Are you sleeping well?'

21. Told by Tom Saunders at a coaching course in 1972.

22. Told to Andrew Ward by his father after an evening with Bob Paisley. The story may have been adapted in the telling but people in football accepted it because it showed Shankly's playing obsession and his canny way of getting on the best side.

he would ask them. He also knew who was having trouble with their drains, whose roof needed repair and whose garage doors had fallen off. He was constantly checking whether jobs had been done for the players. And he was also checking whether the groundstaff had done their jobs properly (Taylor and Ward, 1993: 97–8).

After retirement, it was the day-to-day involvement with the players that Shankly missed the most (Taylor and Ward, 1993: 104).

References

Alister, I. and Ward, A. (1997) *Barnsley: A Study in Football, 1953–59*, 2nd edn, Oxford: Crowberry.

Bale, B. (1996) *The Shankly Legacy*, Derby: Breedon Books.

Bowler, D. (1996) *Shanks: The Authorised Biography of Bill Shankly*, London: Orion.

Darby, T. (1998) *Talking Shankly: The Man, the Genius, the Legend*, Edinburgh, Mainstream.

Giulianotti, R. (1999) *Football: a Sociology of the Global Game*, Cambridge: Polity.

Hodgson, D. (1978) *The Liverpool Story*, London: Arthur Barker.

Hughes, E. (1980) *Crazy Horse*, Manchester: Arthur Barker.

Inglis, S. (1996) *Football Grounds of Britain*, London: Collins Willow.

James, G. (1993) *Football with a Smile: The Authorised Biography of Joe Mercer*, Leicester: ACL Colour Print and Polar Publishing.

Keith, J. (1998) *Shanks for the Memory*, London: Robson.

—— (1999) *Bob Paisley: Manager of the Millennium*, London: Robson.

Kelly, S. (1996) *Bill Shankly: It's Much More Important Than That*, London: Virgin.

—— (1999) *The Boot Room Boys*, London: Collins Willow.

McIlvanney, H. (1995) 'No power, no glory', *Sunday Times,* 5 November.

Paul, D. (1998) *Anfield Voices*, Stroud: Tempus.

Shankly, B. (1976) *Shankly*, Manchester: Arthur Barker.

Swann, G. and Ward, A. (1996) *The Boys from up the Hill: An Oral History of Oxford United*, Oxford: Crowberry.

Taylor, R. and Ward, A. with Williams, J. (1993) *Three Sides of the Mersey: An Oral History of Everton, Liverpool and Tranmere Rovers*, London: Robson.

Taylor, R. and Ward, A. (1995) *Kicking and Screaming: An Oral History of Football in England*, London: Robson.

Thompson, P. (1993) *Shankly*, Liverpool: The Bluecoat Press.

Wagg, S. (1984) *The Football World*, Brighton: Harvester.

Young, P. (1968) *A History of British Football*, London: Stanley Paul.

−4−

Passing Rhythms: The Modern Origins and Development of the Liverpool Way

Stephen Hopkins

A recent major work on the social and cultural aspects of football's development as the global sport, makes the telling point that 'playing techniques, styles and their aesthetic appreciation have been notably absent' from the rapidly increasing literature devoted to the game (Giulianotti, 1999: 129). While the recent growth in academic, as well as popular and journalistic, writing about football has largely concentrated upon elements of fan support, behaviour and culture, there has been a much smaller growth in interest in the way in which the game is played, and the ways in which this interacts with other aspects of any particular club's historical and cultural identity.

This chapter seeks to examine 'the Liverpool way' of playing, with an exploration of the early years and development of the 'modern' Liverpool (under the managers, Bill Shankly, Bob Paisley and Joe Fagan). The intention is not simply to reduce discussion of this rich, complex area to a question merely of tactical formation, significant though tactical variations are. What is of particular interest here is how the 'style of play' is understood by fans (and players and staff at the club, at least to an extent) as a central element of their self-identification; popular myths have developed concerning the 'right' way for a Liverpool team to play, and these are strongly held, transmitted to new generations of supporters and players, creating an unbroken link with the past, and consolidating a complex process of identity construction. In a period of transition in the management of the club, with the arrival in 1998 of Gérard Houllier signifying for some an overdue 'revolution' in the club's management philosophy, and relative lack of success on the pitch, this popular historical memory does not fade away: indeed, if anything, the symbolism attached to Liverpool's playing traditions is perhaps stronger in the contemporary period, as supporters seek a means to negotiate the rapidly changing circumstances of the club, and the game more generally. Although there is not space here to discuss the recent developments, in the much less successful 1990s (see Chapter Seven for aspects of the 1990s management of the club), this chapter should provide some pointers for an appraisal of the elements of continuity and change that have been part of the transmission of the 'Liverpool Way' to the contemporary era.

Equally, there is not space either to trace the early origins of the club's playing style, although some elements of Liverpool's early development are included in Chapter One, and in Kelly (1996). However, as Giulianotti (1999: 137) points out, 'the exact origins of most cultural paradigms or genres are very difficult to establish', and we must avoid the error of attributing linear historical 'lines' to what is, in fact, a complex dialectical process, involving teamwork and individual creativity, continuity and change, in terms of tactical appreciation and style of play. Giulianotti (1999: 137) further argues that 'football people at any one time are brought up to value one or two "traditional" playing styles. A "revolution" occurs in this footballing community when the dominant tradition loses power to a new model'. It seems to me that changing playing styles are rarely as 'revolutionary' as this argument suggests, and that transitions generally occur within a pre-existing historical framework. 'New' styles have to be 'fitted in', both practically and symbolically, to the prevailing pattern of play familiar to the players/supporters, and they have to be made consistent with long-held, collective beliefs regarding the club's playing identity.

Of course, identities do change over time, and occasionally this can be properly described as revolutionary. The transformative effect wrought by Bill Shankly's arrival as manager at Liverpool in December 1959, followed by fifteen years of building a style, on and off the pitch, that became known as 'the Liverpool way', is an example that might well serve to support Giulianotti's argument. We turn to a brief and incomplete look at the way in which the Liverpool way came to prominence, and the evolution of the 'boot room' philosophy during the 1960s and 1970s.

Shankly, Paisley, and the Liverpool Way: The Struggle for Simplicity

Just go out there and express yourself in your own way, but be part of the machine that keeps moving the round thing'. (Phil Neal in Taylor and Ward, 1993: 163).

Many people came here to watch training sessions in those years thinking there was some particular kind of magic, and they'd come down to Melwood [Liverpool's training ground] and we'd allow them to watch and, after the training session, they would feel as though they'd been cheated. They would say, 'Well, you mustn't be showing us it all. You must be hiding something from us.' The whole method was simple. It was based on a rapport with management, good management, good players and the freedom to express themselves. (Tom Saunders in Taylor and Ward, 1995: 286–7).

The stories and anecdotes relating to the genius and charisma of Bill Shankly are legion, and there have been countless attempts to distil the essential characteristics of his approach: in Chapter Three, Andrew Ward has provided a full explanation of Shankly's relationship with Liverpool, the club, the city and its people, as well as a survey of some of the large volume of publications celebrating this authentic hero. Here, it is particularly the approach to playing the game that is of interest.

The watchword of Liverpool's approach under Shankly, and subsequently under Paisley and Fagan, was simplicity. Shankly, in common with many of his contemporaries in the British game in the 1960s, was disdainful of the pseudo-scientific tactical approach to the game, preferring to concentrate on the players and encouraging them to do the simple things correctly. Steve Wagg (1984: 73–100) discusses in detail the painfully slow 'coming of technocracy' to the British professional game in the post-war era. He recalls the frosty reception for the successful touring side, Moscow Dynamo, who played a series of games at the invitation of the Football Association in the autumn of 1945 (see also Downing, 1999). The basis of the 'public condemnation by football people of Dynamo' was that 'masculinity, as well as individuality . . . were felt to have been sullied' through their emphasis upon 'pretty-pretty' passing, tactics and teamwork. Immersed in a British football culture that continued to treat coaching with suspicion well into the 1950s, or even later, the Liverpool staff undoubtedly took time to digest the lessons of football's rapid development elsewhere. The elements of the game that Shankly and the back room staff (which he mainly inherited, the likes of Reuben Bennett or Bob Paisley, who became first-team trainer in August 1959, or promoted from within, like Ronnie Moran, full-back and club captain in 1959, who eventually retired from Anfield in 1998) thought were central revolved around 'good players, playing with freedom within a sensible framework' (Bowler, 1996: 217).

A certain degree of myth-making has built up around the preparations employed at Liverpool; a mystical quality has been attributed, for example, to the regular five-a-sides that dominated training during the season. Undoubtedly, although Shankly was dismissive of tactical devices, particularly those designed to stop the opposition playing, he was nevertheless very keen on a structured and methodical training regime. Intuition, psychology, man-management, all were facets of the Shankly character that were channelled obsessively towards playing the game. However, if the rhetoric of 'scientific' tactics was derided by Liverpool under Shankly, it would be equally wrong to view their approach as unstructured, based only upon some kind of impressionistic 'feel' or simple enthusiasm for the game.

A *collective* approach, based on the understanding that the team is all, and the individual nothing without the team, helped to produce a team ethos founded on self-respect, discipline, trust and dedication to the overall cause. Some have likened the spirit generated as similar to a harmonious family, while more politically minded observers (following Shankly's famous interview in 1975 with then Prime Minister Harold Wilson; see Keith, 1998: 184–210) saw Liverpool's approach as a 'form of socialism'. Here, I agree with Giulianotti's caution concerning the functional position that 'views football culture as a straightforward reproduction of wider social relations' (1999: 128). It is, of course, no accident that men like Shankly, Paisley, Jock Stein, Matt Busby and later Kenny Dalglish and Alex Ferguson were imbued with a strong collectivist mentality, being socialized when and where they were, in mining communities in the West of Scotland or Durham, and yet the teams produced by Liverpool and Manchester Utd over the last forty years, and the styles of play promoted as integral to the respective clubs' identities, have emphasized different, perhaps even contradictory, values. The 'Liverpool way' has privileged pass-and-move, a 'shape' or pattern of play that was efficient and, above all, controlled (mechanistic, according to its critics). Simply, and reductively, where Liverpool's football was primarily based on two touches (control first, and then pass), Manchester Utd can be characterized as one-touch, moving forward quickly, with flick-ons and a greater emphasis upon individual trickery. The point here is that these footballers' and managers' similar objective social circumstances could be shaped and expressed in football, according to different aesthetic appreciations of the 'right' way to play.

To return to the Liverpool way, there were tried and tested methods of preparation, some of which were innovative for the time. Ian Callaghan (1975: 28; see also Ian St John in Taylor and Ward, 1995: 284) recalls the 'sweat box': 'a wooden box formed of boards. A player goes in on his own with four men . . . in each corner throwing balls at him from all angles which he has to control and hit'. The numbered shooting boards were another example of this planning on the training pitch. Roger Hunt also remembers the 'training boards where we had to receive a ball, trap it, shield it, control it, shoot on the turn, all the things that you have to do within a game, match situations, playing under pressure . . . In that sense, it was tactical as well as technical work . . . It was all sharp, quick exercises, pressure things in short bursts' (Bowler, 1996: 216). The significance of these routines was that the players were asked to practice in training, repeatedly, elements of the game that they would be required to reproduce in match situations; later on, during the unsuccessful 1990s, new manager Houllier would argue that Liverpool had lost some of their urgency in training. At least some of the players had come to regard training as little more than 'filling in time' between matches.

To illustrate the continuity that existed in Liverpool's preparation from the 1960s through until the early 1990s at least, it can be seen, from a variety of later players' accounts, that a similar set of exercises and priorities were to be found at Melwood: Alan Hansen recalls (Taylor and Ward, 1995: 286) that 'You used to have a stupid thing – well, I thought it was stupid (at first) – where if you passed it and didn't move two or three yards you were penalized, and that soon taught you that you had to move'. Interestingly, Phil Neal (1986: 81–6), when he arrived at Anfield from Northampton Town in 1974, was 'exhilarated' by Liverpool's insistence on working primarily on ball skills, rather than simply doing stamina work, as he had been used to. Nonetheless, Neal was struck by the fact that training 'never varies, week-in week-out the routine is exactly the same'. While recognizing that this 'repetitive diet' had remained largely unquestioned because it had brought success to the club, Neal couldn't help 'wondering what the atmosphere would have been like had they not been so successful'. He went on to say that he would have preferred more variety in training exercises, but 'as long as the side keeps winning all the powerful voices in the "boot-room" will be able to claim without fear of contradiction that the results on the field fully justify the system. I'd go even further and suggest that something as simple as superstition could be at the heart of the matter . . . It's a very old-fashioned club in many respects'.

Arriving at Liverpool soon after Neal's departure, John Barnes (1999: 90–2) also expected 'some kind of initiation into the mystique of Liverpool playing. Liverpool's secret training methods were part of football's folklore; no one knew what they were but everyone was convinced they existed. Me too . . .'. For Barnes, the five-a-sides that followed 'a very light warm up' came as a relaxation after the regimented Watford style, but he was surprised to learn that they involved 'no tactical work, none whatsoever. All the strategic stuff was done within the small-sided games. Liverpool believed that everything we faced in five-a-sides would be encountered again on match day . . . Liverpool's training characterised Liverpool's play – uncomplicated but devastatingly effective'. Barnes underlines the competitive nature of training ('Cup Finals on a small pitch'), and argues that 'if there was any secret to Liverpool's success it lay in the fact that the fixation with five-a-sides gave us an extra edge on match days. Bigger pitches and goals made us feel we had more room'. Moreover, Barnes touches on another critical aspect of the club's self-perception: despite some redevelopment work, Melwood 'remains pretty basic. It doesn't bear comparison with some of the sumptuous Italian training grounds like Inter Milan's Appiano Gentile . . . It surprised me how rudimentary it was. That was typical Liverpool; all they were worried about was the football. Coming from Watford, which was so organized with a really close community relationship with the fans, it all seemed so different. Anfield's code was essentially: "Run on the pitch and win"'.

In a partially contrasting account, Jan Molby (1999: 61–5), who had spent two seasons at Ajax in the early 1980s before Joe Fagan signed him for Liverpool, was surprised at the relatively relaxed training regime, and the lack of emphasis on tactical variation: 'Compared with what I'd been used to at Ajax it was very low-key. There were no flying tackles, nobody was working very hard. Basically, it didn't amount to all that much . . . All the staff [Joe Fagan, Ronnie Moran and Roy Evans] were joining in, and I found it difficult to take in at first.' One explanation for this apparent difference is that Molby joined Liverpool during the pre-season build-up to the Charity Shield, and they were renowned for starting pre-season slowly. Another, more interesting, explanation stems from the cultural differences between English and Dutch football, and the strength in depth of the respective leagues:

> [At Ajax] you had to play for your life and train for your life. You could be in a team which won 5–0 on a Saturday but, if you didn't perform in training during the week, you wouldn't keep your place. It put everyone under pressure and led to a quick turnover of players . . . Every morning we played possession football, 8-a-side in a very confined space (a small square), one-touch, two-touch, with some shocking tackles going in. It was very high-powered stuff. Some of the training sessions were much tougher than some of the games, which we cruised through (Molby, 1999: 38–9).

In England, not only were there considerably more games to play, there were very few where the players could play within themselves, as Molby had been used to at Ajax: 'We [Liverpool] could go away and be two or three nil up but the other teams just wouldn't give in. They'd keep going because their fans would demand it.'

This also points to another important aspect of the Liverpool way, one that Shankly was especially focused on: continuity of personnel (see Chapter Three and Yeats, 1966: 47). A settled side, playing according to each other's strengths, was the goal, and Shankly was famously unimpressed by players who were injury-prone. Bob Paisley (1983: 31; see also Bowler, 1996: 303), acting as physiotherapist, recalled that Chris Lawler was 'in the middle of his run of over three hundred consecutive appearances. Chris hurt his foot on the Saturday, and in training I told him to take it easy. Bill saw me talking to him and asked: "What does that malingerer want now?"' Later on, Phil Neal played with a broken toe, wearing an enlarged boot, in order to maintain his place. Selecting the right sort of character, as well as the right kind of player, was a crucial part of the Liverpool way; often Shankly would be drawn to those players who viewed their profession as a craft, and took real pride in their work.

There is an unresolved debate regarding the extent of Shankly's tactical awareness, as against the consensus that exists concerning his extraordinary motivational powers. Ronnie Moran (Bowler, 1996: 223) argues that 'tactically Bill was far advanced . . . He would combine a lad who was quick in the head but not so fast with one who could run'. On the other hand, Roy Evans (who joined Liverpool in 1964, but whose playing career was cut short by injury) considers that Shankly was 'idealistic. He wanted perfection. He wasn't a coach, he wasn't a tactician, he was an enthusiast and a teacher. He preached simplicity' (Bowler, 1996: 246). Tommy Smith recalls (Bowler, 1996: 223–4, 231–2; Hey, 1997: 42) that while Reuben Bennett would watch Liverpool's forthcoming opponents, Shankly didn't want extensive dossiers on the opposition, in case 'we frightened our bloody selves to death'; rather, 'if we came up against the best players, someone who could run the show, we wouldn't man-mark him like other teams. We just kept in communication . . . We played to a system. It depended on togetherness and we worked on it in five-a-sides. We never moved up, we kept it dead flat so if anyone ran beyond the back four they'd put themselves offside. We never ran out to catch them'. Here, we also see the origins of the goalkeeper's role as occasional sweeper behind this flat back four, a function performed most effectively by Ray Clemence.

Smith also argues, more controversially, that Shankly was 'the first to go for a 4–4–2 . . . which a lot of people think England [managed by Alf Ramsey] started, but I can honestly say that it was Liverpool that were one of the first teams to play that way. I came across it playing for the England youth team in Switzerland – they used to call it the "Swiss bolt". The boss brought it in for us, and we perfected it'.

However, alongside this emphasis upon continuity, there was also a ruthless approach to players who could no longer maintain the required standard on a regular basis. Ron Yeats, one of Shankly's favourites, acknowledges, 'he knew exactly when to replace you, and I don't think anyone had any qualms about it . . .' (Taylor and Ward, 1993: 145). In came Larry Lloyd, Ray Clemence, Brian Hall, Steve Heighway and Kevin Keegan, in Shankly's 'second' team of the early 1970s. Typically, this ruthlessness was combined with a sympathetic attachment to 'his' players, those that had served the club loyally, and would now have to hang up their boots. As Shankly knew only too well from his own experience, when a player has to stop, there is an irreplaceable void. The most important aspect of this inevitable process of generational turnover is that fundamental principles were not disturbed for any newcomer; they had to fit in to the prevailing pattern without upsetting the equilibrium. Jan Molby (1999: 65–6) shows how this attitude lived on in the 1980s; while nervously awaiting his debut, he pressed Joe Fagan about what his role should be: '"Play", he said "Play. Don't do anything silly, just play within the system" . . .'. For Phil Neal (1981: 145), 'when Liverpool bought me and other players, we were told to play our natural game. Playing with the lads and training with them week after week made modifications to their game and to ours. The newcomers and the old hands learn to work together by combining their skills, not by playing to a set, mechanical pattern'.

The final word on the question of Shankly's attitude to tactical issues can be left to the man himself. Although he went on several occasions, along with other members of staff, to Lilleshall (the FA's coaching centre), Shankly quipped, 'It was an education because everything they did, I did the opposite . . . God Almighty! I could have written a comic cuts book about it! They were trying to tell me that you could make football players! They had a set plan all the time, but when it broke down, there was nowhere to go. Talk in a language the players understand, simplify and clarify . . . We're not too fond of coaching, coaxing is a better word' (Bowler, 1996: 245–6).

If there is disagreement over Shankly's tactical acumen or interest, then Bob Paisley is regarded uniformly by his players as a deep thinker about the game, an excellent (and at times uncanny) judge of a player's physical condition, but generally a poor communicator. There is, however, some argument concerning the extent to which Paisley's image was carefully honed, to perhaps lull opponents into a false sense of security. Stories abound of his uncomplicated tastes, whether in clothes, food or football. His captain, Graeme Souness (1985: 49–53, and 1999: 188–91), recalls Paisley's flat cap and carpet slippers, worn whenever possible because of an injured ankle. In Paris, after the European Cup final victory against Real Madrid, Paisley looked incongruous in the palatial splendour of the team's hotel, and Souness recalls him 'sitting back with a cigar, a glass of whisky and wearing those old-fashioned slippers . . . Completely relaxed and apparently not at all excited'. Before training every morning, Paisley would stop in at a local garage for a cup of tea, while he picked out his horses from the paper, and Souness used to meet him there for a chat. He simply felt comfortable in this kind of uncomplicated daily routine, familiar to millions of other working-class men of his generation. I tend to agree with Stan Hey's assessment that 'it would do Paisley a disservice to try to define him as the last true football man, with its connotations of centre-partings, boot-room camaraderie and home-spun values, because although he embraced all of these, he was also one of the great thinkers and modernisers of the English game' (1997: 183).

After Paisley's death, in an unusual tribute, an editorial in the *Independent* (15 February 1996) made the point that Paisley was:

> A working-class man who made good, but whom extraordinary success failed to corrupt or sour . . . What is truly remarkable about this is the fact that Paisley was never feted in the way that other, far less successful, soccer managers have been . . . He did not have a way with the press, was not actively considered to become an international manager . . . Bob Paisley stands for all those hundreds of thousands of his generation whose intelligence and loyalty achieved much, but whose attributes went largely unrecorded and underestimated. And who did not mind.

Souness (1985: 53) agrees that he was a 'football "intellectual"'. Had he been more articulate he would have been hailed as one of the greatest thinkers and managers on the game'. Stan Liversedge (1995: 48), Liverpool's programme editor for many seasons, and ghost-writer of successive managers' notes, agrees that 'anyone who took Bob Paisley for a fool would have spent his money badly . . . He was a canny fellow, all right — and don't let that woolly-cardigan image fool you'.

A couple of striking examples of this forward-thinking approach, rarely associated with Paisley, come from his autobiography: 'Soon, I think we shall see a European League, and then, with supersonic travel, and the emergence on to the football scene of hitherto non-soccer-playing nations, there could even be a World League by the end of the century' (Paisley, 1983: 95). It is worth noting the date of publication, and the fact that very few of his contemporaries were contemplating these sorts of seismic shifts in the global game. Or, again, as far as the induction of younger players into the game is concerned, Paisley (1983: 102–3) makes a strong case for root-and-branch reform, involving 'the setting up of special schools at which the development of their football talent would run parallel to their general, academic education. It would not be at the expense of normal education but as an addition to it. The lads would have the benefit of their natural talent being nurtured and developed by expert coaches, and not by ambitious and inexperienced schoolmasters . . . The current rules often mean that when a youngster is old enough to link up with a professional club, he has already formed too many bad habits which are difficult to eradicate . . .' It is easy to imagine the pride Paisley would take in the £12 million Academy opened by Liverpool in Kirkby in 1998.

Paisley's image as a 'kindly, avuncular . . . favourite uncle type' (Hey, 1997: 184) should not therefore deter us from his ambitions for Liverpool, and his willingness to gently, but firmly, remind commentators of his prowess. When Liverpool won the European Cup in 1977, and became the first British side to retain it the following year, Paisley (1983: 28) acknowledged that Shankly 'had to take a lot of the credit for what happened . . . But on the other score, there is a bit of credit due to me and the staff, because we changed the whole team over'. Only four of the players involved in 1978 against Bruges had played under Shankly in the first team (Clemence, Heighway, Hughes and Thompson). In 1978, before the defence of the European Cup, Hey (1997: 189) interviewed Paisley, who pointed out as a matter of fact, not immodestly, that 'in their history, Liverpool have now won, or been runners-up in the league, FA Cup and European Cups 36 times. And I've been involved on 26 of those occasions, as player, assistant manager, or manager.' It is not hard to see how this record inspired the players, and despite his apparent uncertainty with the media, he commanded real respect. Souness (1985: 49) argues that although 'he may have been regarded as a fatherly figure by the supporters . . ., let me tell you, he ruled at Anfield with a rod of iron . . . He was a commanding man and there were few who dared mess around with him. If we looked as though we were becoming a little complacent . . . Bob would say, "If you have all had enough of winning, come and see me and I will sell the lot of you and buy 11 new players"'.

In terms of playing style, the Liverpool way was firmly entrenched, and while Paisley was busy integrating players such as Phil Neal (right-back), Joey Jones (left-back), Terry McDermott and Jimmy Case (midfield) into the team during his first two seasons in charge, fundamentally the passing game remained central. Neal (1981: 148–9) underlines two simple foundations of Paisley's approach: "'If the ball's controlled, keep it controlled." By this he means that, if you receive a controlled pass along the ground, give a controlled pass along the ground . . . Another saying of the Boss is that the longer you keep the ball the less time the next man to receive it has. This has become known as the "early ball" game.' A crucial aspect of Paisley's approach was the search for players who could display flexibility out on the pitch, who were intelligent enough to make decisions and communicate with each other during the maelstrom of fiercely competitive matches, and who did not 'hide', but actively sought out responsibility. As Tom Saunders, long-serving Youth development coach, observed, 'I can't recall a time here where players have been looking towards the bench for advice for what should happen next . . . It's a decision-making game, and you want men who can assume responsibility and make decisions on the pitch while the game's going on' (Taylor and Ward, 1993: 174). Neal (1981: 144) makes the point that 'the management put absolute trust in the players. They never clock us in and out but trust us to be a credit to ourselves and the club'.

Ray Kennedy, whom Paisley famously 'converted' from his previous role as a striker with the Arsenal double-winning side of 1971, into a graceful, yet strong midfield passer, was viewed by Paisley (1983: 14–17; see also Lees and Kennedy, 1994) as 'one of Liverpool's greatest players and probably the most under-rated . . . his contribution to Liverpool's achievements was enormous and his consistency remarkable'. The qualities he admired in Kennedy, apart from his origins in the north-east, were his 'ability to open up a game and give you the width of the park . . . He had so much control and was such a good shielder of a ball that an opponent virtually had to knock him over to take the ball off him. He had a great footballing brain, and his striker's instinct in the box never left him'. This stress upon intelligence, and its flexible application on the pitch, were hallmarks of Paisley's favourite players; Alan Hansen confirms that 'Bob Paisley used to say the first two yards of professional football was in the head. When he first said that, I thought, "What a load of rubbish", but the more I played the game, the more I realised he was spot on' (Taylor and Ward, 1995: 287).

In Graeme Souness (bought in January 1978 from Middlesbrough), Alan Hansen (who came from Partick Thistle in April 1977) and Kenny Dalglish (bought from Celtic at the start of 1977/78, to replace Kevin Keegan), Paisley created the spine of a team that had intelligence and drive, and that went on, in 1978/79, to win the League in perhaps the most complete fashion ever. As Phil Neal argued, Paisley had 'developed a team that, at one stage, I felt could possibly run itself. He had so many leaders within the team, particularly the '79 season, when we scored 85 goals and conceded only 16 goals in the league' (Taylor and Ward, 1993:167). This average of two goals per game or above was matched by the Liverpool Championship-winning teams of 1982/83, 1985/86, 1987/88 and 1989/90, and it gives the lie to an oft-repeated claim that this particular Liverpool side put the accent too heavily on defensive qualities, and were too ready to grind out efficient 1–0 victories (of which there were six in the League). In short, the accusation has been that this side was dour, mechanical, and lacking flair. What is at issue here is precisely the question of the club culture and playing style of a team.

Though Liverpool in the late 1970s and early 1980s are seen by many football fans (and even by some Kopites) as an efficient 'machine for winning', while the late 1980s team (of John Barnes, Peter Beardsley and John Aldridge) are contrasted as 'the great entertainers', the truth is much more complex. What is satisfying and aesthetically pleasing to Liverpool supporters may well incorporate elements from both of these stereotypes, but my argument is that 'the Liverpool Way' emphasizes the hard work involved in winning, and then repeatedly winning over and over, season after season. As soon as the Championship or Cup is safely tucked away, the celebrations barely over, Bob or Joe would be moving on, the slate wiped clean, reminding the players that it would be more difficult next year. Dalglish (1996: 143) illustrates Ronnie Moran's deliberately low-key reaction to a hard-won victory, '"I've got a job for another week."' Souness (1985: 52) notes that Paisley 'would moan and grumble . . . and generally bring us down to earth. The only time he would relent and hand round a bit of praise and a few laurel wreaths was when we had actually won a trophy. Next morning it would be back to basics and start all over again'.

Necessarily, if this slightly puritanical ethos is one of the primary aspects of the club's self-image or character, then playing with an ostentatious or devil-may-care flamboyance (*extravagance* is a better term here, conveying a derogatory and condescending impression) is rightly to be mistrusted. It is ludicrous, of course, to suggest that Liverpool in these years did not play with style; it was simply that Liverpool's aesthetic was not the same as, say, Manchester United's emphasis upon glamour (some Kopites refer disparagingly to Manchester United as 'the Glams', among other epithets). When Manchester United finally won the Championship (for the first time since the 1960s) in 1992/3 and then again in 1993/4, it was generally portrayed as a triumph for this glamorous self-image, as a vindication of their club's identity, although in neither season did they average two goals per game.

Paisley, himself, saw the 1978/79 team as 'the best of the Liverpool Championship sides I have been associated with in one capacity or another' (Paisley, 1983: 22). Again, continuity was vital. In winning the Championship in 1965/66, Liverpool had used only fourteen players, the lowest total in the history of the League, with five ever-presents (Lawrence, Byrne, Yeats, Smith and Callaghan). In 1978/79, the total was fifteen, with Clemence, Neal, Ray Kennedy and Dalglish ever-present, Souness missing only one game, and Thompson, Case, Alan Kennedy, Hansen and McDermott all featuring in thirty-four matches or more. For Paisley, this record, while partly a question of luck, has to do with the 'factor of competition, which makes players unwilling to drop out because they're worried about getting back in, particularly when the team is winning' (Paisley, 1983: 118).

Significantly, however, the avoidance of injury cannot be reduced to fortune or the willpower of players, it is also a matter of the correct physical and mental preparation, and here not only was Paisley, as we have mentioned above, a very accurate diagnostician, but he also firmly believed in a training regime that combined established principles (the programme was designed to integrate skill, strength, stamina, speed and flexibility), with the need for flexible responses. Attention to detail was critical, and the desk diaries that accumulated season by season in the manager's office, with entries almost every day, dealing with all types of apparently inconsequential material, 'ranging from weather conditions for a match in September to the fact that a certain player was late for training on a day in March' (1983: 13), provided a mine of information regarding the raw materials available to the staff. This intelligence-gathering was unobtrusive, and not 'scientific' in any dogmatic way, but Paisley enjoyed studying players and their physical and mental responses, and it was no accident that his 'relaxation' was often spent in the company of horse-racing trainers (such as Frank Carr). Souness (1985: 52) provides a good example of Paisley's love of racing and gambling, a passion he shared with many other working men in the city, and several of his players: 'He was certainly keen on the horses and I have even known him come in at half-time – when things were going well – and tell the boys which horse won the 3.30 at Catterick.'

Unlike Shankly, Paisley's obsession with the game was tempered by his methodical approach, and at least one of the players who served under both managers, Chris Lawler, 'found Bob much easier to deal with than Shanks, because he listened to your problems. Shanks would just ignore you' (Hey, 1997: 186; see also Bowler, 1996: 276). With a core of five of the 1978/79 team still available (Neal, Thompson, Hansen, Dalglish, Souness) and the addition of players who became regulars in the early 1980s (Bruce Grobbelaar in goal, Mark Lawrenson at centre-half, Sammy Lee, Craig Johnston and Ronnie Whelan in midfield, and Ian Rush up front), in 1982/83, in Paisley's final season, Liverpool continued to adhere to the same basic philosophy of how the game should be played, and very similar methods for transferring those principles from training ground to match conditions.

Allez les Rouges: Liverpool's Playing Style and European Football

We don't go around with our eyes shut (Bob Paisley in Hey, 1997: 188).

We learned in Europe that you can't score a goal every time you get the ball (Geoff Twentyman in Bowler, 1996: 267).

Liverpool's emphasis upon passing the ball, maintaining options for the player in possession through unceasing movement of, and off, the ball, and defending collectively when the ball was lost, was not necessarily European in its inspiration. However, it is true that Liverpool's style did develop through the assimilation of new ideas and tactical ploys, as they qualified annually for European competition from 1964 until 1985, when, after Heysel, the club was banned from Europe until 1991. It is not the intention here to provide a record of Liverpool's participation in the Fairs'/Uefa Cup, the Cup Winners' Cup or the European Cup (see Hale and Ponting, 1992 and Kelly, 1992), but to offer some thoughts on the more general impact that playing in Europe had upon the playing styles adopted.

Even as early as 1964, Liverpool's first season in the European Cup, the League Champions were exposed to influences that would help shape their approach to the game well into the future. Although a good deal of controversy still reigns over the semi-final elimination at the hands of Internazionale in the San Siro (Bowler, 1996: 228–234; Hale and Ponting, 1992: 18–21), the home leg was judged by many to be one of the finest games of the era. The Inter side, famed for its *catenaccio* defence, and coached by Helenio Herrera, had proved their credentials by defeating Real Madrid in the previous year's final. After the first leg, Herrera was full of praise for Liverpool's tactical nous, but the second leg proved a bitter reverse, with complaints by Liverpool about their preparation being affected by Milanese supporters, and accusations of match-fixing after two of the goals were fiercely contested by Shankly.

Liverpool took at least two significant lessons from this experience; in the future, when playing abroad, there was a strong sense of suspicion regarding the conditions that awaited the visitors, on and off the pitch. Undoubtedly, travel and facilities in the 1960s and 1970s were not comparable with the standards enjoyed by subsequent teams, but there are a number of anecdotes relating to these exaggerated concerns and fears, including Liverpool's decision to take their own food and bottled water, to arrive only the afternoon before the match, and to try to isolate the team from any problems that might arise (Taylor and Ward, 1993: 185–93; Paisley, 1983: 50–70; Souness, 1985: 94–106; Dalglish, 1996: 103–19). These precautions maybe served a dual purpose, in building team spirit in perceived conditions of adversity, and in concentrating the players' minds; eventually, Liverpool were capable of absorbing hostility and intimidation, settling themselves, and imposing their own game.

Second, Liverpool learned the virtues of patience and possession. Arguably, it was through the experience of playing over two legs in European competition that Liverpool refined their playing style, adopting elements of the continental game which were complementary to the acknowledged strengths of the English game. This produced a 'measured aggression' (Bowler, 1996: 232) that emphasized control of the tempo of the match, self-discipline and a ruthless streak. On the pitch, away from home, Liverpool teams attempted to maintain possession in a systematic fashion, often moving the ball around the back four (including the goalkeeper), frustrating the opposition and quietening the crowd. Attempting to 'draw the opposition onto them', Liverpool hoped to exploit counter-attacking opportunities, as they arose, but they wouldn't be unduly concerned if the match was played at a slow tempo. If, by chance, they fell behind, Liverpool learned through bitter experience that they risked more misery by 'chasing the game', throwing caution and discipline to the wind. A 1–0 defeat was not disastrous, and could often be repaid with interest at Anfield. The Ajax defeat in December 1966 (7–3 on aggregate, after a 5–1 reverse in the first leg in Amsterdam) was put down by Shankly, at least in part, to loss of discipline after conceding two goals in the opening quarter of an hour of the away leg, although in hindsight the quality of the Ajax team ought not to be dismissed (Bowler, 1996: 250–1; Paisley, 1983: 54; Callaghan, 1975: 41; Barend and Van Dorp, 1999).

Later on, after a damaging defeat by Red Star Belgrade (4–2 on aggregate, with 2–1 defeats in both legs of the second round tie) in the 1973 European Cup, Bob Paisley attempted to derive the lessons that could be drawn:

> Our approach was a bit frantic. We treated every match like a war. The strength of British football lay in our challenge for the ball, but the continentals took that away from us by learning how to intercept. We discovered it was no use winning the ball if you finished up on your backside. The top Europeans showed us how to break out of defence effectively. The pace of their movement was dictated by the first pass. We had to learn how to be patient like that, and think about the next two or three moves ahead when we had the ball. (David Lacey, *Guardian*, 15 February 1996)

According to Paisley (1983: 59), Dalglish (1996: 107–9) and Souness (1985: 97), the team of the late 1970s and early 1980s, even with two European Cups under their belts (Borussia Moenchengladbach in 1977, in Rome; Bruges in 1978, at Wembley), still managed to commit a similar costly error against Nottingham Forest in the away leg of the first round in 1978/79: 'When we were a goal down we were looking for an equaliser instead of accepting that as a reasonable result in the first leg of a European Cup tie . . .', said Paisley, while Dalglish considered that 'this naive reaction probably stemmed from the fact that we were playing familiar League opponents'. Souness described it 'as one of the biggest lessons I have ever received in European football'.

However, the value of an away goal was also learned after experiencing elimination by Vitoria Setubal in 1969/70 (losing 1–0 in Portugal, before winning the return 3–2) and by Ferencvaros in 1974/75, when a 1–1 home draw was followed by a frustrating 0–0 in Hungary (Ferencvaros are distinguished as the first continental team to win at Anfield in January 1968, 1–0 on the night and 2–0 on aggregate, and also as the only side to beat Liverpool twice over two legs). Dalglish recognized early in the 1980s, when Liverpool defeated Athletic Bilbao 1–0 away after a goalless draw at Anfield, on the way to winning the European Cup for the fourth time, that 'the important thing is that the opposition haven't scored; many good teams have fallen out on the away goals rule'. One of Liverpool's best-ever results in Europe proved the same point, when in the European Cup semi-final in 1981, a 0–0 home draw with Bayern Munich was followed by a thrilling 1–1 result away, with Ray Kennedy scoring with fewer than 10 minutes left, and Karl Heinz Rummenigge's equalizer not enough to stop Liverpool's qualification on the away goals rule. Sammy Lee had famously man-marked Bayern's most dangerous creative force, Paul Breitner, out of the game, illustrating that Liverpool were now also prepared to adjust their tactics to take account of opposition strengths. Souness (1985: 50) recalls that Paisley 'loved that game', and many Liverpool supporters would also have it very close to the top of any list of favourite matches. These lessons from playing in Europe had to be relearned, sometimes painfully, for a new era and by new players, when Liverpool were readmitted to European competition in 1991. For instance, defeat by the single goal at Anfield, in the second leg of a second round UEFA Cup tie, against the moderate Danish side Brondby in 1995/96, had followed what many considered a 'tie-winning' scoreless draw in Copenhagen.

On occasion, of course, Liverpool learned by simply coming up against talented and committed opponents, who outplayed them and deserved their victories. Although comprehensive defeat was rare enough, and the respect given to a team such as Ajax may have appeared grudging, the Liverpool staff were quick to recognize and appreciate quality football. One example of such a defeat was provided by the 1979/80 first-round European Cup exit against the Soviet Union's finest side, Dynamo Tbilisi. The Georgians lost 2–1 at Anfield in the opening leg, but several observers judged that 'only abysmal finishing prevented them inflicting a home defeat on the English Champions' (Hale and Ponting, 1992: 136–7; Paisley, 1983: 60–1; Kelly, 1992: 104–5; Dalglish, 1996: 109–10; Souness, 1985: 98–100).

Although Liverpool had played teams from East Germany (Dynamo Berlin, Dynamo Dresden three times), Poland (Wroclaw), Hungary (Ferencvaros, Honved), Romania (Dinamo Bucharest, Petrolul Ploiesti) and Yugoslavia (Red Star Belgrade), this was the first meeting with a team from the Soviet Union. It was clear that the playing style of the Soviets was not dissimilar to Liverpool's, based as it was upon accurate, economical passing and good movement, controlled build-up play and an ability to interchange positions. Players of the calibre of Chivadze (who scored Dynamo's goal), Shengeliya, Kipiani and Gutsaev also had skills to match the best in Europe. Significantly, this side seemed unruffled by the intimidating reception they received, and they were temperamentally strong, not a feature then associated with East European or Soviet sides. Drawing in Tbilisi

0–0 at half-time, Liverpool still had hopes of scraping through, but a goal by Gutsaev meant Liverpool were forced to attack, and conceded two more late goals on the counter. Bob Paisley alluded to the difficult travelling arrangements and the players being woken by fan demonstrations in the early hours of the morning of the game, but still knew Tbilisi were 'a very confident and skilful side'. Typically, Paisley 'had a long chat over a drink' with Tbilisi coach Akhalkatsi, partly no doubt in an effort to glean potentially useful information, but also because here was a man who clearly shared similar ideas about the way to play football. Dalglish reckoned 'We deserved to fail . . . Liverpool were simply beaten by the better side'; for Souness, despite some gamesmanship, Tbilisi 'were undoubtedly the better side and good value for their eventual . . . victory'. Dynamo lost in the second round to Hamburg, but this excellent team gained some reward in 1981, winning the Cup Winners' Cup against Carl Zeiss Jena.

Since Liverpool's return to European competition, the record has not been particularly impressive. An excellent opportunity to complete the full set of European club trophies, by adding the Cup Winners' Cup in 1996/97, was squandered with a disastrous performance in the away leg in the semi-final at Paris Saint-Germain. Still, it was seen in the late 1990s that with qualification for the Champions' League being a top priority for Gérard Houllier's new team, Liverpool would need to adapt their playing style to such a different format if they were again to take on and succeed against the Continent's most accomplished sides.

Some People Think It's Fun to Entertain: The Liverpool Way in a Changing Football World

> Life at Liverpool was simple. No wild predictions, no arrogance, no petulance (Dalglish, 1996: 143).

> The largest part of our game is still ball control, accurate passing and good movement. And it's also about patience, which demands intense concentration . . . The perfect player hasn't been born, so you have to ensure that you can cover people's weaknesses within the framework of the team (Paisley in Hey, 1997: 190).

In the domestic sphere, Liverpool continued to dominate English football, first under Joe Fagan, who like Bob Paisley had risen through the boot room ranks, and was by no means sure that the manager's job was his destiny but took it on because he was asked to by the club, and then Kenny Dalglish, who became player-manager in 1985 (Kelly, 1995; Dalglish, 1996; McIlvanney, 1995: 56–9). The style of preparation and play didn't change radically, and the football and administrative sides of the club remained under the guidance of most of the same individuals.

Of course, there were new faces on the playing staff from time to time (with John Wark, Jan Molby, Gary Gillespie, Kevin MacDonald, Michael Robinson and Paul Walsh all playing quite substantial roles under Fagan), but in general Liverpool supporters became adept at comparing (rather than contrasting) individuals who performed similar functions within the overall continuity of the team pattern. Defensively, the core of the team under Fagan's managership remained Alan Kennedy, Neal, Hansen and Lawrenson, with Grobbelaar in goal. Remarkably, in 1983/84, four of these five were ever-present in the league, and Neal missed only one game. Part of the explanation for this was undoubtedly the intelligence and experience of these players; as Paisley pointed out, 'If you can win the ball by interception [rather than tackling] it not only cuts down on injuries . . . it also means you can use the ball better because you've got it cleanly, you're not at full stretch, and you're in space.' (Hey, 1997: 190–1). In midfield, Liverpool relied upon the complementary virtues of good passing, strong running, physical and mental toughness, characterized by Souness, Lee, and Johnston, with Steve Nicol, Ronnie Whelan, Molby and Wark all breaking through. Up front, Dalglish and Rush continued to work as a genuine partnership (42 league goals combined in 1982/83, 39 in 1983/84, 20 in 1984/85). Never did a player bear out Bob Paisley's maxim, about the pace of a footballer comprising mental as well as physical quickness, so completely as Dalglish did. His manager stressed that:

> The judgement in Kenny's passing bears the hallmark of great golf shots. And he can read ground conditions the way cricketers can. He has the uncanny knack of knowing a ball will bounce, carry or skid on a particular surface . . . Kenny can make a team spark collectively with his gifted ability to read situations, and offer other players so many options with his wide-ranging distribution and vision. Of all the players I have played alongside, managed and coached in more than forty years at Anfield, he is the most talented. When Kenny shines, the whole team is illuminated (Paisley, 1983: 87–8).

When Joe Fagan, a Liverpudlian by birth (as opposed to the honorary status conferred upon Shankly and Paisley), became manager, he was endorsed by the latter for the telling reason that 'above all, he was not the sort of man who was going to come in with different ideas that could have ruined the club' (Paisley, 1990: 33). It was certainly never held against him that, when offered the chance to sign for Liverpool by George Kay in 1938, Fagan opted to join Manchester City, and then had to wait nine years for his debut! Like Paisley, Fagan was 'reliable rather than flashy' as a player, and was equally dependable as one of the backroom staff. Brought to the club from Rochdale by Phil Taylor in 1958, he was already known to Shankly, who had tried in vain to sign him when manager at Grimsby, and was kept on as reserve-team coach. An undemonstrative and self-deprecating man, Fagan's players generally recall a sense of their manager as one of a number of influential members of the staff (alongside Ronnie Moran and Roy Evans), lacking ego, but determined to overcome 'the fear of disappointing the supporters' (Paisley, 1990: 34).

If this description sounds slightly dismissive, that the Liverpool 'system' was merely kept ticking over under Fagan's leadership, then it should be recalled that in his first year, Liverpool completed a historic treble (winning the Championship from Southampton, the League Cup for the fourth time in a row against Everton, and a fourth European Cup against Roma, in Rome). This 'fine-tuning' also produced another appearance in the European Cup final in 1984/85, and a semi-final exit in the FA Cup, although in the end it was a barren year, Liverpool's first season without a trophy of any shape or size for nine years. Fagan had to make do without Souness, who had decamped to Sampdoria, but exemplified the Liverpool way with his pragmatic insistence: 'Souness has gone; forget about him, we've got a job to do without him' (Ponting, 1996: 198). So, while it is fair to say that the circumstances of Fagan's leave-taking (after the chaos of Heysel) overshadowed to some extent his team's achievements, nonetheless, his role over twenty-seven years at Liverpool ought to be remembered more often than it is.

It is not possible here to detail the beginning or acceleration of the apparent decay of the 'Liverpool Way' in the 1990s, but it is clear that under managers Dalglish (1986–91), Souness (1991–94) and Evans (1994–98), although all three were steeped in the traditions that had brought the club unparalleled success, the football world was rapidly changing, and Liverpool could not remain immune from these developments. The debate regarding the responsibility for Liverpool's relatively turbulent attempts to adjust has recently been joined with a vengeance, with revealing (though, of course, partisan) accounts by ex-managers Dalglish (1996) and Souness (1999; see also Kelly, 1994), as well as by players who each spent a decade or more at Anfield (Barnes, 1999: 237–56; Molby, 1999: 161–99; Hansen, 1999). The significant point here is that all of these accounts stress the deep impression created by the individual experience of the 'Liverpool Way'. For Barnes (1999: 109–17), when he joined Liverpool in 1987, they had 'an instantly recognisable shape that was unique to them . . . Anfield's emphasis was on passing the ball and keeping moves simple. Players fitted into the Liverpool way while giving it an added dimension'. This structure or pattern, what Barnes refers to as a team's 'DNA', was based upon retaining control of the ball, although 'as a footballing breed, the English never treat possession with the reverence it deserves. Possession is almost a dirty word. Liverpool are the best in England at keeping possession, but send them into Europe, against a team like Celta Vigo [who eliminated Liverpool from the UEFA Cup in 1998/99, 4–1 on aggregate], and Liverpool look ordinary'.

All of these ex-players have continued to involve themselves fully in the game away from Liverpool, whether as managers or coaches (Barnes at Celtic, Molby at Swansea and Kidderminster, Dalglish at Blackburn and Newcastle, and Souness at Galatasaray, Southampton, Torino, Benfica and Blackburn, not to mention other former Liverpool players currently or recently in management such as Kevin Keegan, Phil Neal, John Toshack, Ronnie Whelan, Nigel Spackman, Steve McMahon, David Hodgson, John Aldridge, Nigel Clough), or alternatively as media pundits and commentators. (As well as Hansen and Lawrenson, who has also had a spell in management, on *Match of the Day*, other ex-Liverpool players are continually to be found on radio or TV broadcasts: Barry Venison, David Fairclough, Jim Beglin, Ian St John, Michael Robinson, in Spain, to name only a few.) Their contributions are of a variable standard, but they are undeniably informed by their playing experiences, and their opinions on the game often reflect a sense of attachment to Liverpool's playing style. Of course, despite the 'revolutionary' appointment of Houllier, and his fellow French coach, Patrice Berguès, it also remains the case that Liverpool have a large number of their former players still closely involved in the running of the club (Phil Thompson as Houllier's assistant manager, Sammy Lee as coach, Steve Heighway in charge of the Youth Academy, Ron Yeats as chief scout).

There clearly remains something significant with regard to the footballing education received by these men at Liverpool and, despite undoubted differences that exist in terms of the level at which these former players are contributing to the game, it is nonetheless hard to imagine any of them actively renouncing their identification with the 'Liverpool way'. Even those who spent only a relatively short time on the playing staff, or played in the more recent, less successful, era, appear still to have found the experience crucial to their ideas about how they want football to be played.

There is certainly some truth in the suggestion that in the 1990s, as Giulianotti has posited (1999: 142), the increasing 'inter-penetration of sporting aesthetics, techniques and tactics . . . [means] hybridity can only expand as we enter the post-modern milieu of increased labour [player] migration, television coverage and international competition'. However, this apparent convergence in playing styles is mediated by the particular cultural traditions and identities of individual clubs. For Liverpool, the death of Bob Paisley in February 1996 was, of course, felt with great emotion, perhaps the more so because supporters recognized that here, genuinely, was definitive proof that an era in football had passed. Several of the obituaries, including those in the Liverpool fanzine, *Through the Wind and Rain* (no. 30, Spring 1996), drew attention to the enormous changes that had occurred in the football world since Paisley had stepped down as manager. In December 1999, to mark the fortieth anniversary of Bill Shankly's arrival at Anfield, prior to the home match against Coventry many of the players from the 1960s and 1970s paraded in front of the Kop, and there were fulsome, moving tributes paid, with nostalgic reminiscing for older players and supporters alike. However, there was also some ambivalence, not with regard to the great man's legacy, but because such an occasion would inevitably overshadow the first tentative steps that Houllier's young team were taking on the road to re-establishing Liverpool as a footballing force in the land. The club and its supporters are in the process of wrestling with this inescapable dialectic; all associated with Liverpool are proud of a past that deserves to be celebrated, particularly in these days where football's 'history' appears to have begun with the Premiership in 1992, but building for a successful future requires a recognition that the game has changed radically. This has occurred on the pitch, in the styles of play adopted, though perhaps this aspect of modernization has not been as dramatic as the upheavals in the 'social world' in which football exists.

If, when, Liverpool do win the League Championship once more, it will be understood (and felt) by the many thousands who celebrate it, including Gérard Houllier himself, as a continuation of the footballing tradition represented by men such as Bill Shankly, Bob Paisley and Joe Fagan. More importantly, it will also be seen by a large proportion of those who celebrate as a vindication of the wider moral, social and political values enshrined by these men. After all, in order to stay the same, things must change.

References

Barend, F. and van Dorp, H. (1999) *Ajax, Barcelona, Cruyff: The ABC of an Obstinate Maestro*, London: Bloomsbury.
Barnes, J. (1999) *John Barnes: The Autobiography*, London: Headline.
Bowler, D. (1996) *Shanks: The Authorised Biography of Bill Shankly*, London: Orion.
Callaghan, I. and Keith, J. (1975) *The Ian Callaghan Story*, London: Quartet Books.
Dalglish, K. with Winter, H. (1996) *Dalglish: My Autobiography*, London: Hodder & Stoughton.
Downing, D. (1999) *Passovotchka: Moscow Dynamo in Britain, 1945*, London: Bloomsbury.
Giulianotti, R. (1999) *Football: A Sociology of the Global Game*, Cambridge: Polity.
Hale, S. and Ponting, I. (1992) *Liverpool in Europe*, Enfield: Guinness.
Hansen, A. (1999) *A Matter of Opinion*, London: Partridge.
Hey, S. (1997) *A Golden Sky: The Liverpool Dream Team*, Edinburgh: Mainstream.
Keith, J. (1998) *Shanks for the Memory*, London: Robson.
Kelly, S. (1992) *Liverpool in Europe: The Complete Record from 1964*, London: Collins Willow.
—— (1994) *Graeme Souness: A Soccer Revolutionary*, London: Headline.
—— (1995) *Dalglish*, London: Headline.

—— (1996) *The Illustrated History of Liverpool, 1892–1996*, London: Hamlyn.

Lees, A. and Kennedy, R. (1994) *Ray of Hope: The Ray Kennedy Story*, London: Penguin.

Liversedge, S. (1995) *Liverpool from the Inside*, Edinburgh: Mainstream.

McIlvanney, H. (1995) *McIlvanney on Football*, Edinburgh: Mainstream.

Molby, J. (1999) *Jan the Man: From Anfield to Vetch Field*, London: Victor Gollancz.

Neal, P. (1981) *Attack from the Back*, London: Arthur Barker.

—— (1986) *Life at the Kop*, London: Queen Anne Press.

Paisley, B. (1983) *Bob Paisley: A Lifetime in Football*, London: Arthur Barker.

—— (1990) *My Fifty Golden Reds*, Warrington: Front Page Books.

Ponting, I. (1996) *Liverpool Player by Player*, London: Hamlyn.

Rush, I. (1986) *Rush: Ian Rush's Autobiography*, London: Grafton Books.

Souness, G. with Harris, B. (1985) *No Half Measures*, London: CollinsWillow.

Souness, G. with Ellis, M. (1999) *Souness: The Management Years*, London: André Deutsch.

Taylor, R. and Ward, A. with Williams, J. (1993) *Three Sides of the Mersey: An Oral History of Everton, Liverpool and Tranmere Rovers*, London: Robson.

Taylor, R. and Ward, A. (1995) *Kicking and Screaming: An Oral History of Football in England*, London: Robson.

Wagg, S. (1984) *The Football World*, Brighton: Harvester.

Yeats, R. (1966) *Soccer with a Mersey Beat*, London: Pelham Books.

−5−

Kopites, 'Scallies' and Liverpool Fan Cultures: Tales of Triumph and Disasters
John Williams

Introduction

I want to look in this chapter at the changes in support and supporter styles around Liverpool FC from the early 1960s to the present day. I'll talk here mainly about younger (though not always 'youth') male supporter traditions – there is a focus on female supporters of the club in Chapter Nine – though I do draw on the perspectives of older fans, too. I want to stress, strongly, that the overall character of Liverpool fans owes much to the contribution of its often neglected older fans and perhaps especially to its female followers and their welcome and resolute refusal to be excluded from these cultural 'male preserves' in the city (see Chapter Nine, and also Williams and Woodhouse, 1999).

I also want to try to say something here about the connections between local oral traditions, music cultures and football fandom in Liverpool, especially in the formative years of the Kop as a 'singing end' in the 1960s. In doing this I am trying to respond to calls for more work on football fans which concentrates on the specific, local traditions of club support and the 'cultural power' that supporters exert in relation to the sport and to their own clubs (see Clarke, 1991).

In the early 1960s, of course, Liverpool FC was becoming an international focus because of the synergy between music and football in the city and the cultural inventiveness of its fans; in the 1970s the spotlight fell on Liverpool because of the excellence and dominance of the club's extraordinary football team and management; in the 1980s it was more footballing excellence, but also an altogether harsher glare on the character of the city following the fatal hooliganism at Heysel and the crowd disaster at Hillsborough; by the 1990s the focus was on the prospects for reviving the club's football status in a new, global era, but also on the new economics of the sport as the club struggled to adapt to the new era of the game's development, eventually investing in a new business structure, a talented foreign coach and a roster of imported foreign players (see Chapter Ten). I want to try to cover all these issues here. I'll begin with some opening comments on the Liverpool Kop.

The early Kop

Following the arrival of the more media-conscious Bill Shankly and the *footballing* success he brought to the club in the early 1960s, at the slowly modernizing Anfield base the main Liverpool home terrace, the cavernous Spion Kop itself, was about to become something of a focus for national, and even international, celebrity. When the Kop played out its final hours as a standing terrace in 1994, press and TV crews from all over the globe came to record the event. Arthur Hopcraft's early insightful and essentially sympathetic profile of the Liverpool Kop, and of other English football terraced ends of the 1960s – 'the privileged places of working-class communion' (1971: 161) remains one of the classic pieces of pre-Hillsborough football writing about standing football crowds in England. Interestingly, what Hopcraft seemed to find alluring and impressive about terrace life in the 1960s was, by the early 1990s, being quoted at length in official reports as being exactly the reasons why the football terraces had to be left to the past (Taylor, 1990). For these reasons at least, it is worth quoting his description at some length here. For Hopcraft (1971: 162), these great terraces were:

> . . . [H]ideously uncomfortable. The steps are as greasy as a school playground lavatory in the rain. The air is rancid with beer and onions and belching and worse. The language is a gross purple of obscenity. When the crowd surges at a shot or a collision near a corner flag a man or a boy, and sometimes a girl, can be lifted off the ground in the crush, as if by some massive, soft-sided crane and dangled about for minutes on end, perhaps never getting back to within four or five steps of the spot from which the monster made its bite. In this incomparable entanglement of bodies and emotions lies the heart of the fan's commitment to football. The senses of triumph and dejection experienced here are never quite matched in any seated section of a football ground. It is the physical interaction which makes the monster the figure of unavoidable dreams it becomes. To kill off this animal, this monstrous, odorous national pet would be a cruel act of denial to us.

In the early 1960s in Liverpool, and with the Kop in its early pomp, many Liverpool football supporters, mainly working-class men, spent some of their greatest communal moments grasped and flung around in its lurching, soft-sided grip. But the Kop's effects were not always so benign; it could also bite. In December 1966 the usual tens of fans who were treated for injuries, as the giant beast rippled back and forth, were multiplied tenfold as at least 200 supporters were carried out injured from a steaming, packed terrace as Liverpool tried, unsuccessfully, to rescue a first-leg disaster in a European Cup tie against the rising Dutch Champions, Ajax. Inglis (1996: 219), perhaps unfairly, describes the Kop as being 'a fairly unmanageable terrace throughout its 88 year history'. In fact, the Kop was often described by many Liverpool supporters, male and female, as being the 'safest' place in the ground, especially in the 1970s and 1980s (see Chapter Nine). But it could also play with, frighten and damage even its staunchest allies.

Finally, these still great civic spaces in the city, the football terraces at both Liverpool and Everton, acted – as they did in parts of North London and elsewhere in de-industrializing Britain (see Robins and Cohen, 1978) – as a stable point of reference, identification and *belonging* in the early 1960s, in a city which had been torn about by the modernizing planners charged with clearing the Liverpool city centre of its poverty-infested but communal bullrings and back-to-back houses (see Channon, 1976: Ch. 1). With working-class families now decanted from the centre to high-rise blocks along the Everton Valley and to new, isolated and unemployment-blackspot housing estates in Huyton, Netherley and Kirkby on the periphery and outside the city boundaries, the two football clubs acted as collective points of city communion, continuity and neighbourhood solidarity, especially for working-class men. In 1969, the Liverpool city council called a belated halt to its high-rise relocation policy, but by now its slogan of 'City of Change and Challenge' resonated barely at all with those who had seen the Liverpool city centre, and its tough local communities, effectively gutted. Observed one commentator of the time, 'Not only in the major operation of its heart has Liverpool come near losing its soul – drastic surgery *outside* the central area had grave psychological consequences' (Channon, 1976: 31).

Football, Youth Culture and Music in Liverpool in the 1960s

Things other than urban disruption and football were also already stirring, loudly, in Liverpool at this time. This was a heady period, especially for male youth in the city. The so-called 'Mersey Sound', led by the international pop music success of the Beatles, had thrust Liverpool into the world spotlight. The city's football clubs were also enjoying success together – Everton's 'school of science' had won the League title in 1963 – in a way seldom experienced even in the long history of the professional game in Liverpool. Even the new 'modern' Labour Government of 1964 was led by a Prime Minister, Harold Wilson, who represented a Liverpool constituency, Huyton. Wilson also cleverly used his local connections to emphasize the supposed youthful 'energy' of his new administration, especially in his carefully prepared publicity shoots with the ubiquitous Beatles. This was also a period in which British drama, theatre, and popular culture, more generally, celebrated specifically northern working-class traditions, probably for the first time, for example, in the new British 'kitchen-sink' realist TV dramas – including the Liverpool-based successful police series, Z Cars – and in the popular 'realist' wave of British films and novels of the time. Culturally, at least, it was a relatively good time to be young, working-class, a football fan and from Liverpool in the early 1960s.

At the same time, as new traditions for travelling and watching football began to emerge in England in the 1960s, with younger supporters at the forefront, brash young supporters of Everton and Liverpool were already developing an early reputation for football 'trouble'. Early themes here focused on the 'instrumental' nature of Merseyside football delinquency; on theft, for example. A police sergeant in Liverpool told the author James McClure that in the late 1950s and early 1960s, even before 'football special' trains arrived, unwary football visitors arriving in Liverpool by train would be directed by locals into Gerard Gardens or other city housing estates to be stripped by waiting predators: 'We used to have them trooping into St. Anne's Street [police station] without their coats, their boots, and their shoes: their money had been taken off them and everything' (McClure, 1980: 269). A popular club comedian joke in the early 1960s was also that Liverpool FC supporters could be spotted by the 'railway carriage door' they were supposed to wear in their jacket lapel (having wrenched it from its moorings on a football trip).

By November 1964 the national press was reporting that 'shopkeepers lock up when Everton are in town', and local police forces were already promising 'get tough' measures when Liverpool fans were visiting (Dunning et al., 1988). In fact, of course, when Celtic fans came to Anfield for a UEFA Cup Winners Cup tie in 1966, and fought before and after the game, littering the pitch with bottles during it, this was easily the most serious crowd trouble yet seen in the Anfield part of the city. Some of this early English focus on Merseysiders as hooligans was clearly media hype and some was a consequence of the sheer numbers of younger Merseyside fans who were now travelling away with their successful football clubs, unchaperoned, almost for the first time. But some was also the result of the convenient 'export' of aspects of real cultural traditions in the city. Such traditions had been forged out of and around the trading industries and cultures of Liverpool – especially those in the docks – and also the perceived 'necessary' resort by young men, sometimes, to theft and to barter in a city where unskilled labour, high levels of unemployment, routine street-smartness, and merciless masculine status hierarchies were long-established as key recurring features.

At the same time as this more 'subterranean' reputation of Liverpool fans was spreading among some rival fans, the mainstream public 'reading' of the Kop – and therefore of Liverpool supporters at large – was very different. The regular televising of football highlights on the BBC began in Britain in August 1964, at Anfield. The choice of venue was highly appropriate. Liverpool were League Champions, and the club was guaranteed a large and vociferous following, especially as the British pop industry, a growing cultural and economic force in the early 1960s, was then dominated by Brian Epstein, the Beatles, and other Liverpool artistes. One emerging local band, Gerry and the Pacemakers, musicians and also fans of the club, reached the top of the singles charts late in 1963 with a reworking of a grandiose old musicals' standard, 'You'll never walk alone'. The themes of the song – struggle, pride, community, 'hope in your heart' – seemed ideal for the trials and emotions of football fans, and its 'walk on' chorus, slowly, began to be sung on parts of the Kop. (The later, impressive, Kop anthem, the self-penned 'Scouser Tommy', adds images of stirring Liverpool heroism in foreign wars to this seductive mix.) The Liverpool club, with Bill Shankly's enthusiastic support, eventually responded to growing informal pressure by agreeing to play the Pacemakers' version of the song on the p.a. before matches as a means of getting the home fans 'involved' and of intimidating visiting teams. It was, as we now know, enthusiastically embraced by the Anfield crowd.

Other songs followed, especially local pop hits with 'sing-along' choruses, which could be used, simultaneously, to celebrate the city's global, cultural success, as well as being easily adapted for specific local football use. More prosaically, older, familiar tunes were incorporated into local repertoires: 'Ee aye addio', followed by any appropriate 'football' ending and sung to the tune of the playground song 'The farmer's in his den', was a simple, staple part of the Kop's early song book. It is also likely that the long tradition of performing Liverpool comedians, the strong poetry and oral history cultures in the city, as well as the deep-rooted folk song and music hall and public house strands of popular musical performance, based especially around the cultural exchanges made possible by sea trade, all fed the Kop's new reflexive and creative appetites as a performer at the match: as part of the active text of a game. These performance and oral traits – plus the occupational and informal trading and exchange cultures in the city – are deeply embedded parts of the 'local structures of feeling' on Merseyside (I. Taylor et al., 1996). This extension by Ian Taylor and his colleagues of Raymond Williams' original concept is useful in the way that it draws on and combines historical discourses and myths, as well as on local patterns of consumption and employment, gender and 'race' relations and spatial environments, in order to reveal markers of local social formations and identity, and also expressions of local character.

Once the Kop had fully developed its public reputation for innovation and wit – and for its urban vim and vinegar, too – it was soon clear that the production of some of the newer, more inventive, vocal material required more than simple spontaneity and informality. According to Hopcraft (1971: 166), in the 1960s 'The Liverpool crowds have been imitated but never adequately, no other fans being able to match their invention, to say nothing of the sustained indecency'. Much of the singing in the crowd was spontaneous, an immediate response to incidents on the field. But the Kop also soon acquired its own local 'writers' in order to keep the great crowd fed with new songs, as 1960s Kopite Phil Aspinall told Stephen Kelly (1993: 67–8):

We used to make the songs up in a pub. In our case it was always The Albert, next door to the Kop. But there are a number of pubs dotted round Liverpool where the same kind of thing goes on. If the songs were long, we'd have to organize it. We usually do that before the game, while we're having a few drinks. If the words were easy and the tune was catchy, you might be able to start it in that afternoon. Sometimes it would take a few games before it really got going. They're easy tunes in the main, and people soon catch on once they've got the tune. On the Kop it would snowball and everyone would be singing it in three or four minutes . . . I've been drinking in The Albert since the 1960s. We'll be singing most of the night – you know, old Beatles and Elvis numbers – until we get thrown out.

European nights at Anfield soon became established as 'special' occasions when the Kop and its various informal bards were expected to turn out in force – and with new songs. This was in tune with Shankly's own thinking, of course, that foreign teams could be intimidated by the physical prowess and commitment of his players and by the howling reception they received from the 25,000 souls who now gathered under the roof of the home end at Anfield (see Chapter Three). The European night-game crowds in the 1960s also assembled inside Anfield from 5.30 p.m. onwards for these pay-at-the-gate events, so the atmosphere inside the stadium by kick-off time was simply intense. Innovation and the sense of 'border-crossing' and experimentation was more generally in the air at European matches. Liverpool's famous all-red kit was first introduced, in fact, as a 'European' strip in a tie at Anfield, against Anderlecht, in November 1964. Shankly tried the strip on Ron Yeats, the club's towering centre back, just before the match. Convinced the new gear made his players look more fearsome, the manager simply asserted that this should be the club's new strip (Kelly, 1993: 139–40). Anderlecht, a top European club side of the time, were crushed, 3–0.

The Kop also busily collected chants and songs on their own European journeys, of course. The titanic struggles with France's St Etienne in 1977 produced 'Allez les rouges', for example, a song eventually 'revived' for the 'new' Liverpool under French manager, Gérard Houllier. An estimated 25,000 Liverpool fans also famously travelled by bus, plane and train to Rome in 1977 for the club's first European Cup Final victory, with a new song 'Roma', sung to the tune of 'Arrivederci Roma', and penned by Phil Aspinall and his mates on their way to an away game at Newcastle (Kelly, 1993: 68). According to the club's players, themselves still low after an FA Cup Final defeat just days before, it was the sight of the huge bank of Liverpool red in the Olympic Stadium, as the players inspected the pitch, which stirred the side to victory.

The central place for football in the lives of working-class men in Liverpool in the 1960s, and in other working-class cities like it, is easily romanticized now, especially as today's leisure options proliferate (for those who can afford them) and ties of family and place have been so weakened by post-Fordist shifts in patterns of work, by changes in social and geographical mobility and by shifts in gender relations (see King, 1998). Football clubs today are now also more 'available' for support by those who inhabit a space outside the 'traditional' ties of family and neighbourhood. 'Going to the match' then was both a respite from work and from home and also an exploration of friendship, communal worth, and, essentially, of local working-class masculine solidarities both at work and at play (Holt, 1989). But it was also focused strongly on an *aesthetic* – the grace, the style and the pace of professional players – and on spectator *performance* – the physicality, the creativity and harmony of the crowd – in a way which called up qualities and sensitivities in working men which had few other appropriate or satisfying outlets.

Although the Liverpool Kop, in its deep partisanship and darker mode, had 'all the menace of an hysteric's nightmare' (Hopcraft 1971: 164–6), in the 1960s it was also a place where tough Liverpool dockers, factory workers and tradesmen could collectively warm, for example, to the sensuous skills of the slight Hungarian inside forward Varga as he guided Ferencvaros to a rare Fairs Cup win at Anfield during the 1967/68 season: 'More than any other English city', Hopcraft wrote in 1971, 'Liverpool experiences its hope and its shame through its football.'

For Liverpool supporters in the 1960s, such as Alan Edge (1999: 138), it was the case that before marriage and the kids set in with new responsibilities and constraints, watching football at Anfield with close male mates offered three or four years of an 'exclusive arrangement' which tied working men, perfectly, to each other, to their favourite football pub, and, thrillingly, to their own 'spec' on the Kop. But it was not so for *all* Liverpudlians, of course; in a deeply segregated and racist city, there was little space for black people from Liverpool to assert their own allegiance to either of the major Merseyside football clubs (see Williams, 1988; Hill, 1989; and Chapter 6).

Saturday's Kids

At the same time as singing was being established at Anfield, penetrations of the football world by aspects of what was, even by 1964, a rapidly expanding teenage leisure industry also had the effects of exacerbating divisions by age inside football grounds. At Liverpool, as elsewhere, younger fans began, noisily, to colonize the areas behind the goals in the early 1960s. The Kop, however, because of its sheer scale, and also its lack of lateral fencing, managed to incorporate, initially at least, both the new more vocal and more disruptive fandoms of youth, and the more established, older, and more traditional fan styles which gathered around the younger core area. At other venues this was much more difficult to achieve, especially as hooliganism accelerated and as older, 'respectable' fans gradually evacuated these smaller terraced spaces, effectively giving them up to the sorts of masculinist, 'neo-tribal' struggles which were to become such a defining feature of football culture in England for the next twenty-five years (see Dunning et al., 1988). In short, we were about to move into quite new, and sometimes disturbing, football times in England.

The emerging new forms of terrace *patois* were, of course, largely the preserve of the young. The influence of popular musical forms and a more general concern with consumption, style and the exploration of existing local cultural traditions have been a central feature of football's youth cultures on Merseyside at least since the early 1960s. As the maximum wage was lifted in 1961, so the players themselves were also slowly moving into an era of new and more conspicuous lifestyles and, increasingly, onto the stage of impression management and public celebrity (Wagg, 1984).

The generally favourable TV and press coverage provided of Liverpool fans – especially the all-singing, all-dancing Kop – throughout the 1960s and into the 1970s also served to mask, however, some important local developments. By the late 1970s, for example, more and more young Liverpool hard cases had left the by then 'safe and boring' Kop for the 'Anny Road End' at the other end of the Liverpool ground. These 'deserters' were among the most belligerent, but also the most vociferous and most inventive young Kopites, who railed, especially, against the bland media construction of the great Liverpool terrace as a partisan but essentially good-humoured enclosure (including an early 'anthropological' feature on the BBC's *Panorama*). Instead, they sought more immediate football action, set-up as they now were against the visitors' enclosure at the far end of the ground. Exchanges between the Kop and its recalcitrant offshoot at the other end of the stadium became more fractious as the 1980s wore on. If, for the new Anny Roaders, the Main Stand fans were older 'moaners', and the Kemlyn regulars the dull, scarf brigade, 'family' Kopites were, increasingly, just 'gobshites' (Edge, 1999: 142). Some Liverpool fans identify *this* early splintering – rather than the falling 1980s crowds or the later reduction in Kop capacity, post-Hillsborough – as the real beginning of the long-term decline of the Kop as a raucous, impassioned and sometimes dangerously unpredictable home end (Kelly, 1993: 43–4).

The national media image of generally 'peaceful' local derby games in Liverpool – families and friends split only by their football support – helped to continue the national popular profile of Liverpudlians as roguish but essentially collectively *non-violent* football fans. Meanwhile, other terrace 'contests', this time around consumption and style, were hotting up. Regular European football travel for most Liverpool fans from the mid-1960s onwards meant adventure, some lasting friendships, broadened cultural horizons, and many extraordinary footballing successes and memories (Goodwin and Straughan, 1996). For some younger male fans from the city, however, it was also an extravagant dip into the exotic and exposed style pots of Europe.

Going abroad for football at first meant the intoxication of foreign football travel, and bringing back a rival hat or scarf for its rarity value and to show others you had made the trip. Soon, for younger fans, it also offered opportunities for scanning, buying – and sometimes stealing – designer leisure gear not yet available in the UK. Young scousers in Paris for the European Cup Final of 1981, for example, eschewed the usual tourist sites giving priority instead to an ultimately fruitless search for a mythical Adidas [trainers] Centre in the city (Goodwin and Straughan, 1996: 39). As economic depression intensified in Liverpool during the Thatcher years, so too did the determination of those on the margins of the legitimate enterprise culture to continue to strut their stuff; especially as football supporters from the South began to work on well-established North/South footballing divisions by taunting rivals from north of Watford with hefty money wads or even by the 'flashing' of designer underpants! (see Williams, 1991). On Liverpool match trips abroad, while the majority got on with routine football travel, other forces were stirring. Apart from the usual hunt for free food and drink, attractive options for 'work' at matches abroad now narrowed down to two main targets: the travelling 'professionals' took on the jewellery stores; the committed 'casuals' could run easily through a continental sports shop or a men's outfitters. Billy Wilson, a young Kopite at the time, followed style trends in the city like many young men did – probably a little *too* closely (Kelly, 1993: 46–8):

> The late 1970s and the early 1980s were the period of the 'style wars' . . . Sports gear was the essential ingredient, preferably exotic, continental brands. It has been said that most of it was 'lifted' from unsuspecting shops on the continent at away European ties. So, they'd be kitted out in continental anoraks/training tops/cycling tops/sports coats. Then the trainers had to be the correct type to be cool . . . [In] the late 1970s/early 1980s I recall wedge haircuts being very essential to any cool Liverpool fan. After the Italian games in 1984 and 1985 a lot of Italian banners, tops and hats were sported on the Kop . . . I would say that the Kop drops something when they see that other clubs' supporters have copied their ideas, whether it be clothes, banners or whatever . . . Liverpool supporters feel they created this whole 'new-mod' scene, and laughed off counter-claims from London and Manchester.

This interest in stealing at football abroad seems to be an *English*, rather than simply a Liverpool theme (Williams et al., 1989). But the focus by what was always a small minority of Liverpool fans on stealing and 'grifting' around football and elsewhere, is also probably quite a common feature of life in those declining post-industrial seaports which house a large and vibrant unskilled urban underclass. The combination of regional separateness, an intense focus on football as an expression of local aspiration and identity, the centrality of sea trade in local economies, coupled with industrial decline and innovative street cultures draws strong connections, for example, between the dominant 'structures of feeling' of the city of Liverpool and those in 'independent' southern European cities such as Marseilles and Naples (see Bromberger, 1993).

Responses of other Liverpool fans to this kind of behaviour were ambivalent. On the one hand, there was fury at the easy crude stereotypes, increasingly peddled on TV and elsewhere, about the alleged dishonesty of *all* people from Liverpool. These sorts of affront were also opposed later, as we shall see, by Liverpool football fanzines. Such media stereotypes continue unabated in the early twenty-first century along with tired and routine abuse from rival fans that Liverpudlians all 'sign on', live in 'slums', and are, predictably, 'cheating scousers'. On the other hand, although stealing on football trips was never sanctioned by the majority of Liverpool supporters, it probably became grudgingly accepted by many; after all, it was reckoned, this sort of *instrumental* hooliganism was 'better' than fans *fighting*, and at least it never disrupted the game. Targets for theft were also, usually, larger anonymous businesses *outside* Merseyside, and, if abroad, well, the continentals looked as if they could at least *afford* it. Hard times, it was reasoned, produce unavoidable costs.

Orchestrating the so-called 'style wars' back in Liverpool from the early 1980s was *The End* fanzine, inspirational and pseudish offspring of musician/fan Pete Hooton and colleagues, and arbiter of all things stylish in football, music and club cultures in the city (see also Redhead, 1991; 1997). Gradually, the very strong music base of the early issues of *The End* faded, to be overtaken by endless accounts of the designer labels which were 'in', those which were now *passé*, and exhaustive theses on trainers, haircuts and exactly how to wear jeans. Over? On *top* of trainers? Split, flared or straight? Here, too, was contained the identikit profile of the new, true Liverpool 'scally': love of the right (usually Indie) music, and clothes; adeptness at robbing; keen on having a draw (smoking dope), rather than sinking gallons of ale; being scandalized by ignorant 'woollybacks' (from nearby St Helens, Warrington, and especially from 'agricultural' Leeds); and showing open resistance to any media-stimulated form of music or football cultural shift – no Merseyside football fan would ever describe *himself* as a 'casual', less still join some named football 'firm'. Topping all of this was an explicit and appalled rejection of the real hooligan 'gobshites' elsewhere who were still trashing football grounds and attacking 'anoraks' or 'woollybacks' (ordinary fans).

In fact, throughout the 1970s and 1980s hooligan groups at Liverpool, all still tied, unconventionally, to particular parts of the city, were best known elsewhere and in Liverpool itself less for their organization or their general fighting prowess than they were for their alleged dangerousness when faced in Liverpool, for their commitment to 'robbin', for their outrageous expertise in 'bunking in' at away matches and, on some occasions especially later when in Europe, for their full-on project crime (Williams, 1988: 16). In general, Liverpool hooligans were not typically well known at all for the sort of nihilistic and sometimes racist violence and vandalism which, increasingly, characterized some English football hooligan crews – at Manchester United, at Leeds United, and at Chelsea in the 1970s, for example. Away travel, and especially some matches at home, might bring unavoidable and pleasurable contact with 'their lads', of course; but hooligan traditions on Merseyside had never easily sanctioned simply expressive forms of violence around football, especially if they threatened to bleed, uncontrollably, into the staging of the match itself (see, Cotton, 1996; Edge, 1999: 142–4). In the early 1980s, in fact, the Liverpool police, strategically, denied knowledge of any *named* Liverpool football gangs at all, though the fighting which sometimes went on in Utting Avenue outside the away end at Anfield made it clear that some locals were still 'well up' for any serious challenges from outside the city (Williams, 1988: 21).

These notions, and the still dominant public profile of younger Liverpool football supporters as sometimes 'fly' *football* fans, rather than fighting hooligans, are among the reasons why the tragic incidents at the Heysel Stadium in 1985 hit the city so hard, of course, and why they also brought instant – and understandable, if probably ill-judged – assertions from Merseyside that those involved simply 'could not be from Liverpool' (Williams, 1986). In short, this locally valued image of authentic Liverpool 'scals' – promoted in fanzines such as *The End* and among young men in the city, as essentially sharp urban rogues who could 'look after themselves' when they needed to, who could organize their own, illicit enterprise and consumption cultures, and who loved their football – was about to come under some very close scrutiny. Europe was about to go badly wrong for Liverpool.

More generally, this determined *separation* of football – or, at least, *the match* – from 'trouble' at Liverpool, both confirmed and reinforced the notion, still strongly held in the city, that the fans of the club *valued* and protected the sport rather more than was the case in cities such as London, Manchester and Leeds, where hooliganism had been allowed to take a much more central and disruptive hold, especially in the 1970s. This tied in with ideas about the more 'sophisticated' football allegedly played by the Liverpool club in the 1970s and 1980s, which combined the physical attributes of the English game with the patience and technique more usually associated with football on the continent (see Chapter Four). Liverpool FC's place as a fixture in European football competition from the mid-1960s onwards also imbued local football cultures with a sense that the club's fans were both more knowledgeable and, increasingly, more sporting than those elsewhere in England, especially as they welcomed to the city fans and clubs from some of the continent's less familiar outposts. This general sense of the club and its supporters as passionate *and* insightful and gracious about the game was something which was also sustained, of course, by the relatively benign national media image of footballing Liverpudlians, at least in the 1960s and 1970s, as seen through the prism of the Kop.

There is, clearly, a lot of local chauvinism solidly at work here, but all these mythologized traits – these football stories that people told and retold about themselves in the city – also contributed to real local traditions which are still guarded and celebrated at Liverpool, and which are difficult to track in quite the same form elsewhere. This generosity of footballing spirit lives on at Anfield. Visiting goalkeepers continue, almost always, to be applauded into the Kop goal, and sections of the home crowd, almost always, show their respect for 'good football' played by the opposition. Booing home players, or jeering at ex-Liverpool players who return to Anfield with other clubs is also generally condemned among the club's fans and is asserted to be 'not the Liverpool way'. Few Liverpool players, in any case, have left the club in acrimonious circumstances in order, provocatively, to 'better themselves' elsewhere, unless, of course, they went abroad.

An example of this local feature came after another damaging Liverpool home defeat in 1999, this time by the then newly-promoted Watford. It produced the 'usual' Kop response of warm applause for the visitors. The reception drew approving comment from Watford manager, Graham Taylor, but it also resulted in a public appreciation of the grace shown by Liverpool fans in defeat, written by Peter Drury for the *Independent* (20 August 1999):

> It remains a rare pleasure to visit a match at Liverpool FC. The Kop makes it so . . . Nobody booed when the Watford team-sheet was read out; everybody clapped when the Watford goalkeeper ran towards them for the start of the second half. Then at the end – and here was the highlight for anyone who clings, anachronistically, onto ideals of mutual respect, sportsmanship or simple decency – they stayed behind to applaud their victorious visitors . . .
>
> On the Kop they love Liverpool but they understand that, without an opponent, there isn't a game. Without Watford and Swansea, and even Everton and Manchester United, Liverpool is a pretty pointless entity. Pointless is precisely what Saturday became for Liverpool. Happily, the Kop offered that pointlessness some meaning.

Drury exaggerates, of course, the 'sporting' ethos of the Kop: his comments seem much more in tune, in fact, with the more middle-class notions of fair play associated with sports such as cricket and rugby union, rather than with the desperate desire to win, at almost all costs, vividly expressed on almost all football terraces in the North virtually since the game was professionalized in the late nineteenth century (see Holt, 1989). Nevertheless, his account is properly appreciative of values which are still cherished by many Kopites: namely, a willingness to concede to a deservedly better or fighting performance by the opposition, perhaps especially if it is from a skilled foreign foe or from a battling and courageous domestic underdog. This sporting cosmopolitanism, especially in relation to foreign clubs and players, coexisted, however, with powerful forms of 'domestic' racist exclusion in the home crowd: as visiting *foreign* black players might, on occasions, be lauded by Liverpool fans for their skill and vision, so *local* black people – black *Liverpudlians* – saw, and occasionally experienced, the Kop as an exclusive and hostile space (see Chapter Six). In the mid-1980s, racism and xenophobia were about to loom large in the Liverpool story abroad.

Heysel: the end of Europe

Getting a handle on the seriousness of hooligan cultures in terms of their effects on 'ordinary' Liverpool fans in the 1970s and 1980s is not always easy. Up until 1980, crowds at Anfield continued to top an average of over 40,000, reaching club record levels of 47,221 as late as 1976/77, and during an extraordinary and unprecedented period of individual English football club success. In nineteen seasons from 1972/3 Liverpool won an astonishing eleven League titles, finishing out of the top two clubs only once. In 1980/81, as the club 'slumped' to fifth place in the League while still winning the European Cup for a third time, Anfield crowds fell to an average of 37,547, and stayed broadly around the same mark (below 40,000) throughout the 1980s, even as League Championships and European and domestic Cups were delivered to Liverpool 4, as if by order.

Was this drop in attendances a sign of a 'hooligan effect'? Possibly, though after the deep shock of Heysel in 1985, and even though some long-time fans probably stopped attending matches, Anfield attendances actually went up in the 1985/86 'double' season, against the background of what was initially an open-ended ban on all English clubs from European competition, and a national slump in English match-attendance figures. The 1980s fall in Liverpool home attendances was probably associated more with the troubled image of the sport and the effects of economic depression in the city, even as numbers of fans at Anfield drawn from *outside* Liverpool were probably already rising (Williams, 1997). Everton's average home crowd, rather more locally drawn than Liverpool's, collapsed in 1983/84 to below 20,000, the lowest figure at Goodison since before the First World War, though it soon recovered again as Everton then produced a Championship team in 1985.

Watching matches only at home can, of course, insulate one from the worst effects of hooliganism. The 'fun' was definitely in travelling away. There may be some generational effects also at play here. For Alan Edge, for example, the dreaded 'hooligans' at football were simply 'bastards' who had quite maliciously spoiled the traditions and experience of supporting football for older fans who had also loyally followed the club, home and away, in the 'peaceful' eras of the 1950s and 1960s, before match transport or even motorways were at hand (Edge, 1999: 141–5). For some younger male fans, of course, the prospects for some argy-bargy with the police and rival fans was increasingly just part of a 'lively' afternoon at the match. For all those in between, the aggressive tribalism which now characterized fan conflict at the sport was simply something to observe and to be both avoided and endured.

Accounts presented since that time of Liverpool hooliganism in the 1970s and 1980s read like a nostalgia call for thin adventure yarns in which fights just 'happen' and young girls are even casually 'gang-banged' in the back of football coaches (Cotton, 1996). How serious was it all? Writers such as Scraton, for example, actually seem totally confused by the hooliganism question, at one point bemoaning the racism, sexism and homophobia of the terraces (but not the violence?) in the 1980s (1999: 10), and the next, offering what others (Lea and Young, 1984) might describe as a 'left idealist' argument about media-orchestrated moral panics and national statistical trends on football hooligan arrests in the 1980s which are taken to confirm that the State and its agents had simply 'exaggerated' the hooligan problem all along (Scraton, 1999: 30).

In a sense, the tragedy at Heysel in 1985 temporarily stilled the views of those who merely dismissed hooliganism as a media 'fabrication', or else as just the universal and timeless, harmless rituals of working-class 'lads' (though such accounts were not slow to return later. See for example Armstrong, 1998). There was pious bile after Heysel from the hated (in Liverpool, certainly) bucolic, little-Englander Thatcher Government, of course, which clearly could see no role for itself in creating the public climate which was so ripe in England for the existence and promotion of the sort of casual xenophobia and machismo which underpinned events there and which had led indirectly to the deaths of 39 mainly Italian fans. (Racism, of course, was hardly unknown in Liverpool.) Instead, talk among Mrs Thatcher's Ministers was soon of bringing more (middle-class?) families into football, of identity cards for all fans, and of new police campaigns aimed at finally bringing the hooligan to heel (see Giulianotti, 1994; King, 1998).

In Liverpool, itself, sentiments after Heysel were mixed, ranging from deep shock and real shame that some people from the city were directly involved in such an appalling football tragedy, to open anger at the predictably spiteful and vicious press coverage that football, and especially the city, attracted as a result of the disaster. The city's strong self-identity, its semi-Celtic local culture, its long-term industrial decline and depopulation, and its social, cultural and geographical relative isolation from the mainstream of Englishness, all allied to a formal and deep popular opposition to the politics of national government in Britain in the 1980s, turned Liverpool in on itself for mutual support after Heysel, as would also happen again later following the disaster at Hillsborough (Walter, 1991).

Initially convincing claims that London-based racists might have had a hand in events in Brussels surfaced soon, but they were never proven, and knowledgeable Liverpool fans 'on the ground' were also unconvinced by this explanation of events. There was understandable local anger, at the quite abject performance of UEFA officials in siting the Final match at such a poorly appointed stadium in Brussels, and at their ill-advised arrangements for ticket sales and distribution for what was, after all, the blue riband match in European club football. Peter Robinson, the Liverpool club's Chief Executive, had warned UEFA beforehand that the stadium and its ticketing arrangements were unsatisfactory, possibly dangerous, by English standards. No heed was taken of his remarks.

Suggestions in the press and on TV from fans returning to Merseyside, however, that Italian fans simply should not have been in adjacent pens to Liverpool supporters and that *this*, and flimsy lateral stadium fencing, was the major reason for the tragedy, came uncomfortably close to victim-blaming. Were we, perversely, demanding at Heysel the sorts of spectator pens or unclimbable fences which actually contributed to killing fans, later, at Hillsborough? Violence aimed by AS Roma fans at Liverpool supporters after the previous Final in Rome in 1984 was also, plausibly, raised as a possible contributory cause. This may well have played a part. But citing this was also as if proposing that violent retribution might have been *reasonably* sought by Liverpudlians on *any* available Italian in 1985, even those drawn from Juventus in the *North* of Italy.

Difficult to accept, too, were chauvinist claims by some returning Liverpool fans that the inept Belgian police were *really* to blame because they were simply too *cowardly* to intervene against earlier Juventus hooliganism, or in the exchanges between rival fans which took place before the fatal charge (see Williams, 1986). In short, Heysel clearly had plenty of the ingredients of what now passed pretty much for *accepted* young male supporter rituals at English football, if not elsewhere in Europe. Taken abroad, and placed suddenly out of context in a crumbling stadium and with a hesitant police force, and disaster was in the offing. Pete Hooton, himself, saw it all unfold (Taylor and Ward, 1993: 243–4):

> It was the type of skirmish that you'd seen 100, 200 times before, on grounds all round the country, over a fifteen year period and you thought to yourself, 'Well, that's a skirmish and within a couple of minutes there'll be a police-line there and they'll force both sets of fans back and there'll be a no-man's land of 50 metres.' That didn't happen. That's when people started to think, 'What's going to happen here?' . . . There was no one taking control . . . People realised the police were actually scared. It was a sense of, 'There'll be a bit of trouble.' I don't think anyone thought of walls collapsing anyway, but you've got to apportion blame to Liverpool fans because they charged over . . . It was a sense of *fait accompli* in a way: 'This is our end, get out.' It wasn't getting controlled and people panicked.

Comments such as these offered the context for setting Heysel against the backcloth of more than fifteen years of routine football violence by English football fans at home and abroad (see Williams et al., 1989). As Hooton suggests, however, it was difficult to take the moral high ground on Merseyside by arguing that scousers had 'only' really ever been abroad on football and 'robbin' escapades, and that the *real* English hooligans actually resided in small 'woollyback' English towns and in London. This was especially difficult, too, when published Liverpool fans' despatches emerged later, reporting on both their 'shopping' abroad *and* their own minor football tussles on foreign soil (see Cotton, 1996).

In the main, however, it was certainly *true* that the Liverpool club and its fans had had a 'good' record at football abroad, especially when compared to the violent and sometimes racist trashings dished out by other English crews over many years (Williams et al., 1989). Many Liverpool fans were also completely estranged from the England national side in the 1980s – Ireland was favoured by many, and the England team was, in any case, southern-based, and was profoundly *her* (Thatcher's) team – and so Liverpudlians had relatively little to do with the extreme England hooliganism on the continent in the 1970s and 1980s (Williams, 1986). But Heysel? Well, no matter what the real intentions in Brussels, this was now something on quite a different scale.

One positive outcome of Heysel was the setting up in Liverpool, in 1985, of a new, non-club-based, national supporters group, the Football Supporters Association (FSA), by long-standing club supporters Peter Garrett and Rogan Taylor. The FSA was also the springboard for a new national supporter fanzine movement, which later sprinkled some of its authors among the established football writers and in sports television (Haynes, 1995). The FSA was also central to the public debate about the second major football disaster involving Liverpool supporters in the 1980s: this time the club's followers were clearly involved as *victims* rather than as alleged perpetrators.

Heysel, on the face of it at least, had done little to disrupt the established *football* pattern at home. Although all English clubs – including new Champions, Everton – were banned from Europe, in 1985/86 Liverpool won the domestic 'double' for the first time, and under new player-manager Dalglish began to build another impressive team for the late 1980s. Only a surprise FA Cup Final loss to lowly Wimbledon prevented another Liverpool 'double' in 1987/88. But the club was soon faced by another spectator tragedy of such proportions that not even the trauma of Heysel could offer adequate preparation.

Hillsborough: new nightmares

For those who have followed the Hillsborough case – and in Liverpool, even now, it is seldom ever really off the public agenda for football followers at Anfield, and for others – certain key phrases about the Inquiry hearings covering the afternoon of 15 April 1989 have now taken on an almost totemic resonance: 'the 3.15 p.m. cut off point'; 'accidental death'; 'defective camera 5'; 'disgraceful lies'; 'missing video tapes'; 'the truth'; and so on. TV coverage has also put some of these phrases into the national domain. Nevertheless, it is still incredible just how many people seemed to know so little of the important detail of the incidents in Sheffield, at least until the Jimmy McGovern ITV drama about the tragedy was screened in 1996. Hillsborough also remains sensitively high in the public consciousness of the city because of the highly moralistic way it has been linked by the national press and TV with wider social issues in Liverpool, including the alleged excessive 'sentimentality' of people in the city, but especially perhaps the social context of the later Jamie Bulger killing – poverty, parenting, family dysfunction, etc. – and with Liverpool's alleged endemic problem of crime.

I do not want to rehearse again here in detail the events of 15 April 1989, or to look at length at what happened to the families of the bereaved later. That can easily be followed elsewhere (Scraton, 1999; Scraton et al., 1995; Taylor et al., 1995). It is relevant, however, to try to say something more about the wider context of Hillsborough, outside of football.

More specifically, the promises of broadly collectivist social policies for wealth-creation and of 'one nation' welfarist social policies in Britain had already grown distant and hazy by the late 1960s, and by the 1980s the earlier consensuses around notions of local and regional 'civic pride' and around a sense of collective 'social cohesion' seemed to have been substantially dislodged, as policy aims, by national government strategies which lay a much more profound stress on the importance of ownership and choice in the private sphere and on individual striving for personal success of the kind most closely associated with 'Thatcherite' social and economic policies.

If, under the twin pressures of commodification and privatization in 1980s Britain, public spaces were neglected and 'a narrower range of "strangers" are met in public space, and, increasingly, experiences of public life are with a more homogeneous group of others' (Brill, 1989: 30), then these developments suggest an important theoretical and socio-political connection between disasters of that period in public places in England of a kind little made in the press coverage of Hillsborough, or in the report of the official Inquiry into the disaster, chaired by Lord Justice Taylor (1990). In this sense, according to Ian Taylor (1991: 12), for example, such disasters – on public ferries; on the railways; in the London Underground; at football matches, etc. – were all

[C]learly an expression of a kind of careless inefficiency and neglect for the public interest which characterises the British service industry in general. The Hillsborough disaster was the product of a quite consistent and ongoing lack of interest on the part of the owners and directors of English league clubs in the comfort, well-being and safety of their paying spectators: this particular failure within football that I am condemning is a generalised problem in English culture – the lack of regard by authority (and thereby what we now call 'service providers') for the provision of well-being and security of others.

If the wider context for the tragedy is, properly, a debate about public policy and public provision in Britain, in *footballing* terms Hillsborough was much more about the direction and management of the sport and of its spectators. The disaster was not of course *caused* by hooliganism, but it was certainly fundamentally *about* what had become routine collective responses to problems which were now regularly produced by some fans at English football. How else could the necessary balance between safety and security be so badly wrong at a major football match in Britain as it was in the late 1980s (see Ian Taylor, 1991)?

Once police hesitancy and mismanagement of Liverpool supporters outside Hillsborough had led to the ushering in of the fateful unsupervised group of fans who were simply seeking a decent vantage point for the game but who now added to the overcrowding in unescapable pens, the very design of the Sheffield stadium offered little scope for remedial action at that late stage. Given the awful, but hardly unimaginable, catalogue of police mistakes on the day, Hillsborough was simply like many other English football grounds of the time – a potential death trap. The general chaos, horror and lack of preparedness for something on this scale at football, and early police presumptions that what they were seeing must be *hooliganism*, not unfolding disaster, meant that the seriously injured (who might now be saved in similar circumstances) then had little chance of survival (see Scraton, 1999).

If the disaster itself was avoidable and tragic, the treatment later by the police of the families of the dead and injured was little short of inhumane and repellent (see Taylor et al., 1995). Personal and professional damage limitation – the attempted rationalization, or 'cover up' – soon swung brutally into action. What was truly shameful here, to many observers, were the police attempts to continue to fly the drunken fans/broken gate stories about alleged Liverpool 'hooligans' – later aided by the *Sun* – and seemingly to treat the bereaved like little more than contemptible rubbish. After all, these were just football supporter families (many people on Merseyside would add 'from Liverpool' here), people with no obvious power to organize or to question the police case, or even their own desperate treatment at the hands of the South Yorkshire force. 'They *can* be rubbished', must have been the thinking from some of these public 'servants'. How little these senior police officers knew (see Moneypenny's Afterword at the end of this book for more on the fans' struggle).

Ironically, of course, many of those supporters who died in Sheffield would have been among the very first in the ground, arriving early to get a good 'spec' behind the goal. They would, in fact, have been among the very *last* supporters to have been 'on the ale' on the day. Many Liverpool and Forest fans at Hillsborough *had* been drinking, of course. This was English FA Cup semi-final day, after all, traditionally a major day for a football 'bevvy', as most young (and older) male fans still know. Insistent police questioning on this aspect implied that simply having a drink somehow made quite innocent fans culpable for their own deaths.

But Jimmy McGovern's Hillsborough TV drama documentary also takes obvious, but important, liberties on this and on other points, presumably for dramatic and possibly 'political' effect. According to the TV drama-doc, apparently, *no* fan goes ticketless to Sheffield, or even for a single pint before the match, as the police later pummel away grotesquely with questions to bemused and broken parents and relatives about football and drink. Drinking, in fact, is strategically *expunged* by McGovern from the culture on this day. Nor do we get any sense from the TV version – though we do get it from the real ordinary police constable statements which emerged much later – of quite how *damaged* relations had generally become between some young male supporters and the police at football at this time. This, sadly, was just one of the reasons why police responses were so completely inappropriate on the day.

In fact, until quite disastrous policing decisions intervene, McGovern's TV depiction of an ultimately tragic football day, arguably and oddly, in fact looks much more like the spruced up 'new' football experience of the late 1990s than it does an account of the then sometimes deeply troubled sport and the macho posturings 'across the barricades' more characteristic of policing and fan cultures at English football in the 1980s. One learns nothing here, for example, about how or why these ugly, sunken football pens – real death traps – had come almost to be accepted by many fans then, and in one of our most 'modern' football grounds.

Some other context, which reveals much more about troubling aspects of the general character of the sport and of prevailing footballing masculinities at that time and before, is probably also important here in order to understand exactly how the police – but also we ourselves, as fans – could get it quite so badly wrong at football in 1989. This sort of necessary broader contextualization, with its realist account of then existing English male terrace culture, is present in some academic accounts of Hillsborough (see for example Taylor, 1991), but it is arguably, still missing from some of the later, established descriptions and explanations of events on 15 April 1989 which are still more strongly favoured on Merseyside (see for example Scraton, 1999; Scraton et al., 1995).

Fans at Liverpool today

Today, of course, following the public inquiry into the disaster in Sheffield, most of the brutal perimeter fences have gone from major football grounds and so, at the big clubs, sadly, have the terraces. The Liverpool Kop finally succumbed to seats on 30 April 1994, its emotional last stand made against ungracious visitors, Norwich City; another 0–1 defeat. When Minister for Sport, Tony Banks, commented in October 1997 that he might look again at the question of bringing back 'safe' terraces, he was taken immediately to task by the Hillsborough Family Support Group in Liverpool, who spoke of the important progress on safety and on hooliganism at football since 1989. The *symbolic* shift to seats is probably also important here; a sign of the sport finally moving on from a generally troubled period in the 1980s. This was, perhaps, more strongly felt in Liverpool than elsewhere.

By the end of its standing days, in fact, the Kop was but a pale ghost of earlier manifestations, licensed as it was after Hillsborough to hold only 16,480 standing spectators, way below its early 28,000 capacity. The 12,000 fans who are now allowed to *sit* on the new Kop were soon accused, locally, of assuming the general demeanour of an *audience*, waiting to be engaged by events on the pitch, rather than a passionate and committed *crowd*, urging the team on and straining to be involved as the day's drama unfolds. The Kop's bards still work hard at their new songs and chants – a whole raft of new material emerged to greet new, foreign players in 1999 – but it *is* much more difficult in the seats to rouse fellow supporters into song. Noticeably, too, very few local, unaccompanied teenage fans of the sort who made up an important part of the Kop's original standing and singing core now attend at Anfield. Can they afford to? Would they want to sit?

Most longstanding fans at Liverpool probably share the deep ambivalence about 'new' football expressed in Kevin Sampson's excellent seasonal diary for 1997/ 98: they are glad that away games are not quite the bear pit they could sometimes be in the 1980s, but they are also saddened that the culture has lost some of its passion and edge from that time (Sampson, 1998: 46). Certainly, Simon Inglis's (1996: 224) assessment of the new Kop as, 'exceptionally well designed and logically arranged . . . providing clear circulation routes throughout', was hardly likely to set supporters' pulses racing in this new era.

Generally, football supporters in England are also dealt with by the authorities rather differently now. Like it or not, they are a little more *cared* about these days. Fans probably think about their own safety a little more now, too, though the rolling, standing Kop in its pomp, offered for many a sense of collective security and belonging which is quite lacking from the highly individualized experience of watching from seats (see, Chapter Nine). But the seated Kop is no middle-class enclave, far from it. Nor does it lack for wit or for seeking out inspiration for laughter in the course of a match, something noticed by the new manager, Houllier. Although memories of the old standing terrace are themselves highly mythologized, the Kop *is* less collective and less spontaneous today; it misses its ribald and fluid young core, from where most of the early songs sprouted. These days, attempts at songs often roll forlornly around small banks of seats all over the Kop, most of them not taken up by the whole. The Kop, perhaps inevitably like most football 'ends' – and public culture itself – is also cruder – and more cruel – today than it was in its prime.

But new sorts of abuses of *spectators* also emerged in the 1990s. If there was a Thatcherite contempt for the public and for public services and spaces a decade before, now, in times of relative plenty for the sport, there came a new contempt, this time for the much trumpeted football *customer*. Clubs followed the letter, but hardly the spirit, of Lord Justice Taylor's post-Hillsborough recommendations on seats and new facilities at football. He envisaged access for all fans and at reasonable prices, something which is certainly possible today (Taylor, 1990). The reality, in the 1990s, was very different, as ticket prices soared and 'excluded' fans, including many in Liverpool, turned to TV coverage in order to try to remain 'connected' with their local clubs (Williams, 1999; Williams and Perkins, 1999). Despite these effects, towards the end of that decade, most Liverpool home games sold out in advance, and the club began to discuss moving to a new 70,000 seat stadium nearby (see Chapter Ten).

'Post-fan' Liverpool Culture

In Liverpool today, at least in the 'post-fan' (Giulianotti, 1999) reflexive realm of local supporter fanzines, four 'supporter' issues, apart from spiralling ticket prices, were major talking points in the 1990s in the main fanzines, *Through the Wind and Rain* (TTWAR) and *Red All Over the Land* (RAOTL). One, inevitably, is Hillsborough and its aftermath, which was covered, extensively. A second is a near-obsessive concern in the fanzines – especially in the local TTWAR – with the *media image* of the city of Liverpool and, as part of this, with relations with Manchester United, the new, and much nastier, 'Everton' for the late-modern period. A third is a more general theme concerning the alleged changing character and geographical spread of Liverpool supporters – and their need to be better schooled into more 'appropriate' forms of fandom. A fourth is the question of how the club could best respond to the new economic realities of football in the 'global' age. I have said quite a bit about Hillsborough already. Let me now end by saying, briefly, something on each of these other key themes.

The sourness of the Liverpool/Manchester United relationship is widely traced, in Liverpool at least, to an alleged lack of media respect for the great Liverpool teams of the 1970s and 1980s, and the corresponding supposed fawning by the media over much less successful United teams of the same era and since. Relative recent economic and social decline in Liverpool is also liable to play a part here, especially as Manchester has profited in recent years. It is clear, however, that this media effect was something also deeply felt by players at Liverpool during this period, and it was used by coaches at the club to motivate the team, especially in matches against United (Souness, 1999: 84). In the 1990s, media treatment of United became 'caught up' somewhat by the real success of the Manchester club under Alex Ferguson, though this did not really diminish some Liverpool fans' focus on United as a convenient local hate-figure to supersede even Everton.

In the mid-1980s, negative sentiments between United and Liverpool followers reached something of an extreme point, with fans and even on one occasion *players* suffering attacks at the fixture. By the early 1990s, events at Hillsborough had quelled the use by Liverpool fans of the inflammatory, so-called, 'Munich song', which referred to United fans and staff killed in the 1958 air tragedy (see, TTWAR, No. 11, 1991). This improved relations between Liverpool and United fans for a time. But in 1995 another watershed was probably reached when the Kenny Dalglish-managed Blackburn Rovers arrived at Anfield needing a win on the final day of the League season to win the Championship and thus deprive Manchester United of the title. Some Liverpool fans openly wore Blackburn shirts at the match and cheered Alan Shearer's opening goal for the visitors. Scuffles broke out among home fans on the Kop as small pockets of Liverpool supporters, enthusiastically, supported the opposition. A late winning goal for Liverpool was greeted with only stifled cheers in the crowd, and apparent gloom on the pitch – until it was learned that United had failed to win, thus giving the title to Blackburn after all; but more importantly not to United.

These incidents reveal something of the real complexities of football club support and enmities, of course, and they also point to some of the ambiguities of the Liverpool fans' approach to United. For example, most Liverpool supporters refuse to take up the more generalized distaste for United – by sharing an identity with rival supporters in singing anti-United songs – on the grounds that this both condemns Liverpool to a common, 'other' status, and reveals publicly an unhealthy and obsessive concern with their regional rivals. Some fans born in Liverpool also insist on continuing to hold up *Everton* as the 'proper' focus for fan enmity, thus stressing the continuing importance of *localism* for authentic club support. At the same time, however, Liverpool football fanzines have been full of pages of snippets of press coverage of United and Manchester (TTWAR's *Mancwatch and Satanic Curses*; *Neighbourhood Watch* in RAOTL, etc.) which are used to 'confirm' the alleged media obsession with United, for example, at the Manchester based North West edition of the *Mirror*, known locally in Liverpool football circles such as these, as the *Daily Manc* (see, TTWAR, *passim*).

This kind of fanzine coverage, which also defends the city more generally from alleged media bias, is of course one way of trying to 'shore up' support for the club against the affections of those who come to support the club from *outside* Liverpool. It is also, in part, a response to anti-Liverpool invective from the much more vicious United fanzine, *Red Issue*. But it also reflects something deeper about the city's character and conscious 'separateness' during recent hard times, when it has been such a focal point for the effects of damaging shifts in economic and industrial trends and policies – which have been much less powerfully felt in

Manchester – and for the harsh, and often unfair, glare of the media on a range of incidents connected to the city, spanning the Toxteth riots, and the Heysel and Hillsborough football disasters through to the Jamie Bulger case.

The alleged changing *character and geographical spread* of Liverpool supporters in the 'new' football era has also been something of a focus for Liverpool fanzine insights. This is especially interesting because the two main Liverpool FC fanzines are made up of one edited locally, in Bootle (*Through the Wind and Rain*) and one edited outside the city, in Loughborough (the appropriately named *Red All Over the Land*). Fans come from all over Britain and beyond to watch Liverpool home matches these days, of course. In 1997, around one in six (16 per cent) Liverpool season ticket holders lived more than 50 miles from Anfield; the figure for Everton was just 6 per cent. Of Liverpool season ticket holders, 73 per cent were born within 20 miles of the club, compared to 87 per cent of Everton fans who were born close to Goodison. Only one-quarter of those season ticket fans who travelled 50 miles or more to Liverpool home matches were actually locally born (Williams, 1997). Everton *seemed* a more local club than Liverpool. Clearly, some fans travelling to home matches at Anfield were returning to the city; but many more were signalling the status of Liverpool as a national, and international, club second only in this respect in England to Manchester United.

Routinely, on match days now, Liverpool fans from Scandinavia and on occasions from Germany, especially, are identifiable in local pubs or on the Kop. Small groups of British *Asian* Liverpool fans, mainly drawn from outside the city, are also a new feature on the seated Kop. The Liverpool club also has an International Supporters Club, numbering some 60,000 members, and chat on Liverpool fan web sites is frequently sprinkled with contributions from Liverpool followers around Europe and in South East Asia and the Americas.

There are a number of issues at stake here: one is the social and geographical origins of fans; another is maintaining the quality and supposed 'uniqueness' of Liverpool support; a third is the emergence of a new kind of consumer/fan at Anfield. Symptomatic of these sorts of concern is a letter to TTWAR (No. 33, 1997: 30). Here, the 'sit back and entertain us' section of the new Kop is taken to task for its general lack of support and its booing and moaning at home players. These are, the writer concludes, 'probably the same people who are emblazened with every piece of merchandise going'. In TTWAR No. 37 (Winter, 1997) a regular contributor's tirade against 'out of town supporters' provoked a 'Tebbit-test' response in No. 38 (1998: 51) from a London-based Liverpool supporter of 25 years' standing, who admits that he 'never once realised that because I had the audacity to be born outside the city I should be excluded from Anfield – presumably unless I pass some test of knowledge or loyalty'. In No. 41 (Winter, 1998: 51) an *Asian* Liverpool supporter – the fanzines are one of the few cultural spaces in the city where 'race' is featured even slightly as an issue in relation to the club –

welcomes the new diversity in the club's support and new attitudes towards racism, before concluding that:

> Seeing some of the passionless, uninformed, camera-clicking, burger-eating Liverworld bag wavers calling themselves 'supporters' now, I sometimes wish it was like the old days! Anfield is not a theme park, but some people are treating it like such. No wonder the atmosphere is crap.

In TTWAR No. 36 (Autumn, 1997: 25) a contributor summed up a number of related supporter/style issues when he asked:

> Where has the 'knowledgable' supporter got to? You know, the ones we used to be praised to the skies for? Well, it looks as if they've buggered off someplace. Priced out of the game, or simply disenchanted – and he's been replaced by MISTER LIVER-WORLD . . . Their lack of knowledge and lack of patience is doing my head in . . . I've worked out a foolproof plan for identifying these idiots, should you have the misfortune to be sat next to one at the match. They're sneaky, and they always wait until the game starts. A replica shirt is a clue, McManaman or Redknapp on the back makes it clearer, and the Liverworld bag between the feet is a complete giveaway. If they're wearing those trainers that look like mini-spaceships, act fast and ask a steward if you can move, there and then.

RAOTL, predictably perhaps, has a slightly different take on the issue of the club's support. For one thing it has a regular feature aimed at reporting on and promoting singing at Anfield, usually listing in a table the 'performance' of Liverpool fans home and away. It also regularly carries the lyrics to famous songs at the club. All of this is likely to be regarded as education too far for TTWAR, which assumes a much more knowing, a more local, and more 'organic' readership than does the non-local RAOTL. The latter's approach to the traditions of the club are also much more *formally* conceived, and could probably only come from *outside* Liverpool. RAOTL agonizes over the sensitive issue of loyal 'out-of-town' supporters (good) and new travelling 'day trippers' (bad). It *is* concerned about recent developments at Anfield, and it feels some hearts and minds instruction in Liverpool traditions is required for new recruits. In an article called 'Sing your own songs', in RAOTL No. 30, (1998: 37), 'Johnny Red' has his sights on members of the club's official International Supporters Club (ISC) as likely instigators of embarrassingly 'bad' singing at Anfield. He recommends, without apparent irony, a Liverpool fan induction process:

> Due to the numbers involved in starting this crap singing, their accents and the way they were dressed, I would hazard a guess that they were an ISC branch on a day out . . . I had the idea that some sort of Liverpool fans code of practice could be drawn up by

the ISC which outlines the history of the club, the fans, the Kop, etc., and various dos and don'ts. I feel that the club has an obligation to maintain our traditions or we will slide even further towards blandness . . . This could be done in the form of an 'education pack', or slide show. This may sound desperate, but something has to be done . . . We have always had the most knowledgeable and sporting fans; we are in danger of losing that reputation and something needs to be done now.

This regular emphasis in Liverpool fanzines on the real cultural *knowledge* of true fans which is set against the empty and wanton *consumerism* of new arrivals links well with the final 'supporters' issue I want to mention briefly here, namely, the alleged craven commercialism of the Liverpool club, and the recent ownership and economic policies at Liverpool. These matters have received some recent fanzine coverage on a number of fronts. There has been fury, for example, about the 'McDonaldization' of the Kop; a branch of the burger chain was controversially included in the Kop rebuild, and the famous giant yellow 'M' now adorns the great stand and even promotes a family area in the new Kop seats. In TTWAR (33, Winter, 1997: 34) an appalled correspondent suggested that:

> Stewards should patrol the Kop with a big net pulling out anyone under 12 with a painted face or with a Liverworld bag, and eject them immediately. You have to be cruel to be kind. I won't harp on about commercialism, and Robinson doesn't give a fuck anyway, but the arse who permitted the 'M' on the side of the Kop should be dragged through the streets by dogs.

In similar commercial vein, a statue of the great Kop hero, Bill Shankly, which is outside the club shop, carries a crass reminder of the club sponsors' support for its construction. At Anfield, these days, one assuredly enters the branded territory of brewing giants Carlsberg and club kit sponsors Reebok. Concern over recent club kits has also focused on the overbearing role of sponsors in introducing non-traditional Liverpool colours – green, black, even blues – into club products (see, TTWAR, 15, Winter, 1992: 6).

The symbolic and topophilic importance of the stadium and the sanctity of the totems of the club are deeply important to football supporters, of course (Bale, 1994: Ch. 6). This is certainly true at Liverpool. Steven Kelly, committed editor of TTWAR, responding to readers' requests in 1997, perhaps tellingly, for more *humour* in the fanzine replied instead with a stern reminder that

> The corporate infestation of Liverpool is not a laughing matter, and to trivialise everything in a, 'Oh well, what can we do, let's have a laff', sort of way is the '90s equivalent of fiddling while Rome burns. This club MEANS something to me, and to you, too, hopefully. Laugh away while they screw every last penny out of you, while they demean everything of significance to a great football club and its marvellous supporters. I'm

sure Reebok, McDonalds, Carlsberg, Sky, Moores, Robinson and Parry will say, 'Keep laughing suckers' . . . Recognize the reality of football in the late 20th century, and come to the conclusion that something must be done soon. (TTWAR 35, Summer 1997: 8).

Actually, TTWAR is, darkly, very funny indeed; but it is also, importantly, *deeply* serious. These sorts of crucial issue, along with possible structural changes in the sport, continue to be debated passionately in both TTWAR and, less convincingly, in RAOTL. Ideas for a European Super League, the spread of Rupert Murdoch's TV/football business interests, the alleged 'takeover' of the sport by 'accountants' (including Liverpool's Rick Parry) and the new investment in Liverpool FC by the Granada group in 1999, are all regarded, in these *culturally* knowledgeable football circles, with deep suspicion. At Liverpool, however, perhaps more than at any other British football club, the new and corrosive corporate era for football can be comfortably set against a recent and 'better' past, when action *on the pitch* is fondly remembered as all by which the measure of a football club was properly made. As *Prometheus* told readers of TTWAR (No. 40, Autumn, 1998: 41):

The sad, but inescapable, truth is that the game has already changed out of recognition in a very short space of time. We are still nostalgic for the Shankly and Paisley eras, when what you achieved on the pitch determined whether you were considered a contender for the greatest club in the world. The hard work, creativity and industry of the players and back room staff were enough to put us in a super league all of our own. These days, performances on the pitch seem to matter less than share dividends and corporate marketing strategies. You, there! Just pay up and shut up . . .

Nostalgia burns brightly here, of course, as the writer is happy to point out. TTWAR, especially, is an articulate, informed and an unapologetically *political* forum where the Liverpool club's past is constantly set against a less satisfying present. It proffers a profoundly local and *masculinist* cultural space – there is barely a female contributor, though little *explicit* sexism either – and it is one which also, predictably, privileges certain types of fan in the debate about authenticity: the subtext, almost always, here is that the *real* fans of the club are male, young, probably working-class and ideally local (see Chapter Nine). But this is also a voice which is an important and very *necessary* counter to the commercial output of the football club to which it is so utterly devoted. However, for all their insight and passion, for all the extraordinary knowledge and respect the fans at Liverpool have for the traditions of the club and for its great managers and players, it is not always easy to detect in these debates among fans about the 'beautiful game', a clear and workable vision of a preferred *future*. Mapping a reasonable future for *all* fans is something which is extremely difficult to prefigure, of course, in these days of the global economics of sport. The recent past? Now, *that* still beams on this Red side of Merseyside – like a veritable beacon.

References

Armstrong, G. (1998) *Football Hooligans: Knowing the Score*, Oxford: Berg.

Bale, J. (1994) *Landscapes of Modern Sport*, Leicester: Leicester University Press.

Brill, A. (1989) 'An ontology for exploring urban public life today', in *Places*, Fall: 25–30.

Bromberger, C. (1993) 'Allez L'OM, forza Juve': the passion for football in Turin and Marseilles', in S. Redhead (ed.) *The Passion and the Fashion*, Aldershot: Avebury.

Channon, H. (1976) *Portrait of Liverpool*, London: Robert Hale.

Clarke, A. (1991) 'Figuring a brighter future', in E. Dunning and C. Rojek (eds) *Sport and Leisure in the Civilising Process*, London: MacMillan.

Cotton, E. (1996) *The Voice of Anfield*, Chorley: Sport in Wood.

Dunning, E., Murphy, P. and Williams, J. (1988) *The Roots of Football Hooliganism*, London: Routledge.

Edge, A. (1999) *Faith of our Fathers: Football as a Religion*, London: Mainstream.

Giulianotti, R. (1994) 'Social identity and public order: political and academic discourses on football violence', in R. Giulianotti, et al. (eds) *Football, Violence and Social Identity*, London: Routledge.

—— (1999) *Football: a Sociology of the Global Game*, Cambridge: Polity.

Goodwin, J. and Straughan, L. (1996) *Reykjavik to Rome: Everton and Liverpool Fans in Europe*, Birkenhead: Picton.

Haynes, R. (1995) *The Football Imagination: the Rise of Football Fanzine Culture*, Aldershot: Arena.

Hill, D. (1989) *Out of his Skin: The John Barnes Phenomenen*, London: Faber & Faber

Hodgson, D. (1978) *The Liverpool Story*, London: Arthur Barker.

Holt, R. (1989) *Sport and the British*, Oxford: Oxford University Press.

Hopcraft, A. (1971) *The Football Man*, Harmondsworth: Penguin.

Inglis, S. (1996) *Football Grounds of Britain*, London: Collins Willow.

Kelly, S. (1991) *You'll Never Walk Alone: the Official Illustrated History of Liverpool FC*, London: Queen Anne Press.

—— (1993) *The Kop: the End of an Era*, London: Mandarin.

King, A. (1998) *The End of the Terraces*, London: Leicester University Press.

Lea, J. and Young, J. (1984) *What's to be done About Law and Order?* Harmondsworth: Penguin.

McClure, J. (1980) *Spike Island: Portrait of a Police Division*, London: Arrow.

Paul, D. (1998) *Anfield Voices*, Stroud: Tempus.

Redhead, S. (1991) *Football with Attitude*, Manchester: Wordsmith.

—— (1997) *Subculture to Clubcultures*, Oxford: Blackwell.

Robins, D. and Cohen, P. (1978) *Knuckle Sandwich*, Harmondsworth: Penguin.

Russell, D. (1997) *Football and the English*, Preston: Carnegie.

St John, I. (1967) *Boom at the Kop*, London: Sportsmans Book Club.

Sampson, K. (1998) *Extra Time*, London: Yellow Jersey Press.

Scraton, P. (1999) *Hillsborough: the Truth*, Edinburgh and London: Mainstream.

Scraton, P., Jemphry, A. and Coleman, S. (1995) *No Last Rights*, Liverpool: Liverpool City Council/Alden Press.

Souness, G. (1999) *Souness: The Management Years*, London: André Deutsch.

Taylor, I. (1991) 'English football in the 1990s; taking Hillsborough seriously', in J. Williams and S. Wagg (eds) *British Football and Social Change*, Leicester: Leicester University Press.

Taylor, I., Evans, K. and Fraser, P. (1996) *A Tale of Two cities: Global Change, Local feeling and Everyday Life in the North of England*, London: Routledge.

Taylor, J. (1998) *Body Horror*, Manchester: Manchester University Press.

Taylor, P. (1990) *The Hillsborough Stadium Disaster 15 April 1989: Final Report*, London: HMSO.

Taylor, R. and Ward, A., with Williams, J. (1993) *Three Sides of the Mersey An Oral History of Everton, Liverpool and Tranmere Rovers*, London: Robson.

Taylor, R., Ward, A. and Newburn, T. (1995) *The Day of the Hillsborough Disaster*, Liverpool: Liverpool University Press.

Wagg, S. (1984) *The Football World*, Brighton: Harvester.

Walter, T. (1991) 'The mourning after Hillsborough', *Sociological Review*, **39**(3) : 599–626.

Williams, J. (1986) 'White riots: the English football fan abroad', in A. Tomlinson and G. Whannel (eds) *On the Ball*, London: Pluto.

—— (1988) *Football and football hooliganism in Liverpool*, Leicester: Sir Norman Chester Centre for Football Research, University of Leicester.

—— (1991) 'Having an away day', in J. Williams and S. Wagg (eds) *British Football and Social Change*, Leicester: Leicester University Press.

—— (1997) *FA Premier League National Fan Survey, 1996/97*, Leicester: Sir Norman Chester Centre for Football Research, University of Leicester.

—— (1999) *Is It All Over: Can Football Survive the Premier League?*, Reading: South Street Press.

—— (1999) 'Safety and excitement at football: post-Hillsborough football spectator culture', in *Fire, Safety and Service Recovery in Sports Stadia*, Preston: University of Central Lancashire.

Williams, J., Dunning E. and Murphy, P. (1989) *Hooligans Abroad*, London: Routledge.

Williams, J. and Perkins, S. (1999) 'Ticket pricing, merchandising and the new football business', London: Report for the National Football Taskforce.

Williams, J. and Woodhouse, D. (1999) *Offside? the Position of Women and Football in Britain*, Reading: South Street Press.

6

From Barnes to Camara: Football, Identity and Racism in Liverpool
Dave Hill

Out of His Skin

It was a wet, windy autumn night in east London, but a bleaker one in Liverpool. I was in my car listening to the live BBC radio broadcast of the season's first Merseyside derby, giddy with rage and frustration over what I was hearing. Alan Green's commentary was not the problem. The cause of my consternation was the sound from the crowd, the unbearable eruptions of abuse from massed Evertonians every time a particular Liverpool player got anywhere near the ball.

That player was John Barnes, playing against the men from the other side of Stanley Park for the first time in the red shirt. When this match took place – October, 1987 – Barnes was already an exceptional figure in the English national game thanks both to the shining talents he'd already displayed for Watford and England, and to his unusual background as the son of a senior figure in the Jamaican military. Now, as the Evertonians' baiting rose to successions of crescendos, Barnes was also turning into the powerful symbol of a disorder within football culture, something which those inside the game seemed unable to even recognize, let alone begin to cure – racism, in many forms.

In a small way, I helped make Barnes into that symbol. First, following a second derby a week later which was similarly disfigured (there were four that season altogether), I wrote an article in the *Independent* newspaper arguing that the reactions Barnes had triggered since joining Liverpool brought sharply into focus the unchallenged prevalence of racism within English football at large and also its peculiar manifestations on Merseyside. How strange, I observed, that the city of Liverpool was the home of one of the longest-established black communities in Britain, yet its two great football teams had somehow remained almost totally white during a twenty-year period in which black players had become conspicuous at just about every other professional club in England. And this was in spite of a clear passion for the game among ordinary black Liverpudlians who played for amateur teams and followed the professional game on TV and in the press, but were almost never seen on the celebrated terraces or in the stands of Anfield or Goodison Park.

There seemed much more to find out, and plenty to be said about it. Yet, although Barnes's treatment had inspired debate in the Merseyside media, the only strong voice heard nationally was Green's who, to his great credit, condemned the 'racial stuff' on air during that first derby. Other broadcasters and virtually all the press ignored it: apparently, such crowd behaviour was to go on being accepted as 'part and parcel of the game', even when so extreme that it dominated it.

The more others failed to tackle the matter, the more intent I became on doing the job myself. I wrote a proposal for a book and my literary agent duly set about trying to sell it. Initially, she sent the idea to a number of conventional sports publishers. There were no takers. Yes, they said, they'd love to do a book about Barnes, who, to the intense of annoyance of terrace taunters up and down the land, had been the star of a series of brilliant displays by an all-conquering new-look Liverpool team assembled by manager Kenny Dalglish. But the publishers wanted an authorized biography, almost certainly a standard 'ghost job', and that wasn't what I had in mind at all.

It's worth remembering that this was in football writing's BFP period – Before *Fever Pitch* – when football books with pretentions to proper journalism were few and far between: Eamon Dunphy's *Only A Game?* (1976) Hunter Davies's *The Glory Game* (1972), Arthur Hopcraft's collection of essays and profiles *The Football Man* (1971) . . . that was about it. Furthermore, the book I wanted to write was never going to be one that John Barnes himself would wish to associate himself with, and for entirely understandable reasons. Even if any contribution he might have wished to make to it had been emollient and diplomatic to a fault, the book as a whole was certain to reflect badly on the club he had just joined, its famous local rival, many fans of both, and on the city of Liverpool itself whose cosy 1960s image as a city of good-natured scallywags was already badly damaged. First, there was the stigma of mass unemployment. In its wake the Toxteth riots – and the inquiry chaired by Lord Gifford which followed – put Liverpool's race relations under the national spotlight for the first time. And then, of course, there was the grim disaster at the Heysel stadium in Brussels, where violence by followers of Liverpool before the European Cup Final led to the deaths of thirty-nine mainly Juventus fans.

Given all this, had John Barnes assisted me in my enterprise it could only have brought a heap of trouble on his head. This would have been particularly unfortunate given that the project had been inspired by my sympathy and admiration for this remarkable player. I made a half-hearted approach to his then agent, just to be polite. I was pleasantly relieved when, as expected, I was rebuffed. I had gone through the necessary motions. Now I was free to write the book that really needed writing while leaving John Barnes equally free to say completely truthfully that he'd had nothing to do with it after it came out.

This, in fact, is exactly what happened when *Out Of His Skin: The John Barnes Phenomenon* was published in September 1989. It had finally been commissioned by that most literary of publishing houses Faber & Faber and for the decidedly modest (though very welcome) advance of £4,000. Of this, the usual ten per cent went to my agent and most of the rest was eaten up by the cost of tickets, train fares and overnight accommodation in some of Liverpool's less glamorous hotels. It was, in other words, never going to be a money-spinner for me. It did, though, sell nearly 15,000 copies – quite a respectable performance – and, best of all, it created a small but rather satisfying stink.

The book told the story of John Barnes against the social background that made his move to Liverpool so significant and his experiences there so revealing. To me, Barnes's impact at Anfield had the effect of exposing and dramatizing submerged racial issues on Merseyside and in English football at large. My thesis was that while there was never any formal anti-black policy at Anfield with regard either to players or supporters, the customs and traditions of the club had made it extremely difficult for anyone with a dark-coloured skin to thrive or feel comfortable there. There was, in other words, a sinister hidden underside to the compelling mythology around Liverpool Football Club which had evolved in the era of Bill Shankly and which contributed to and reflected the wider rough-diamond romance of Beatle City.

This mythology surrounding Liverpool FC was a powerful and, in many ways, a wonderful thing. It had had me under its spell since about the age of eight when, despite being from a modestly middle-class home in a small town in Somerset, I was captivated by the football ethos of a proletarian northern city personified by the 'hard-but-fair' reputations of Ron Yeats and Tommy Smith, the exuberance of Emlyn Hughes, the eccentricity of Tommy Lawrence, the flair of my first hero Peter Thompson on the wing, the wry, rugged populism of Shankly himself and, of course, the Kop.

Much of my infatuation with the Liverpool football team was down to the seductiveness of that certain Liverpool style conveyed through the media to me as a child just as vividly by figures as diverse as John Lennon and Jimmy Tarbuck and even by The Liver Birds. But one of the wonders of my pursuit of the John Barnes story was that I was confirmed in my belief that this was a style rooted in substance. Close to twenty years on from the day in 1970 when I sat at the bottom of the stairs in my parents house and wept over Liverpool's shock exit from the FA Cup at the hands of lowly Watford, I found myself talking to ordinary Liverpool people who were just as witty, warm and irreverent as was advertised by the Liverpool legend. My boyhood idealization of Liverpool FC still had some justification because so many of the good things I'd always believed about the city were still true. The trouble was, there was another, less attractive truth as well. This was what the John Barnes phenomenon laid bare.

A New Liverpool?

So, what is the purpose of this rather lengthy recap? A small part of it is to establish that, despite being far from Liverpudlian or, these days, even a supporter of Liverpool FC (more a fascinated sympathizer, really) I have at least some credentials for the task of making sense of issues around 'race' and racism as they arise in the often unique context of Merseyside football. (I'm not black, either, since you ask, although the most gratifying compliments I've received from black people, including one or two professional footballers, was that they wouldn't have known that from reading my book.) But the main reason for starting this chapter by looking back to the events of the 1987/88 season is to evoke a sense of contrast between the situation then and the rather different situation now.

It is only thirteen years since John Barnes was, unforgettably, photographed back-heeling bananas off the pitch at Goodison Park, and he has only just hung up his boots to become chief coach at Celtic. Yet the events and passions triggered by his first appearances in a Liverpool shirt might easily be mistaken for ancient history. That is certainly the first impression created by considering the long list of black players who have subsequently turned out for the Reds.

Under Graeme Souness, Dalglish's eventual successor as Liverpool manager (following Ronnie Moran's brief spell in charge), Barnes was followed by two of the most unlikely black guys to wear a Liverpool shirt: Michael Thomas, whose last-gasp goal for Arsenal had deprived the Anfield club of the 'double' at the end of the 1988/89 season; and David James who, being a goalkeeper, played in one of the positions black footballers have always been least likely to occupy (despite the first black pro in England being a goalkeeper, Arthur Wharton). As well as these, the Souness regime also brought Mark Walters down from Glasgow where (also under Souness) he had been the first black player to turn out for Rangers. Then, when Souness gave way to the leadership period of Roy Evans and his subsequent co-manager Gerard Houllier, Evans brought another black goalkeeper into the squad. Tony Warner never got further than the subs' bench at Anfield and eventually became first choice at Millwall following a spell in Scotland. But it is important to mention him, not least because he was locally born. The first of other black additions arrived thanks to the cheque book: Irish international defender Phil Babb, Cameroonian international defender Rigobert Song, striker Stan Collymore and Paul Ince, the first black player to captain England.

Most recently Houllier has provided Liverpool fans with a new favourite by importing the Guinean-Frenchman Aboubacar 'Titi' Camara from Marseille. Although – at least as I write – Camara has not secured a regular place in the starting line-up, he has endeared himself to the Liverpool crowd with his strength, his skill on the ball and, significantly, his on-field personality. He may be very different from them, but he has something important in common with Liverpool figures of legend in that he seems slightly larger than life. In a symbolic way, Camara has also shown himself to be larger than death. Not only did he run out to play from the kick-off against West Ham in October 1999 despite learning of the death of his father earlier in the day, he scored the only goal of the game.

The sight of Camara turning with outspread arms to celebrate his strike seems to me a rather beautiful image in the context of a Liverpool fan culture marked more deeply than most by mortality and the need to come to terms with it. The Spion Kop, of course, takes its name from a hill in South Africa where many troops from the Liverpool area perished during the Boer War, and the song 'Scouser Tommy' has its catastrophic images of soldiers from the city under fire in foreign fields. The contrasting legacies of Heysel and Hillsborough speak pretty much for themselves. Similarly, Bill Shankly's tongue-in-cheek remark on the relationship between football, life and death is too famous to need repeating here.

Liverpool fans won't need reminding that not every black player joining the club has been a big success. The erratic James became a notorious liability at times – 'Calamity James' to some. Walters and Thomas had their moments, but Collymore's intermittent golden ones were dulled by the pall of disturbance and disappointment he seems to cast wherever he goes. Babb went in and out of favour before being cast into the reserves, and not everyone is convinced about Song, who was transferred to West Ham United late in the year 2000. As for Ince, he arrived at Anfield handicapped by past exploits with Manchester United. Intent on being 'the Governor', he appears to have lived up to the nickname more off the pitch than on it, where his leadership ambitions were actually required.

But these chequered exploits are in no sense evidence that blacks and Liverpool Football Club don't mix. The fortunes of these players were no more nor less uneven during the difficult late 1980s and 1990s than those of the white players, be they white English, Scottish, Irish, Scandinavian, North American, Eastern or Western European. And on the upside, the best years of John Barnes will be remembered just as long as will the teenage feats of Michael Owen, while Camara has already achieved a small yet special place in Anfield folklore. The overall picture is perfectly clear: since the tempestuous months which followed Barnes's first appearance in 1987, black players have written themselves into Liverpool's history and will continue doing so, a transformation which looked a very long way off as little as fifteen years ago.

Meanwhile, a similar metamorphosis has occurred at Everton, despite those many Goodison fans who took such dismal delight in celebrating their white 'purity' by comparison with Barnes's supposed contamination of their Anfield counterparts' racial profile. Again, each story is different. Everton's first black signing, the Nigerian World Cup star Daniel Amokachi, was well liked, even though he struggled. (Was this simply because he added a little novelty interest to a prosaic and fitful side? Or was there also something slightly self-conscious – even a little penitent – about Evertonians' embrace of this big-hearted failure, especially following their ill-treatment of Barnes?) Joe Royle's managership saw the arrival of defender Terry Phelan and also Earl Barrett from Royle's previous club Oldham Athletic. Royle also blooded Bradford-born Danny Cadamarteri who was embraced for energy, commitment and his ability to come up with something unexpected, though his star faded under Walter Smith. Smith experimented unsuccessfully with Ibrahima Bakàyoko and began the 1999/2000 season hoping for better from Abel Xavier, a versatile Mozambican defender signed from PSV Eindhoven who quickly entered the Pantheon of Preposterous Haircuts. Smith also provided the club's first bona fide black hero in ex-Arsenal striker Kevin Campbell, whose goals rescued the Blues from relegation in the FA Premier League basement dogfight of 1999.

These developments among the playing staffs of the two big Merseyside clubs are impossible not to notice. It is, perhaps, especially remarkable that Campbell returned to English football from Trabzonspor after being the object of racist observations made in public by the Turkish club's chairman. Once upon a time Everton would have been one of the last clubs he'd have turned to following such an episode. But what do they signify about the bigger story of Liverpool the city, Liverpool the club and their relationships with people who don't fit the description 'white'? When John Barnes ghosted down the wing leaving defenders tackling shadows and received the adulation of the Liverpool crowd, did it mean he had made racism disappear just as dramatically as his arrival had exposed its full virulence? Did his irresistible form and the easy affability of his contacts with ordinary Liverpool people mean that every Liverpool supporter who'd ever shouted the word 'nigger' would think long and hard before doing it again? Had Anfield, for so long regarded as hostile territory by black Liverpudlians, suddenly been remade as a place of welcome, a place where they could at last become part of that Liverpool identity which the Kop had done so much to define and which I was so beguiled by as a child? Was local black talent more likely now to be recognized and nurtured by the club's scout network and youth development programmes?

Some certainly hoped that all these things were so. But was that much too wishful thinking? Was it more pertinent to ask whether Anfield's acceptance of John Barnes actually gave apologists for racism a most convenient argument for redoubling their insistence that the best way to deal with it was to ignore it? (After all, they might point out, that's what Barnes himself was doing, wasn't it?) And could it be that the subsequent importation of a few talented black individuals into a couple of famous football teams simply created an illusion of 'colour-blindness' that helps conceal the same dynamics of suspicion and exclusion festering underneath?

In the bright, sometimes blinding, light of what might be called 'New Football' all these questions deserve careful consideration – including the ones which more sophisticated observers of racism's workings may consider so naive as not to be worth asking. While the idea that one brilliant footballer can somehow wipe away the ingrained antipathies of an entire football fan culture with a few dazzling dribbles and a clutch of classic goals is perfectly absurd, no one should underestimate the implications of either what Barnes achieved or what he was obliged to endure.

Football's Anti-racism

As recently as the mid-1980s, racism was the subject that no one in positions of influence or authority in football could be bothered to talk about. Today, it is talked about constantly in the sporting media, whether because Leeds fans think it's 'a laugh' to sing songs about gas chambers to Spurs fans, or because white Englishman Neil Ruddock makes a wisecrack about garlic on the breath of black Frenchman Patrick Vieira. Racism, and how to combat it, has become part of the debate about the extraordinary renewal of the national game, along with the virtues of all-seater stadia, the dominance of Sky TV, the spiralling of wages and the influx of foreign stars. Racism is now at the centre of football debate, and this amazing transformation can largely be traced back directly to the trials and the triumphs of John Barnes on Merseyside.

The first and clearest evidence of this came with Lord Justice Taylor's report on the Hillsborough disaster. Its principle purpose, of course, was to investigate the nightmare at the Leppings Lane end and make recommendations about supporter safety in the future. But in the process of furthering the rehabilitation of football supporters – a process begun by the disaster itself – after decades of blanket demonization, the Taylor report drew attention to those unattractive aspects of football crowd culture that had previously been ignored. Consequently, racist chanting became a criminal offence. Would the subject have been addressed quite so urgently if the club whose fans had perished at Hillsborough was not also the club whose most exciting player had been very publicly subjected to some of the most extreme racial abuse ever see in England? Probably not.

That was just the beginning. Before long, in 1993, the 'Let's Kick Racism Out Of Football' campaign was jointly launched by the Professional Footballers' Association and the Commission For Racial Equality with the backing of most professional clubs, the main supporters' organizations and the then newly formed FA Premier League. This was the first phase of what evolved into the Kick It Out campaign which sought to address other manifestations of racism in football as well, such as racial abuse by players and discriminatory employment practices at clubs. Racism, in all its forms, also became the subject of an ambitious report by the government's Football Task Force, published in March 1998, which recommended a stiffening of the law and more vigorous forms of action at all levels of the game from junior and park football right up to the giddy heights of the FA Premier League.

But how did the situation evolve in the particular circumstances of Merseyside? There are several angles on this. Where black professionals are concerned, it is plain that Barnes's success at Liverpool smoothed the way for the flow of black players into the Anfield dressing room and, indirectly, into Goodison Park's as well. This would certainly have happened anyway, but the fact that Barnes had proved such an impressive ambassador for 'blackness' – whatever that was taken to mean by those who felt threatened by it – must have made it easier for others who followed.

This can only be a good thing, and not just for the top rank of black professionals who can nowadays think of Liverpool (and Everton) as possible employers rather than clubs whose supporters were among the most vocally racist in the country. Sceptics may be right to claim that a preponderance of black players in a team may be evidence of nothing more substantial than the kind of racial tolerance that can only be described as skin deep. Even so, the breach of the glass barrier which so heavily impeded black participation prior to Barnes has a symbolic importance which should not quickly be dismissed. It matters that Liverpool look different these days. It matters because of the wall-to-wall whiteness of its great teams in the past, and it particularly matters because those teams, even the ones with hardly a single scouser in them, were seen to personify other qualities seen as constituent of an authentic Liverpudlian working-class identity: tough, canny and spartan rather than fragile, guileless and flash – the very failings the football culture so often presumed to be synonymous with blackness.

Of course, there is a general sense in which the conspicuous addition of black players to the Liverpool team profile simply contributes to another racial stereotype perpetuated by sport, the one which deems that blacks are inherently more athletically gifted and therefore less intellectually able, and which contributes so insidiously to the underachievement of black boys at school. On the other hand, the sheer variety of black players who've performed on the big Merseyside stages has helped challenge the received wisdoms held by so many whites of earlier generations. Every black player who made his name in the 1970s seems to have put up with the assumption of white managers, coaches or fellow players that they might have flair when the sun was shining, but didn't have the blood or the bottle to scrap for an away point in mid-February. Only a total dope would make such assumptions now. Michael Thomas and Paul Ince might not have been everything Liverpool wanted them to be, but no-one could accuse them of being too soft for a ruck in the mud.

But so much for the symbolism of black bodies in red shirts. While that symbolism carries a force for good, which ought to be acknowledged, it cannot be held to represent the end of racism as an issue for Liverpool FC. My most poignant feelings when watching John Barnes at the start of his Liverpool career came from the realization that, even in his pomp, his place in the affections of too many Liverpool fans was very fragile indeed. It could all have been so different. Rumours, since denied, that he'd rather have joined a London club accompanied his arrival. The first few home games at Anfield had to be rescheduled thanks to a problem with the sewers. This was just as well for Barnes: who knows what sort of shit he might have had thrown at him by the more committed bigots among his new home 'fans'? Instead, he turned in three marvellous away performances, so by the time he made his Anfield debut the bulk of the home faithful were falling at his feet.

At the time Barnes himself was in no position to make these kinds of point. But he makes it very bluntly in his recent book (*Barnes: The Autobiography*, 1999: 95-6):

> For me the solution was simple – deliver on the pitch to make the fans love me. The Kop would have slaughtered me with racial abuse if I had faltered on the field. I knew that . . . What a target I would have been. The Kop treated out-of-form white players cruelly, so they would have crucified a struggling black. A bad aura already clung to me because Liverpool fans believed I only came because Arsenal did not step in. Had I played badly, it would have been hell for me. Pure hell.

Barnes also knew as well as anyone that a racist fan is quite willing to tolerate a 'black bastard' as long as he's doing a good job for his team. You don't have to know too much about either football or double standards to be sickened by the fact that many of the same fans who valorize a black star in their own team have no hesitation in hurling racial abuse at the black stars of opponents, especially if their own black star isn't playing. Liverpool fans did exactly that during John Barnes's first season when the Reds travelled to Norwich City for a League match in April 1988. On arriving at Carrow Road I learned that Barnes was out through injury, and felt immediate sympathy for Norwich's black winger Ruel Fox. I knew that Barnes's absence would be taken by a vocal element of Liverpool's travelling supporters as a licence to racially abuse Fox. When this duly occurred, it was no less repellent for its utter predictability.

Other incidents during the same season revealed an awareness among Liverpool supporters of precisely that type of double standard within their own ranks. A fairly bleak example arose during an away match at Luton Town. Travelling Reds supporters had been forced to slip in among the locals due to Luton's notorious ban on away fans. Black players were long-established at Luton – Ricky Hill,

Brian Stein, Mitchell Thomas – and were represented in the team that day. Meanwhile, Barnes was in the Liverpool side. When he got the ball a number of Town fans started up the regulation gorilla grunting, and a nearby Scouser felt moved to respond: 'Ah shurrup, will yer?: youse have got niggers of yer own.'

Then there was the game away to Watford, where Barnes received a friendly welcome from the fans of the little club he'd previously served so well. Thanks mainly to Peter Beardsley, who played beautifully that day, the game was won for Liverpool well before the end and Barnes was substituted. One Liverpool fan showing, I'd like to think, an ironic appreciation that Reds' fans were really no better than Everton's underneath the surface, responded by appropriating one of the racist chants Evertonians had used in the Merseyside derby games: 'Liverpool are white!' he cried, as Barnes left the field. 'Liverpool are white!'

As for Barnes, himself, he already knew that his adoration by the racist patrons at Anfield was highly conditional. It was also, quite literally, impersonal: 'I was fairly circumspect about all the adulation, about all the cries of "we love you, we love you". Liverpool's fans did not love John Barnes, the person. They worshipped John Barnes, the no. 10 who plays for Liverpool' (1999: 96). This realism was borne out in the later years of Barnes's time with Liverpool. After serious injuries had robbed him of his pace he re-emerged as a different kind of player under the Roy Evans regime. During the 1995/96 season he performed well in a central midfield 'holding role', a key component in a system he was widely credited with helping to devise, built around striker Robbie Fowler and Steve McManaman in a 'free' role. This team almost did great things. But not quite. And later, when its form slumped, Barnes bore the brunt of the more critical fans. While some had longer memories and admired Barnes for fighting back to fitness, others reached for insults unpleasantly adjacent to the standard clichés about black players: he was lazy, he was soft, he wasn't trying hard enough. Old habits die hard.

Liverpool 4 versus Liverpool 8

Those who at the time indignantly insisted that even if terrace racism used to be a feature of the Anfield atmosphere it wasn't any more, because Reds' fans all loved Barnes, would do well to reflect upon these sentiments, and on the player's own feelings on the matter, even at the time of his greatest triumphs. But the truest and most damning measure of how far Liverpool FC had to travel as an institution, if it was to be truly accessible to every Liverpudlian, was the reaction to Barnes mania among the city's black football lovers. Whether watching their amateur league games from the touchline, or chatting with them in the pub or in their homes, the story from these black scousers was always the same: they don't want us there – not as players, not as supporters, not at all.

Presented with this perception, a number of white Reds' fans (and one former player) were quick to belittle it back in the 1980s with the standard disclaimers: 'They've got a "chip on the shoulder" or "They won't mix".' But the black scousers' stories were all the more persuasive because they seemed to illustrate a theme of social exclusion which ran not just through football. Like anyone with half an eye for a city's racial landscape, I noticed very quickly the almost total absence of black people from Liverpool's streets and shops as well as from almost all its residential areas – rich and poor alike – outside the 'south end' postcode of Liverpool 8 and its fringes. Nor was this just my personal impression: reports and surveys into employment and housing swiftly confirmed that in most parts of Liverpool black Liverpudlians were nowhere to be seen.

Liverpool's two great soccer stadiums seemed to exemplify this informal apartheid, and with it the city's most distressing paradox: on the one hand it had acquired so much of its personality from being one of Britain's most vibrant and cosmopolitan seaports; on the other, the deep-rooted black element of this historic cultural mix seemed to have been erased from the city's otherwise attractive collective identity.

The black scousers I met felt this exclusion keenly. These included several members of an impressive multi-cultural park team called Almithak, who told stories of uncomfortable experiences with the intimidating citadel that was Anfield in the past. Some recounted going to the ground as fans – Liverpool fans – and becoming marginalized and terrorized – if not by direct threats and insults from other Liverpool fans around them, then by the waves of abuse aimed at visiting black players such as Cyrille Regis or Garth Crooks. Others talked of being spotted as talented schoolboys and invited to train with other promising lads under the aegis of the Liverpool youth system. At first they were pleased to be noticed, but later found their noticeability invited less gratifying attention: coaches insisting they played on the wing even though their position was midfield or centre-back; white players cheerfully calling them 'Sam' – short for 'Sambo'.

Incidents like these may not have been motivated by malice. But in some ways it might have been easier if they had. At least with an out-and-out racist a black person knows the score. But being assailed by unthinking, even benignly-meant, white racist assumptions about inherent aptitudes (sporting or otherwise) and acceptable nicknames, can be trickier to deal with, especially if you are far from your own patch and in a minority of one. Different individuals responded in different ways. Some took issue with their treatment, and were rewarded by being tagged 'chippy'. Others just drifted away. In either case the sentiments were much the same as those of alienated would-be black Liverpool fans. Or Everton fans, for that matter. Emotionally, culturally, even geographically, they were always made to feel completely out of place.

I found this was especially true among black Liverpudlians from the environs of Liverpool 8 – a 'bad area' as white taxi drivers often called it when driving me there – and this deep legacy of suspicion had been firmly cemented by memories of the few black players who had turned out for either Merseyside club before the arrival of Barnes. There had been two for Everton. One was a local player called Cliff Marshall who made a handful of appearances but never established himself. The other was striker Mike Trebilcock. To me at least his story is a bit of a mystery. Although he was dark, he was not very dark – possibly of mixed race – and was never described to me by anyone, black Scousers included, as an example of a 'black player'. However, he was certainly thought of one by racist Liverpool fans. Kopite John Mackin, writing in the Liverpool fanzine *Through The Wind And The Rain* (Issue 13, Autumn 1993) recalls 'a peculiarly graphic song about [Trebilcock] which beggars belief now'.

Trebilcock was signed for a small fee from Plymouth Argyle and never became a regular first-choice player, but he appeared in the 1966 FA Cup Final against Sheffield Wednesday because England international Fred Pickering was unfit. The game provided the nation with one of it's more dramatic Wembley showcases, won 3–2 by Everton thanks to a late goal by winger Derek Temple, following a desperate Wednesday defensive mistake. The drama of those closing moments clearly accounts for much of the reason why that final is remembered for Temple's winner. Yet it still seems very odd that the scorer of both Everton's other goals has been all but forgotten. It was Trebilcock, of course. And given this contribution on that famous day, it seems odder still that he moved from Goodison soon after and, if my information is correct, went to live abroad.

I have not properly researched the stories of Marshall and Trebilcock and must therefore resist leaping to conclusions. But I can speak with more conviction about the experiences of the only black player ever to have represented Liverpool prior to John Barnes, and the bitter legacy they left among the city's black people. Howard Gayle was not just a black guy; he was a black guy from the 'wrong' part of Liverpool. As a player, he was quick, skilful and brave. As a person, he was young and raw and had resolved, long before he joined Liverpool Football Club, that if anyone ever called him a 'sambo', a 'nigger' or a 'coon' he wouldn't take it lying down. To Gayle, that wasn't being 'chippy' – that was following the basic rules of self-defence and self-respect.

At first, Gayle progressed well. Bill Shankly predicted he would become the first black player to represent the full England team. But his career at Anfield never developed in the way Shankly envisaged. Gayle eventually made his first team debut under Shankly's successor, Bob Paisley as a substitute in a home game against Manchester City in October 1980. After that he returned to the reserves until, in April 1981, found himself thrown, completely unexpectedly, into a European Cup semi-final second leg, away to Bayern Munich. In the first leg at Anfield the German team had secured a goalless draw, and Liverpool's position for the return had been made all the more precarious by a long injury list. As a result the inexperienced Gayle found himself on the substitute's bench – but not for very long. Only a few minutes into the match Kenny Dalglish limped off and Gayle was sent on to replace him.

For most fans the significance of that match lies solely in the result: with a display of typical endurance and escapology, the Reds snatched a one-all draw and so went through to the Final in which they won the European Cup for the third time. But for Howard Gayle, and those many black Liverpudlians who knew him and his family or simply wished him well, the night has a bitter legacy. It wasn't because Gayle didn't perform. On the contrary, he was tremendous, playing almost alone up front and running the Germans ragged. Everyone who saw him thinks so, including his team mates. Yet shortly before the end of the ninety minutes Paisley took him off – the substitute was substituted.

Why did Liverpool's manager take this unusual step? The conventional view is that he did it because Gayle was exhausted and looked in danger of getting sent off. Paisley himself says as much, writing later about these events. Gayle's performance had been all the more impressive for being produced in the face of relentless provocation from the German defenders and the racial abuse of the crowd, yet as the final whistle neared it was clear that Gayle's temper was becoming frayed. Even very fair-minded fans believe that Paisley's decision was wise. But Gayle and his supporters back in black Liverpool read something else into the decision. A substitute substituted despite playing a blinder? A black player withdrawn because his temperament was judged too brittle? Would Paisley have done the same thing, they mused, if Howard Gayle had been white?

Maybe he would, maybe not. Maybe he was wrong, maybe he was right. But Gayle's suspicion that he'd been slighted was intensified by the club's subsequent refusal to offer him the contract he desired or the opportunities he felt that he had earned. He felt he deserved better. As well as impressing in the cauldron of the Olympic Stadium, he'd also shone in League matches towards the end of the season and scored in a one-all draw away to Tottenham. The *Guardian*'s Robert Armstrong sang his praises and those of another newcomer, a striker from Chester by the name of Ian Rush: 'Both have shown they possess the nerve and flair required for the big occasion.' Yet Gayle soon became convinced he had no place in Paisley's plans. True, there were other pretenders to first-team places, Rush included. True, Paisley seemed to have already decided that wingers weren't to be part of his plan. But Gayle felt there was more to it than that. He was eventually transferred and, during a spell with Birmingham City, fulfilled at least part of Shankly's prediction of national honours by representing England three times at under-21 level in 1984. But his career never fulfilled its early promise.

Some insist that racial judgements played no part in this story: Gayle, they say, was probably just not good enough and, furthermore, he was a 'difficult' character; sardonic, touchy and too fond of dubious company. But for some white

Liverpudlians any black guy from the 'wrong' part of town is, by definition, dubious. And for some within the club Gayle's disinclination to put up with racial comments or find certain racial 'jokes' funny marked him out as 'difficult' and 'touchy', whereas Gayle himself had learned to live his life by different standards. And, to much of black Liverpool, the treatment of Howard Gayle was damning evidence that even when a black player had proved that he was good enough to play for Liverpool at the highest levels, somehow a way would still be found to squeeze him out. It is not a fanciful theory. After my book had gone to the printer I was introduced to a Danish football reporter who had once asked Paisley during an interview why Liverpool was almost alone at that time in having no black players in its first-team squad. According to the reporter, Paisley's reply was direct and also revealing about the limits of his own North East and Liverpool 'football' upbringing: 'We don't trust them', he was alleged to have replied.

Liverpool FC Now

All of this took place around twenty years ago, and Liverpool Football Club looks a great deal different today. Howard Gayle's disaffection has not been forgotten by those who felt it by association, but his name may well mean nothing to new generations of black Britons, whether from Liverpool or elsewhere. Barnes has left his mark, and even though (thanks to injury) he lost his spark – and the support of some of the Anfield crowd – towards the end of his Liverpool years, his contribution to one of the finest Liverpool teams ever will not be easily wiped away. Now, under the Houllier revolution, the Liverpool team is more cosmopolitan than ever while, in keeping with national trends, its supporters now travel to fill expensive Anfield seats from further and further afield. Thanks to these upmarket demographics of 'new' football, the ground has been opened up to some ethnic minority groups. Even in the mid-1980s a small number of affluent Chinese Liverpudlians were regular attenders, and they've now been joined by a small but noticeable influx of 'middle-class' young British Asians, mostly from outside Liverpool.

Yet none of these developments seems to have lessened the separation between the club and a sharply marginalized section of the city's population. Liverpool might claim that the 1.4 per cent 'non-white' supporters they attract (according to the *1997 FA Premier League Fan Survey*) is a tiny bit bigger than for most other FA Premier League clubs and not much further behind Arsenal – league leaders in this respect with 4.1 per cent – than anybody else. But it is still a tiny figure in a city with such a long and variegated multi-cultural history. And even if it gets a little bigger in years to come, it probably won't be due to attracting the custom of many local black fans. FA Premier League ticket prices are now beyond the range of even quite affluent citizens. Even if a fear of racism fails to deter the people of black Liverpool from turning up at Anfield, given that so many are economically disadvantaged they are likely to be priced out of the market anyway.

Meanwhile, on the playing side, appearances still suggest that local black football talent is more likely to be recognized outside Liverpool than within it. It is, perhaps, ironic that Everton have made the greater efforts to reach out to Merseyside's black citizens. They've recently appointed a young education and community officer, Alan Johnson, who is from Liverpool and is black. It is doubly ironic that Johnson has found through his work that black kids living in and around Liverpool 8 are mostly Reds' fans, partly because Liverpool are seen as the more successful club, and partly because of the legacy of Barnes.

At the same time, Liverpool FC continues to have next to no effective 'grass roots' community mechanisms which really reach into the black parts of the city. And all reports suggest that the racial constitution of youngsters recruited to Liverpool's football youth schemes is almost as uniformly white as ever. There may be black players on the park, and that may be more important than some sceptics are inclined to think. Beyond that, though, the subtle, often unconscious, dynamics of exclusion seem very little altered.

All this helps to put the John Barnes legacy into a clearer perspective. In sharp contrast to Howard Gayle, he was fortunately placed to break through the barriers against black participation. His outstanding talent was, of course, vital. But so, too, was the fact that, in Kenny Dalglish, Liverpool now had a manager – still a player-manager, in fact – who was drawn from a different generation and who knew from his own playing experience that black players were no more nor less deserving of Liverpool's 'trust' than white ones. And Barnes was well equipped to handle his situation on a personal level too. The product of an impeccably middle-class Jamaican background and, it seems, all the confidence that went with it, Barnes looked down on racist fans and players alike as ignorant and pathetic – and therefore found it easier to rise above the fray. Life for Howard Gayle had never been that way.

Whatever their respective merits as players, the differing fortunes of Gayle and Barnes help crystalize the bigger picture of Liverpool FC and issues around 'race'. The discomforts and uncertainties of Gayle in the dressing room reflect those of other black Liverpudlians about the entire institution that is Anfield. Barnes, on the other hand, showed both how racist behaviour might be suspended, even challenged, yet also how conditional the acceptance of a black player by his home crowd can be.

In a way, the two men represent the themes of continuity and change also identified by supporters and academics alike. In the Liverpool fanzine *Through the Wind and Rain* in 1998 (Issue 41: 51), for example, an Asian Reds fan from Birmingham commented on the 'casually racist hard core' of Liverpool support pre-Barnes, which made it 'more intimidating going to Anfield than away games'. He goes on:

The hypocrisy that grew around the time of John Barnes's signing and the condemnation of Evertonians' behaviour was irritating and encouraging. Irritating because a lot of Reds opposed his move, and I knew they'd have been the same if he'd signed for Everton. Encouraging, because people were waking up to the fact that racism was unacceptable. I hoped this would be a turning point and that black people would be encouraged to attend games. It didn't really happen in any significant numbers, and problems persisted.

Les Back, Tim Crabbe and John Solomos in their recent article on 'Racism in football' (in Adam Brown (ed.), 1998 *Fanatics!*) make a similar point. 'It is clear', the authors observe, in talking about racist abuse by Evertonians at those first Merseyside derbies in the 1980s that spurred me to write my book, 'that while John Barnes was the referent in each of the key chants . . . their targets were the predominantly white Liverpool supporters'. They continue:

> Everton fans were making a statement about the perceived normative identity and racial preferences of Merseyside which could only work if those preferences were shared by the Liverpool supporters . . . The intention was to 'wind up' the Liverpool supporters on the premise of a shared antipathy towards 'niggers' which is located within a common understanding of the racial characteristics associated with the Scouse identity. (Back et al., 1998: 78)

The general climate at Anfield on matchdays has certainly changed a lot, too, since the 1980s. The overt baiting of visiting black players is no longer an obvious feature – though opposing *foreign* players, black and white, can still get their share from individuals when local passions are roused. But no matter how many black players appear in a red shirt, and no matter that more and more of Anfield's seats are now occupied by the backsides of affluent folk from Liverpool and from out of town, some of those who make the atmosphere inside the ground – who make the ground *their* ground – almost certainly still regard being white as a prerequisite for being Red. Until that is challenged effectively – and changed – New Football at Anfield will go on looking too much like Old Football did to those it disdained to embrace.

References

Back, L., Solomos, J. and Crabbe, T. (1998) 'Racism in football: patterns of continuity and change', in A. Brown (ed.) *Fanatics! Power, Race, Nationality and Fandom in European Football*, London: Routledge.

Barnes, J. (1999) *John Barnes: the Autobiography*, London: Headline.

Davies, H. (1972) *The Glory Game*, London: Weidenfeld and Nicolson.

Dunphy, E. (1976) *Only a Game?,* London: Kestrel.

Hill, D. (1989) *Out of his Skin: the John Barnes Phenomenon*, London: Faber & Faber.

Hopcraft, A. (1971) *The Football Man*, Harmondsworth: Penguin.

Hornby, N. (1992) *Fever Pitch*, London: Victor Gollancz.

Williams, J. (1997) *FA Premier League National Fan Survey, 1996/97*, Leicester: Sir Norman Chester Centre for Football Research, University of Leicester.

7

The Fall of Liverpool FC and the English Football 'Revolution':
John Williams

The End of Football History?

For an unprecedented twenty-five years, from the mid-1960s to 1990, under the football management of Bill Shankly, Bob Paisley, Joe Fagan and Kenny Dalglish, Liverpool FC were *the* dominant force in English football and, for seven years from 1977 to 1984, unquestionably the strongest club side in Europe. Leeds United in the late 1960s and early 1970s and, briefly, Everton in the mid-1980s posed challenges to this domestic ascendancy, but it was only as Arsenal, and later Manchester United, began to emerge as major footballing powers in England in the post-Hillsborough period from 1989 did Liverpool's stranglehold on the game in England really begin to loosen.

At the same time, football in England in the early 1990s had begun to hum to the new rhythms of global capitalism and to an increasingly internationalized market for both players and coaches. As this new era rapidly took hold, demanding new responses, Liverpool Football Club was still mired in the aftermath of the single biggest post-war football tragedy in Western Europe. The club turned, instead, once again to those familiar verities focused around the traditions of single-minded, but by now rather anachronistic forms of club administration on the one hand, and, on the playing side, to the still powerful aura of the club's famed 'boot room' coaching dynasty.

In this chapter, then, we want to examine some of the specifics of the recent decline in the fortunes of Liverpool FC against the background of wider shifts in the English game. We want to stress here the *relative* nature of this decline, of course; Liverpool's worst finish in the FA Premier League since 1992 has, after all, been a respectable eighth. We, nevertheless, *do* want to argue that a combination of the recent transformation of European professional football and the relatively static response by Liverpool FC to such shifts are important matters in understanding recent changes in the game and also the Liverpool club's drift from national and European club dominance. We want, then, to focus here, especially, on the *management* changes and continuities at the Liverpool club in the 1980s and 1990s, but we also want to try to locate these changes in terms of wider shifts in the business and management of football clubs during this extraordinary period of the game's development in England. Our argument is that Liverpool was, in some important senses, both temporarily numbed to, and 'overtaken' by, wider developments in the sport, changes which prefaced a much more intimate and necessary connection between the football and 'business' sides of the routine activities of top football clubs. In the new, more globalized era of the sport's development, Liverpool FC is now trying to reposition itself once again, not just nationally as a football club but also in terms of its function as a global 'brand' or 'sign' in the important international market place for transcultural sporting identities. This is crucial, as media sports signs – symbols, logos, texts – are increasingly at the leading edge of the recent 'culturization' of global economics because of their value to media systems, their capacity for flexibility and inter-connectedness, and the ease with which they flow through global networks (Rowe, 1999: 70–1).

We Think we'll Manage

There has actually been very little *academic* work on football club administration, coaching and football *management* in England. Stephen Wagg's (1984) marvellous and underused account of the development of English football into the TV age does most to reveal and explain important changes in the functions and role of the football manager in the post-war English game. Most recent academic work on football, however, has concentrated either on supporter cultures (e.g. Brown, 1998) or on the new economics of the sport (e.g. Morrow, 1999). Giulianotti's (1999) recent sociological work on football at least has a chapter on *playing* the game and on the diffusion of coaching styles, but it has little to say on football management per se. King's (1998) impressive work on the social transformation of the English game has virtually nothing useful to say about management and coaching. Recent accounts on football management drawn from psychology are aimed at a 'popular' audience and lack depth and a strong analytical frame (see Sik, 1996). They read rather like the (better) work of journalists on this issue (Lambert, 1995). Sarah Gilmore's (2000) interesting recent work on football managers, nevertheless, approaches the issue from the straitjacket of discourses drawn from management studies. Recent *anthropological* accounts of the world game have little useful to say about football management and football coaching at all (Armstrong and Giulianotti, 1999).

Despite this general lack of academic focus on management, coaching and playing the game some commentators, such as the French anthropologist Christian Bromberger (1993: 120) do, interestingly, argue that club styles of play reflect local milieus. Bromberger argues that, aesthetically, for example, 'the styles of

Olympique Marseilles and Juventus are strongly opposed, each reflecting a particular vision of the world of mankind and the city'. He discusses the value system of Juve – the so-called 'three Ss' of simplicity, seriousness and sobriety – and argues that this is rooted in the industrial rigour and discipline of the Agnelli family who own the club and the Fiat automobile empire (see Giulianotti, 1999: 140).

This is a similar point to the one we have been trying to argue for at various moments in this book. That is, that the character and style of a club such as Liverpool FC owes something to local 'structures of feeling' in the city of Liverpool itself. The approach, positioning and role in the city of the football club has been shaped both by the close but 'friendly' rivalry with Everton, the ethnic and occupational make-up of Merseyside and the cultural practices and values of the city itself, and *also* by the particular 'communitarian' values brought to the club, especially by the coaching and management dynasty established under Bill Shankly from 1959. In this instance, then, we would argue that the 'sense' of the football club comes more from the approach to managing, coaching and *playing* the game and from the relationships established between club staff and supporters and the specific *playing* traditions at Liverpool FC, especially since the early 1960s, than it does from any particular philosophy of club *ownership*.

This sort of claim, of course, fails to answer a crucial question, namely, what accounts for success at a top football club? In general football texts and coaching manuals, in England at least, the answer to this question tends to be reduced either to the mundane citing of 'hard work' and discipline, or to mythologized references to the specific 'chemistry' of teams, or to the undefinable attributes of individual players or managers, rather than to any specific *organizational* features or to established *processes* which might, for example, link fans, players and clubs. Although we would reject aspects of their overly narrow comparisons between football clubs and 'other' kinds of business, a slightly more sophisticated approach to this issue is offered by the economist Stefan Szymanski and business consultant Tim Kuypers, who have recently tried to identify what provides top football clubs with what they call 'competitive advantage' (Szymanski and Kuypers, 1999: Ch. 6). Only twenty-three clubs have won English League titles since 1888. Four clubs alone have won more than half of all League titles (Liverpool, Manchester United, Arsenal and Everton). Liverpool have won an unrivalled eighteen championships, including eleven between 1973 and 1990, the last time the Merseyside club won the championship. What marks out *these* clubs in particular, apart from their size and fan base (which is in fact a relatively weak indicator, in any case, of club success)?

Szymanski and Kuypers argue that these 'winning' football clubs have, or have had, *distinct capabilities* which, by their nature, are exceptional attributes which cannot be easily reproduced elsewhere. They identify *four* such capabilities (1999: 194–245), as follows.

First, *strategic assets,* in a business sense, refers to a scarce resource which provides an advantage in competition which, once possessed by one firm (club), cannot be possessed by others. This constitutes a monopoly over a necessary input in the production process: e.g. raw materials obtainable only from a particular location, or else some specialized equipment. Examples in a sporting context might be an outstanding player or more likely an inspirational and astute football manager. We have argued that Bill Shankly and his coaching staff at Liverpool provided such an asset, though Szymanski and Kuypers also warn that the advantages accrued here are unlikely to extend long beyond the end of any manager's tenure. At Liverpool, of course, a set of practices with regard to preparation of players had been laid down, had been institutionalized at the club and, also, a coaching *team* had been groomed to succeed Shankly. Moreover, senior players at the club were also charged with responsibility and leadership in a way which was probably uncommon elsewhere (Rush, 1996; Souness, 1999). Finally, the approaches established at Anfield also marked out the club's coaching staff as reliable early *identifiers* of necessary strategic assets (players) which could then be purchased cheaply from other firms (clubs). Shankly bought both Ray Clemence and Kevin Keegan from lowly Scunthorpe United for small fees. Each went on to become world-class players for Liverpool in the 1970s. Alan Hansen, Liverpool's kingpin defender for the whole of the 1980s, was plucked, at 20, by Bob Paisley from Partick Thistle for just £100,000.

The second strategic advantage identified by Szymanski and Kuypers is *innovation.* This they define as the ability to generate incremental improvements to existing products. Successful football clubs are likely to have a greater capacity to innovate than their rivals, and at a lower cost. We have seen, already, Liverpool's early capacity to buy players cheaply and to *improve* its purchases. Such innovations are likely to be quickly imitated in business, however, and so they are limited in the advantages they are likely to offer. But, in an era when involvement in *European* football competition was limited to a small number of clubs from each country, Liverpool's routine involvement in European competition from 1965 right up to the Heysel ban of 1985 also provided extensive opportunities for cross-fertilization of systems and ideas which came much less frequently to other English clubs. We have described in chapter four the ways in which routine local chauvinisms and anxieties about foreign travel at the club were mixed with a real openness on the part of the coaching staff at Liverpool specifically to *European* football experiences. These led to admittedly ad hoc innovation and adaptation on the playing and coaching side at the club throughout the 1970s and 1980s, something which contributed to Liverpool's combination of English and 'continental' playing styles.

The third strategic asset highlighted by Szymanski and Kuypers is that of *reputation.* This the authors define as a distinctive capability which comes from the established position of a product in the marketplace. A good reputation makes a product more attractive to consumers: they know what they are buying. Reputation is a hard capability to replicate or imitate. The authors point to the history and glamour of Manchester United in this respect, arguing that reputation is something which can only be acquired, if it can be acquired at all, in specific conditions and over a long period of time. But in the 1970s and 1980s the popular image of Manchester United among many top British *players*, at least, was that it was indeed a high-profile 'national' club, but one which was essentially underachieving. Professional ideologies strongly pointed at that time to top player transfers to *Liverpool* in order to win trophies, but to *United* perhaps for wages, publicity and profile. Significantly, for example, the sacking of United manager Dave Sexton in 1981 was widely attributed *by* the media *to* the media and to his failure to develop an attractive 'public image' (Wagg, 1984: 193).

All of this meant that in the pre-global football era at least, the routine playing success of Liverpool offered the club pretty much an open hand in the choice of the top British players they wanted; simply in *professional* terms, few players could afford to be seen to turn down a move to Liverpool. Perhaps only players at Manchester United and at local rivals Everton were effectively 'off limits' to the Reds at that time. This strong professional ideology, linking Liverpool FC with footballing success, also probably accounts for the larger number of rather more *cerebral* football players – Dalglish, Hansen, Souness, Lawrenson, Barnes – who, importantly, were the core of the dominant Liverpool teams of the 1980s. Coaches at Liverpool were also happy to let good *players* decide on basic strategies, and so were relatively unthreatened by the arrival at the club of players with ideas or strong *football* personalities. Following the establishment of freedom of movement of players in England in 1978, the advantages in this respect of more affluent, and *successful*, clubs such as Liverpool increased further. This reinforced the seldom believed claims at the time from Anfield that there was no complex, technocratic secret to the club's success: it was simply about signing the best players and letting them play (see Hansen, 1999; and Chapter Four).

The fourth strategic asset offering competitive advantage to clubs or firms is *architecture*. This, according to Szymanski and Kuypers, is a unique *organizational* structure, sometimes associated at football clubs perhaps with the manager and coaches, the players, or sometimes with the relationship between the team and supporters, or with the institutions of a club. Taken *together* these organizational advantages amount to a 'powerful source of competitive advantage, distinctly associated with Liverpool and never emulated elsewhere' (Szymanski and Kuypers, 1999: 204). The authors go on to argue that the coach's mythologized 'boot room' at Anfield was a unique and key source of *institutional* architectural advantage at Liverpool in the 1970s and 1980s.

We will return to discuss the 'boot room' and its fate at some length later in this chapter. What I want to do here is to look briefly at how Liverpool FC has responded *as an organization* to the challenges posed by the rapidly changing dynamics of professional football over the last fifteen years of the twentieth century – that is, I want to concentrate in the years following the Heysel disaster in 1985. It was from around that time that some of the strategic advantages discussed above finally began to unwind at Liverpool, even as the club continued in its domestic footballing dominance, for a few years at least, under new manager Kenny Dalglish.

After Heysel

On the *administrative* side of club affairs at Liverpool, local businessman and Conservative Party and Sports Council figurehead John Smith was confirmed as the Liverpool FC Chairman from 1976. Smith's powerful business expertise, and his network of contacts in political and sporting circles in Britain and beyond, were aimed to be the new stimuli for a more strategic and 'corporate' approach to club policy-making. In December 1976, for example, Smith announced that Liverpool FC were about to launch a unique export drive designed to sell the club overseas and to market its goods all around the world. It all *sounded* impressive, but the available technology and the resources allocated here were very modest. Liverpool FC, like most other top English clubs of the time, was barely 'selling' itself *domestically* with any degree of rigour or sophistication, never mind tapping into available *international* markets. Moreover, the low base from which the club had begun its supposed commercial reconfiguration was also made clear in Smith's very prescient comments on what was going to become football's new 'commercial age':

> Clubs cannot manage on their takings through the turnstiles. Every other means of expanding revenue has to be used for clubs to exist. Sponsorship is one of the biggest. We are the only club in the UK and, I believe, the only one in Europe not to have perimeter advertising around the ground. So we can offer what no other club can offer – exclusivity (quoted in Keith, 1999: 146–7).

At the same launch the long-serving club secretary Peter Robinson, who had largely guided Liverpool quite brilliantly at home and abroad up to the devastation and the six-year footballing exclusion from Europe brought by the Heysel Stadium disaster in 1985, was also offered a new seven-year contract at Liverpool and a new, rather strange, title of general secretary. Post-Heysel, and following the even deeper trauma of the Hillsborough tragedy in 1989, Robinson and his staff seemed determined to try to continue the core aspects of the previously successful recipe of what then passed for normal club/fan relations at Anfield. This involved, centrally of course, the continued delivery to Liverpool fans of a winning football team. But it also included a willingness to try, initially at least, to maintain reasonable ticket-pricing policies at Anfield in order to cater for a local audience badly hit throughout the 1980s by Thatcherite policies and by economic depression (Parkinson, 1985; Williams, 1986). Even in the new national thrall for football in the 1990s, Robinson was initially very nervous about increasing match ticket prices in a city where wages were generally low and *local* passion for football was very high.

It meant, too, the perpetuation of what seems to have become the 'modern' Liverpool FC tradition of a general quite low regard for those addressing the club's public face; stories, among fans, of the poor treatment of supporters, visitors and journalists approaching the club in this period are legion. It was not unusual, for example, for foreign visitors to the club to be left, untended and ignored, outside Anfield. Press talk about the lack of basic hospitality at Anfield was also rife. Insider accounts written about the successful Liverpool teams of the 1970s and 1980s also stressed how the club's coaches had warned *players* about courting publicity by talking too much to the press, an apprenticeship which would later dog players who went on to become managers, as they faced a much more demanding 'media age' of the game's development (Souness, 1999: 221).

Added to all this was the internal resistances and structural inertia to the processes of simple administrative modernization – in ticketing, in merchandising, in routine customer services and in public relations, for example – which were increasingly becoming commonplace at top football clubs both in England and in Europe. Liverpool's successes in the 1970s and 1980s extended over such a lengthy period, and depended so completely on events on the field and the club's strategic ability to attract top players – something which seemed quite secure at that time – that it was easy for Liverpool's staff and directors to assume that the model which had worked so successfully for so long would simply continue to deliver. But the world of football, on both the playing and the administrative sides, was actually already changing rapidly.

After 1984, it would be fifteen years before another English club, Manchester United – and by this time one owned by a PLC and with a team packed with *foreign* players – would triumph again in the European Cup (now the rather more taxing and definitely more lucrative Champions League). Laudably, in many respects, the tenacious but essentially paternalistic hold on the ownership of the Liverpool club by the Moores family, owners of the locally based Littlewoods empire, meant that the raw free market ideologies which would sweep more boldly through the sport in the early 1990s were unlikely to take a strong early hold at Liverpool (see King, 1998). Indeed, the extraordinary work with bereaved families by the Liverpool club and its staff around the aftermath of Hillsborough in 1989 was a clear reminder of the very caring, *human* bonds which still tied the club to its supporters, perhaps especially to those actually residing in the city of Liverpool (Williams 1999a; Walter, 1991). Nevertheless, it was also clear that on both the administrative and football sides of the club little cognisance was yet being taken of wider shifts which were already occurring in some of the central practices involved in running a very large European football club.

This general, strenuous emphasis inside Anfield on very 'traditional' work, largely on the football side and inspired by Shankly's legacy and ideas, at the expense of even quite modest developments on the coaching and preparation side and elsewhere, was understandably championed by some Liverpool fans as both a healthy sign of continuity and a proper focus on established *footballing* priorities. This strategy was seen as a welcome bulwark against creeping 'impression management' in football and the growing emphasis on the language of commerce, and on the role of new business elites in the sport (see King, 1998; Wagg, 1984). Manchester United's later struggles against the predatory Rupert Murdoch, for example, were watched with something approaching ghoulish glee on Merseyside. But it also actually meant a crucial falling-behind in the day-to-day necessities, both on the field and off it, of a late modern football club of Liverpool's size, traditions and ambitions. As John Smith's 1976 comments suggest, Liverpool FC had actually led on some early basic commercial issues, and not always to the liking of the club's supporters. Liverpool was the first club in England, for example, to strike a deal for shirt sponsorship, with Japanese high-tech company Hitachi, in 1978. But there was little sign of a wider strategy here designed both to modernize the club and build on its key distinct capabilities which had been built up throughout the 1970s and 1980s. Thus, by the mid-1990s, and as a simple measure of what was by now the club's relative infrastructural and commercial 'Luddism' in this respect, there still existed no reliable computerized – or otherwise systematized database of Liverpool FC's 25,000 season ticket holders, the club's core supporters and investors. Names and addresses of the club's major sponsors, the fans, were kept on dog-eared cards in a series of boxes.

The Liverpool club's general approach to administration, then, supreme in the club's halcyon days when 'business' in the European football context essentially meant bums on seats, guarding the sanctity of competition, working routinely with TV outlets, and dealing with the travel and the staging of matches, seemed increasingly out of step, in fact, with some of the significant new developments running through the European game in the 1990s. This was especially so regarding matters of club structures, the growing complexities involved in television deals, the necessity of effective national and global marketing, the spreading international market for football players, new approaches to player conditioning and coaching, and the growing importance of extra-UEFA international club relationships (see Williams, 1999b and Chapter Ten).

Added to this, if – as King (1998: 207) argues – in the new 'global' era football *cities* were to be the new driving force in the world game, with top clubs helping to denote which cities are politically and economically important and thus worthy of investment by international capital, then the city of Liverpool in the 1980s was some way from being the sort of nascent regional powerhouse likely to be favoured by top football clubs. Liverpool's poverty and militant municipalism, for example, and its docks-centred casual employment and substantially employer-absent branch economy, were stacked against effective local or regional entrepreneurial development (see, Parkinson, 1985: Ch. 1) There was little prospect on Merseyside, then, for the sort of small firms and cultural-industry development in centres such as Manchester, or for the sort of neo-Thatcherite football-related commercial development which was to feature so strongly later under entrepreneurs such as John Hall in Newcastle (Williams, 1996). Poorly managed and rapidly depopulating, and with a large, unskilled workforce which was overly dependent on the failing docks, and with few new private-sector white-collar service jobs attracted to the city, Liverpool in the 1980s was an unattractive commercial proposition for both foreign and domestic capital (Parkinson, 1985).

Administratively, Liverpool FC, by now a multi-million-pound business and with fans spread worldwide, retained a simple, hierarchical structure with little in the way, for example, of devolved responsibility to effective departmental heads. By the end of the millennium, astonishingly, the club remained the only one in the FA Premier League – probably the only major football club in Europe – still to have no official internet website of its own. It eventually 'piggybacked' on an existing fans' site and later, with Rick Parry now to the fore, moved into business with the Granada media and leisure group to better exploit the club's lucrative internet rights. In short, both in 'business' and in playing terms, the game was very quickly moving on in the early 1990s as Liverpool FC, still stunned by Hillsborough and its traumatic aftermath, and still rooted in some of the tried and successful methods of the past, clung on to a general system of operation that had fixed them at the top of the European football tree, but in quite a different phase of the sport's development.

Eventually, as relations between top clubs in the FA Premier League themselves threatened to fragment in the face of new opportunities for developing TV football markets, Rick Parry, the then FA Premier League Chief Executive and one of the architects of the new league – and also a longstanding Liverpool *fan* – was recruited by the club in 1996 in an attempt to try to pilot it successfully into the new global era. In the same year, and reflecting the obvious tensions in the collective hierarchy of the FA Premier League clubs, a Harris poll of UK TV football viewers was predicting, admittedly implausibly, that already-dominant Premiership champions Manchester United might earn up to £380 million a year from go-it-alone pay-per-view football coverage (Giulianotti, 1999: 93).

Peter Robinson, still an important figure at Anfield, remained at Liverpool as an influential director as Parry initially struggled to get to grips with his new challenge and with Robinson's own powerful legacy. Robinson finally retired from

Liverpool in the summer of 2000. Parry found himself saddled with an administrative set-up at Liverpool which was still geared for a period already twenty years in the past but one which was, in fact, even more extravagantly out of its time because of the failure of the club to grasp properly the *real* pace of change, for example, in the expanding use of new technologies.

Liverpool FC, then, despite the early promises from John Smith back in the 1970s, had also underestimated the growing importance of new football markets and the necessity for new forms for relationships with supporters for those top football clubs still bent, in the late 1990s, on stable European footballing success. The club still lacked effective liaison structures and was slow in terms of developing a forward-looking vision of how links with fans and other partners at home and abroad might best evolve in the age of 'new' football. Both an enthusiastic modernizer, and a man with a strong feel for the club's very special traditions and local relationships, Parry had joined a ship which seemed uneasily stranded between the compasses which had helped plot a marvellously successful course in the club's recent, but nevertheless now 'distant' past, and the need for very new charts and equipment for the tricky navigation that, unquestionably, lay ahead. Parry, above all else, is according to a city analyst 'Someone who knows the value of football to television companies.' (*Guardian*, 12 July 1999). Following a later tie-up between the Granada media and leisure group and the club, engineered by Parry, a spokesman for Granada commented, ominously, 'The worlds of football and television are in some senses symbiotic' (Gibson, 1999; see also Chapter Ten).

King Kenny

While *administratively* Liverpool FC was moving slowly and cautiously in the 1980s, specifically on the *footballing* side of club affairs, continuity was – unsurprisingly – also strongly stressed. It was a celebrated and brilliant Liverpool player, Kenny Dalglish, who had picked up the club's football managerial reins in the immediate aftermath of the Heysel disaster and Joe Fagan's retirement on the morning of the fateful European Cup Final against Juventus in 1985. Dalglish was steeped in the recently established Liverpool traditions under Shankly and Paisley of ebullient team spirit, signing 'good' players, a rejection of the 'star treatment' even for key performers, and an 'uncomplicated' approach to match preparation and tactics and strategies of play (see Dalglish, 1996: 51–61; see also Chapter Four). But he was also drawn from a very different footballing generation than that of his predecessors. He was already comfortably well-off as a top player and he extolled more the newer, politically conservative and 'privatized' virtues *outside* the game of providing for his immediate family, of 'executive' leisure – in this case, predictably, golf – and a willingness to explore commercial opportunities, than he did the older more communitarian values of, say, a Shankly, Paisley or

Fagan. If this was also, as Stephen Wagg (1984) has argued, the age of the football manager in the full glare of publicity, Dalglish, a very private man if one with a cruel and biting sense of humour out of the public eye, was clearly ill-equipped for the increasingly pressing requirements of the national sporting stage (see also Hansen, 1999, Ch. 9).

There were obvious strengths inside the institution Dalglish took over in 1985, but there were also growing signs of the traditional 'Liverpool way' now beginning to look a little dated, at least when judged against some of the new developments coming on-stream in the sport. Even for cerebral players at Liverpool, for example, such as key defender Alan Hansen, 'team spirit' was still a vital part of the club's success (Hansen, 1999). Ian Rush's later accounts of the intense team bonding at Liverpool and the drinking cliques inside the club in the mid-1980s, was also a marker on the *general* nature of the occupational culture inside many top British football clubs at the time (Rush, 1986; 1996).

The 'best' Liverpool social sessions of the 1980s were held once the *serious* football action was deemed to be over, but they still could be impressive affairs. On 18 May 1982, for example, Liverpool travelled on the day to relegated Middlesbrough for a final Tuesday night fixture, the League title already having been secured once again. By the middle of the afternoon Rush and his senior colleagues were in a Teesside pub, downing lager. 'It was the first of quite a few pints I sank in the next couple of hours. And the rest of the lads were enjoying themselves too.' The squad stumbled back to their hotel rooms for coach Ronnie Moran's 4 p.m. room-check. The match ended in a disjointed 0–0 draw. 'Apparently the Middlesbrough players had got wind of our afternoon session', reported Rush. 'They were half embarrassed at playing us.' (Rush 1986: 99). After the last match of the next season 1982/83, Liverpool left on a short tour of Israel. In Tel Aviv, the night *before* the first tour game, a group of the younger Liverpool players got badly drunk. Rush fell over in a bar and a 'free fight' broke out *between* the players over who had 'pushed' him. The next morning, equipped with shiners and facial gashes, a group of Liverpool players, including the tyro Rush, were up before a stern Bob Paisley, but no further action was taken.

Drinking by players on this scale was no novelty in English football, something confined to Liverpool; far from it. Tony Adams's recent 'confessions' show it was certainly still central to the occupational culture of top English football clubs even a decade later (Adams, 1998). Moreover, Liverpool were still, arguably, the top football club in Europe in the early 1980s, when Hansen and Rush were also fast approaching their prime. But, traditional British team spirit and strength, and this kind of chaotic and abusive treatment of the body, were unlikely to triumph for too long in the new football era. Indeed, when England lost to host nation Sweden in the 1992 European Championships, England manager Graham Taylor complained that the Swedes and other football nations were no longer intimidated by the collective physical power and 'togetherness' of the English. They were now, simply, technically superior and athletically better prepared. They now played the 'English style' *better* than the English (see Williams, 1999b).

Perhaps another small but important symbolic indicator of Liverpool's general approach even to major matches in the 1980s was that, distressingly for the new young Liverpool boss, Dalglish was forced to conduct his first formal managerial press conference immediately after the Heysel disaster in a club *tracksuit*. This was because the Liverpool players had travelled to and from Brussels for the European Cup Final in tracksuits and had returned to Merseyside immediately afterwards (ibid.: 133–4). The press conference called at Anfield to announce Dalglish's appointment, even as the dead were being assembled in Belgium for identification, was described later by one writer as 'Possibly the crassest piece of public relations in football history' (Kelly, 1999: 173).

Even for lengthy trips for crucial European club matches at this time, to distant parts of the old Soviet Bloc, for example, Liverpool persisted in training at Melwood on Tuesday morning, making the gruelling trip in the afternoon/evening, playing the match often the following afternoon, and returning to England immediately after the match. This seemed to work, it was argued: why change it? On the related and important *medical* side of club affairs, up to now taken care of by the recently retired Bob Paisley, Ian Rush also agreed (apparently approvingly) in the mid-1980s that Liverpool FC broke all the accepted rules (Rush, 1986: 145):

> Liverpool operate just about exactly the opposite to the way most people believe a football club should be run. Take the medical side of the club, for example. We have all the latest equipment at Anfield, costing thousands of pounds and we don't have anyone qualified to use it! Ronnie Moran and Roy Evans, our two coaches . . . just read the instructions on the various pieces of equipment and operate it from there. It's hard to imagine, I know. Millions of pounds worth of footballers being treated with less fuss and less knowledge than your pet dog would expect at the vet!

It was soon clear to new manager Dalglish that much of what was available, in terms of guidance or training, on exactly *how* to manage at a club such as Liverpool in the late-1980s remained very much at the *intuitive* level. Dalglish, for example, would have to make the potentially difficult move from player to club manager simply with the support of the club's extraordinary backroom staff. His instant promotion from player to player-manager would be impossible in, say, Italy or Germany, where football coaches are required to be formally qualified for their jobs. As a push towards more professional status and better preparation for football managers in England, but also as a response to some of the glaring *technical* deficiencies in the English game, the technical director of the FA, Howard Wilkinson, wanted to introduce similar sorts of FA-controlled accreditation here (see, Lambert, 1995: 55). Dalglish's 'qualifications' for the managership at Liverpool in 1985 were that he was arguably the most talented British player of his generation, he had a shrewd knowledge of the game and, crucially, he *knew* Liverpool Football Club. On his first day in his new job back at Anfield, however, he was also, tellingly, mystified by what it was the manager of Liverpool FC actually *did* at the club, especially in the closed season. Sitting in his office with 'wee uncle', the legendary Bob Paisley, the following exchange took place (ibid.: 134):

> 'What am I doing sitting in here', I asked Bob. 'There's nothing happening. The phone's not ringing. There's nobody training. All the players are still on holiday'.
> Bob said: 'That's part of the job at this time of year'.
> 'Oh', I said.
> It didn't sound too good to me. I just sat there and talked to Bob about football, which in itself was an experience.

Dalglish, later described the Liverpool manager's job as, 'never complicated . . . one of the most straightforward jobs in English football' (Dalglish, 1996: 180). This was because Peter Robinson and John Smith still dealt with major financial, and most other football administrative, matters at Liverpool. The job of the Liverpool manager was to pick the team and to *let them* win football matches. Technical preparation was minimal: not even set pieces – corners or free kicks – were practised in the club's training. Dalglish even picked as his team captain the nervously introverted and largely silent Hansen, simply because he felt the Scot was 'lucky' (Hansen, 1999: 40). Perhaps because of this deceptive simplicity, Dalglish soon seemed to get to grips with football management, Anfield-style. Astonishingly, he not only guided his squad to the club's first, and only, domestic 'double' – League Championship and FA Cup wins – in his first season in charge in 1985/86, but he also later successfully, if briefly, rebuilt the Liverpool side around a new generation of exciting attacking players between 1988 and 1990, including, especially, the talented Jamaican-born winger, John Barnes (see Hill, 1989 and Chapter Six).

The Boot Room Implodes

The famous Anfield 'boot room', was, in physical terms at least, little more than a cubbyhole at the Anfield ground, containing four kit hampers and a couple of cupboards, and wall slats where the players' boots were stored on hooks. This was profoundly a *man's* space, a shop floor environment, in what was a supportive but harsh culture; current assistant manager Phil Thompson remembers, for example, the beer and topless calendars in the boot room, renewed each November, and a source of considerable attraction to the club's young apprentices (quoted in Kelly, 1999: 60).

The mythology of the boot room began under Shankly when coach Joe Fagan helped out with coaching and support at local Runcorn-based non-League club Guinness Exports. By way of thanks, the Runcorn club sent crates of beer and Guinness across to Joe at Anfield, thus providing the early fuel for animated in-house discussions about club training, players and systems but also providing the opportunity for the club's coaching staff to entertain visiting managers and coaches after home matches. Shankly himself not a drinker save occasionally to quell his nerves about flying, was not a boot room regular. This was a place, instead, where his lieutenants and sergeant majors could pore through injuries and illnesses, discuss the morning's training, and run the rule through the new recruits while looking for developing weaknesses in the long-servers.

The boot room was the professional touchstone of the Liverpool club's playing success for some twenty-five years; a place where the club coaching staff would also meet on Sundays to discuss players, coaching and tactics, and, after matches, to suck in knowledge from other clubs about coaching techniques and 'likely' players in lower divisions (Dalglish, 1996: 143). In the early days of the original boot room, before the advent of the players' lounge and the requirement that players join wives and sponsors after the match, senior players also popped their head in for a natter and a beer with the coaching staff before setting off home. Other 'outsiders' were also allowed access. Tom Saunders, staff coach with the FA and head teacher at Liverpool West Derby Comprehensive, a man steeped in schools football in England, joined the Liverpool club full time in 1970, primarily to organize the recruitment and development of young players. Opera-loving Saunders also watched future match opponents for Shankly and Paisley and, lacking some of the rough edges of the shop floor, he was also a crucial link between the youth and coaching side at Liverpool – including the boot room – the manager, and the club directors.

The boot room itself was eventually demolished, after Dalglish had left Liverpool, as part of the Anfield stadium rebuilding programme, and under pressure from UEFA, ironically, for the provision of a larger *media* interview area at the club. If the boot room was essentially about sharing and soaking up football information, the Liverpool club, since Bill Shankly at least, had never placed great store by doing any more than simply humouring the national press. Dalglish, himself a single-minded and sometimes wilfully obtuse character, especially in his dealings with the media, but also a man who suffered from a severe lack of self-confidence, was accused by some critics of having destroyed the 'threatening' *institution* of the boot room during his spell as manager – a charge he later strenuously denied (Bowler, 1996: 276). Dalglish had actually installed a bar in his own office at Anfield, thus crucially re-directing some of the important post-match drink and gossip among coaches and managers *away* from the boot room base of Liverpool coaches Ronnie Moran and Roy Evans. Whatever the motivation for this development, it was probably the first concrete sign of a real shift in the successful Anfield coaching dynasty which had been inspired from the late 1950s by Bill Shankly.

As the exciting late-1980s Liverpool team quickly began to wane, with key players – Nicol, Rush, Hansen – beginning to age, and Dalglish's new signings – Speedie, Rosenthal, Carter – failing to match up to stringent Anfield standards, self-doubt and gloom began to envelop a clearly strained Dalglish. In 1989 the Hillsborough tragedy and its aftermath in Liverpool hit the manager and his family hard (see Chapter Five). He reported later that he had contemplated resigning his job early in 1990 following a 'creepy' return with Liverpool to Sheffield in front of an empty Leppings Lane terrace, where Liverpool fans had perished only months earlier (Dalglish, 1996: 179). Instead, he hung on until March 1991, before leaving, suddenly, after a coruscating FA Cup replay with Everton, pleading accumulated stress rooted in coping with the terrible aftermath of the 1989 disaster. The manager and his family, essentially very private people, had been key, and almost ever-present, figures in the public mourning which had engulfed the city in the months following the tragedy. After a cursory and largely uninformative press conference at Anfield, Dalglish and his family left immediately for a holiday the United States, leaving long-serving coach Ronnie Moran to step briefly into the Liverpool managerial breach.

Soon, another ex-Liverpool player and Dalglish colleague, Graeme Souness, an excitable and aggressive, but successful, player-manager at Glasgow Rangers, would take over at Anfield. He joined a club which was, arguably, still struggling as an organization to deal fully with the effects of the events of 1989, as well as with the pace of change in 'new' football as an industry, with six years' exclusion from European football competition, and with the very special pressures brought by a quarter of a century of near-constant footballing success at the highest level (see Chapter Four).

Dalglish himself summed up the philosophy of the Liverpool boot room as: 'Give the opposition very little and get as much as you can out of them' (Dalglish, 1996: 143). Szymanski and Kuypers (1999: 240) describe the boot room at Anfield as a: 'distinctive capability . . . [an] 'architecture', a source of competitive advantage derived from the network of relationships inside an organization, which not only benefits the individuals involved but also enhances the organization itself'. Souness remarked on the importance of the boot room, not only for club talk, but for 'documentary' records, of a kind which were probably innovative in the early years of Bill Shankly's tenure. Paisley, Moran and Fagan kept detailed written records of events at Melwood, the club's training ground. According to England international Phil Neal, a policy of custom and practice reflected in comments such as 'Have a look, see what we did last year' was a common response among the club staff to try to right a slump in form or an outbreak of injuries (quoted in Kelly,

1999: 116). For Souness, the boot room was important for its 'continuity . . . that stems from a set of volumes stored at the ground and kept up to date without fail every day. It is the football bible as far as the Anfield staff is concerned, and contains the answer to almost every problem, and every situation which could arise in the day-to-day running of a successful club' (*Management Week*, 14 December 1990). The boot room was also important for its *symbolism*: it stood for a set of values which evoked notions of occupational solidarity and *democratization* – coaches and other staff 'chipping in' – as well as the idea, in an increasingly commercialized and commodified realm, of the club as a closely knit 'family', characterized by traditions of generational inheritance.

On the basis of accounts such as these, Szymanski and Kuypers, in their review of strategic advantages in English football clubs (1999: 239–40), concluded that:

> The boot room, then, appears to have been some kind of database for the club, not merely of facts and figures, but a record of the club's 'spirit', its attitudes and its philosophy . . . The boot room might be thought of as the equivalent of 'reputation' in the context of an organization, an established set of traditions which oblige newcomers to adapt themselves, to fit in, largely because the very success of the organization makes rebellion or radical departures lack credibility.

The Souness years

Graeme Souness's accession to the manager's job at Liverpool in early 1991 chimed well with what were then wider prevailing free market ideologies of management which were the product of the then dominant Thatcherite political philosophy in Britain – Souness was himself a publicly keen admirer of Thatcher and her neoliberal policies. Known for his opulent style, Souness, no typical British footballer he, married a divorced heiress, sought exclusive private education for his children (at Millfield school) and, unusually, openly left Liverpool FC in 1984 for the less successful Italian club, Sampdoria, simply because of the better money on offer in Italy. Known inside football as 'Champagne Charlie', his general approach to life fitted, glaringly, less well with aspects at the time of the wider culture and politics of the city of Liverpool or, indeed, and more importantly, with what had become some of the accepted approaches to management and coaching at Liverpool Football Club.

Souness was a respected, rather than a loved, ex-player at Liverpool, and he was a man with a formidable reputation for toughness both in sport and in business. Indeed, Souness's approach to playing the game – his calculated violence and intimidation, mixed with cunning and great skill – was indicative of the extent to which the uncertain ethics of business and gamesmanship had increasingly intruded into football and become assimilated into the conventional wisdom of the game and sanctioned in its ideology (Wagg, 1984: 148–9). He had been welcomed back to the club by most Liverpool fans precisely because of his uncompromising competitiveness and supposed winning mentality, expressed in his turbulent recent successes as manager of Glasgow Rangers. Above all, he was welcomed to Anfield because of his *Liverpool FC* heritage. He was unlikely, nevertheless, simply to 'fit in' with the established management traditions at Anfield.

It was soon clear that Souness felt the club he had rejoined was still immersed in the nostalgia of past playing achievements, and he strove for change on the playing and coaching side. He was critical, later, of the lack of real commitment from the senior professionals at the club who, he felt, were either already past their best playing days (the injured, overweight and reluctant Barnes) or were allegedly too concerned about testimonials or a last football pay day (Nicol, Whelan, Rush) (Souness, 1999: 85–9). The new manager obviously felt he had inherited a team which had little backbone for a fight on the field, and which was already going alarmingly backwards so soon after its early 1980s European football dominance in which he himself had been a key figure as a player.

Originally recruited and publicized as a 'boot room' disciple, but one who had also a modernizer's steely glint to the club, Souness quickly moved unwanted players on and also brought in new players to the club on what were, by this stage, rocketing salaries. This was the moment when the new FA Premier League commercial boom in English football was getting under way and new TV income from BSkyB was already boosting the bargaining power of players and their advisers (Williams, 1999b). With established players on agreed contracts and new arrivals pocketing higher wages, this buying and selling strategy produced further disharmony in an already unhappy Liverpool dressing room. Also, the earlier internal 'boot room' discussions about what *exactly* the club needed and precisely *which* players the club might sign – something which had already begun to recede under Dalglish – now virtually disappeared in a much more hierarchical managerial set-up under Souness. Finally, almost for the first time since Bill Shankly had taken over at Liverpool, first-team players were allowed to leave the club – Staunton and Beardsley, for example – to go on to comparable playing success elsewhere. Their replacements – Dicks and Clough – little matched up to the loss of these established internationals. Talented youngsters coming through the Liverpool production line – McManaman, Fowler, Marsh, and the Dalglish signing, Jamie Redknapp – tempered the effects of these sorts of negative player 'exchange' sufficiently for Liverpool to win the FA Cup under Souness in 1992. The competition in this cup campaign had been weak, however; this was but a temporary glow.

Souness, a man who had of course played at the highest level abroad, also began tending seriously to Liverpool players' diets for the first time, and he moved all the club's training activities and its day-to-day focus away from Anfield to the

Melwood training ground. This sort of detailed attention to the preparation of players was naturally to become much more common in England, especially following the arrival of foreign coaches in the late 1990s. This necessary modernization of day-to-day routines at Liverpool also meant, however, that the daily visits by players to Anfield and the collective coach ride to Melwood for training, during which the elusive and vital Liverpool 'team spirit' was mainly sparked, also disappeared. Players now arrived for training alone in cars. 'Boot room' meetings, partly as a consequence, also became less central to the coaching and playing culture of the club. Finally, Souness had also taken over at the club at a time when it lacked real stability and enough top quality on the playing side, and when it was also missing effective boardroom leadership and real vision and dynamism in the area of club administration. In short, the club as an *institution* was clearly ailing, and it had been for some time. David Fairclough, a player with the club in the late 1970s who had, unusually, like Souness played abroad, had seen signs of Liverpool's demise a decade earlier (in Kelly, 1999: 241):

> I felt that the boot room had run its course. It might sound controversial, but having seen and done things abroad in Switzerland and in Belgium, and seen how the game was changing, I thought when I was in Switzerland that Liverpool, even though they were still European champions, were falling behind. I could see the game changing. I thought, ultimately, Liverpool would have caught up by the time I got back, by broadening their vision a little bit. I don't think Liverpool or English clubs were aware of what was going on on the continent . . . It is a European game now, and Liverpool have this attitude that 'We are Liverpool, we are the best, why should we change things, we've won trophies.' . . . We should have been more aware . . . I think Liverpool were a bit blinkered.

In 1993, under Souness, there also occurred a crucial *symbolic* moment for the club and a sign of the power of new money in the game. Wracked by defensive lapses, Souness moved to sign Tim Flowers, an emerging and talented young goalkeeper at Southampton. Ten, even five, or perhaps even *three* years before, Liverpool would comfortably have secured their man, drawing on their distinct capabilities of *reputation* and *innovation* to pull the young player on board. Now Flowers *rejected* a move to Liverpool in favour of Dalglish's offer of high wages and ambition at the Jack Walker-funded provincial Blackburn Rovers, where the goalkeeper went on to win a Premiership title in 1995 and England recognition under Kenny Dalglish. Symbolically and materially, this was a crushing reverse, and along with poor playing results added to the growing sense that the Liverpool club was in decline as others were quickly emerging, and also that the Liverpool manager, in the parlance of the boardroom and the press, had 'lost the confidence' of some of his senior players and also some key members of the Liverpool board.

Souness was eventually accused by fans, Liverpool coaches and the press of traducing the legacy left by Shankly and those who had followed him, and of riding roughshod over the by now mythologized Anfield 'boot room' footballing philosophies. Although the club *was* changing, change was clearly necessary. The truth about Souness, however, is that he had arrived at the club as its distinct capabilities were already being allowed to drain away. But Souness was also simply a poor man manager and, unlike many of his predecessors, at best an inconsistent judge of top players. He had also *played* at Liverpool with some of the squad he now had returned to the club to manage and, unlike Dalglish, he found this difficult personally. He had made actually quite modest – though prescient – changes to player preparation at Liverpool, even if a much more intensive training regime at the club was blamed by fans for a dramatic increase in player injuries.

As Liverpool's results worsened in the early 1990s, and as Souness's own health and his stock with club supporters and local commentators declined further following more ill-judged signings, the writing was soon on the wall. The public exposure of his commercial links with the *Sun* newspaper in 1992 – which was still fiercely boycotted across Merseyside following its insensitive and distorting Hillsborough coverage – added rancour to the inevitable parting. After the sort of dithering which was to become characteristic of the Liverpool board's hesitant management style in the early 1990s, Souness's resignation was eventually accepted by his close friend and now club Chairman David Moores following a shattering home FA Cup tie loss against Bristol City in January 1994.

Definitely Maybe: the Time of Roy Evans, 1994–1998

Damaged by the Hillsborough-related mistakes of an acerbic and apparently insensitive manager, and also by the 'modernizing' discourses and techniques and the ill-judged transfer and man-management practices of Souness, the Liverpool club turned, once again, in 1994 to what seemed the greater certainty and stability offered by a recognized boot room disciple. Bootle-born Roy Evans, twenty years on the Liverpool club coaching staff, stepped up, perhaps reluctantly, to take charge, ostensibly to try to re-engage once more with earlier, more successful Liverpool traditions (Hopkins and Williams, 1999). Briefly, it seemed it might prove an unlikely master-stroke.

Increasingly, in these so-called 'new times', when the predominant vocabulary inside the game is one of markets and 'brands', the very notion of a working relationship with a football club which spans, as it did for Evans, more than thirty years in all, and the sense of historical continuity, loyalty and integrity, and even duty, which that can evoke can appear outmoded and anachronistic. Evans was the sort of servant who personified the historical commitment and the collective spirit of a British football club – as well as, admittedly, sometimes the ingrained paternalism of some football club Chairmen.

Any serious audit of the Roy Evans years at Liverpool needs to acknowledge at least two important things. First, the scale of the problems he faced in rebuilding the club after its post-Hillsborough demise under a drained Kenny Dalglish, and the chaotic revolution 'led' by Graeme Souness between 1991 and 1994. Secondly, the very real quality of the team that Evans, Doug Livermore and long-time coach Ronnie Moran constructed on the basis of the 3–5–2 (or wing-back) system, particularly in 1995/96 when, but for a dark November when too many points were dropped against poor opposition, even the vaunted 'double' of League and FA Cup might, once again, have been within Liverpool's reach.

Under Evans, but with John Barnes closely in support on and off the field, Liverpool re-established their national credentials as *the* passing team in England in the mid-1990s. They kept possession of the ball better than any other side, they passed the ball relentlessly, they committed fewest fouls, and they played the purest football, in keeping with the club's long-established collective ethos of simplicity and teamwork. In his careful support and development of emerging young 'scousers' such as Steve McManaman and Robbie Fowler, especially, Evans also reinvigorated local traditions for nurturing young players at the very heart of the club's ambitions. The intelligent and talented McManaman, especially, had lost his way under Souness; under Evans he became the creative hub of an exciting new team. For all this, the club's League Cup Final triumph of 1995 against First Division Bolton Wanderers represented merely the barest of rewards.

Evans, a traditional English club *coach*, rather than a football manager, was essentially a nice man who lacked the cunning and disciplinary ruthlessness of some of his Anfield teachers. His approach to the football press, for example, suggested a dangerous openness and naiveté. 'If you get too close to one newspaper you can give yourself problems', he reasoned. 'If you stay reasonably honest with the media, they will be reasonably honest with you' (quoted in Lambert, 1995: 126). Evans *liked* his footballers, and he wanted to be their friends. In Bill Shankly's day, by way of contrast, if you were a player and merely injured you effectively ceased to exist, because you were of no use to the club (see Chapter Three).

Maybe Evans had always hated the necessary cruelty of this kind of approach to football club management. He was publicly criticized by the media for being 'too close' to the players, though after the destructive and abrasive management style of Souness, a renowned half-time teacup thrower, a new direction in this respect was also probably necessary (Lacey, 1998). The Liverpool approach under boot room product Evans was also a mystery to some new foreign players at the club. Abroad, if a player was dropped from the team the coaches talked to him, explained his deficiencies and worked on his weaknesses to try to get him back in favour. The psychology of man-managing intelligent, and sometimes sensitive, athletes was a central component of running a successful football club on the continent. At Liverpool, players left out of the first team were not typically faced with explanations or shows of real support. They effectively disappeared from view until they had magically 'found' their form once again.

Evans was certainly dogged during his time in charge at Anfield by recurring accusations about other aspects of the 'laxness' of his regime; his younger stars were dubbed the 'Spice Boys' by the media for their alleged penchant for celebrity culture and the high life. They were, damagingly, compared in this regard to the allegedly more 'focused' young players who were then emerging under the fierce and puritan management of Alex Ferguson at Manchester United. Some of Evans's more senior players, especially the expensive and perplexing Stan Collymore – a man 'lost in the mist of his own mind' according to one of his previous managers, Alan Smith (quoted in Sik, 1996: 115) – also seemed completely unwilling to come to heel, at one point flatly refusing to play for the club's reserve team. For many commentators, Evans seemed a weak character who had problems facing up to difficult decisions.

In point of fact, although lacking the disciplinary steel of some of his predecessors, Evans was in many ways simply following the tenets of the regime established under the Liverpool boot room dynasty when, as we have already seen, players were never route-marched, but were treated as 'adults', and senior professionals would be expected to keep in check their own socializing and the potentially dangerous excesses of younger members of the squad (Souness, 1999: 88). Published accounts of life at Anfield by later 'drinkers' recruited by Souness – the laddish Neil Ruddock, for example – showed that aspects of the occupational culture identified by Ian Rush during the 'good times' at Liverpool in the 1980s were still in place during the hard times later. But, under an increasingly puritanical and watchful media eye, as new methods of player preparation were emerging, and at a time when the sport was massaging it's own new glossy image as a 'family' product, Evans seemed to be struggling for good sense and judgement among some of his talented, and monied, younger players, but also for reliable *senior* dressing room leaders in this last important respect.

This was a very different era, of course, from the one in which Evans himself had been guided as a young coach. In the 1960s or early 1970s, few players at Liverpool ever spoke to Bill Shankly or Bob Paisley about *financial* rewards; players were recruited, simply, because they *wanted* to play for the club. Money could be dealt with later. Few players refused the offer of a contract at Liverpool. Even in the late 1980s, the club's own players were still very limited in their options for career movements – where could they go after Liverpool? Also, players' salaries were still firmly managed, they were as yet relatively unaffected by agents, TV income, or the very high wages already offered by some clubs abroad. By the mid-1990s, however, the celebrity status of top footballers, the more open international market for players, and the contracts and wages now offered even to moderate performers in the new TV age, meant a whole new set of concerns for football managers and club officials (see Williams, 1999b; Morrow, 1999). In this new post-Fordist occupational culture for players, where flexibility and mobility were the watchwords, players moved more frequently, and showed little loyalty to their clubs, or supporters, and expected little in return. The Bosman transfer ruling later offered players even more scope for reflexivity and shaping their own careers, irrespective of club and supporter claims on their loyalties (see, Williams, 1999b; and interview with Houllier; and also Chapter Ten). Significantly, Steve McManaman, perhaps the key Liverpool player under Evans and a local boy who had spent his entire career at the club, 'waited' on a Bosman transfer in 1998/99, eventually leaving for record wages at Real Madrid, with no transfer fee payable to Liverpool.

All of this growth in the power of players, their alleged lack of club loyalty, the penchant of Liverpool stars for the high life, and the laxness of Evans's regime, was used as the damning background to the abject defeat of Liverpool in a poor 1996 FA Cup Final against arch-rivals Manchester United. The Liverpool players had turned up for the match, in full media glare, sporting ostentatious cream 'designer' suits and 'Tarantino' sunglasses. This publicly languid approach and the Liverpool capitulation in what was arguably the club's most important match of the 1990s, simply provoked more media and supporter hostility aimed at Evans's alleged indolent and fabulously wealthy footballing underachievers.

In the following season, 1996/97, the experienced John Barnes, still a key ally of Evans's inside Anfield, was sent by the Liverpool club to observe the famous Ajax youth system. Barnes was apparently destined to continue aspects of the boot room ethos at Anfield, even in these very changed, and for Evans, troubled times. A new £12 million Academy for youth development was established at the club soon afterwards, under ex-player Steve Heighway. But, further alleged player indulgences, and inevitable defensive frailty and failures on the field, finally provoked the frustrated Evans, seemingly, to dispense with his entire playing strategy which he had built up so carefully since 1994. The key symbolic moment marking out this shift probably came with the signing, in 1997, of an experienced midfield ball winner, a 'hard man', but a technically limited and ageing player with a discipline problem: exit a slowing but still astute John Barnes, to be replaced at Liverpool by an already failing, self-styled 'Guv'nor', England international midfielder Paul Ince.

What followed in this belated new Evans approach was a decline from the seriously flawed excellence of the Liverpool squads of the mid-1990s to a much more anonymous and less fluent team later. The emergence of the mercurial Michael Owen, in 1997, served only to mask real weaknesses elsewhere, especially in defence (see, Cornwall, 1999, on Owen). At the beginning of the 1998/99 League season, and under pressure for more managerial change, but *without* sacking the loyal and liked Evans, the Liverpool club announced a surprising new direction. Evans and Gérard Houllier, ex-French national team manager and ex-Technical Director of Coaching in France, were unveiled to a disbelieving press as the new *joint* managers of Liverpool FC. The beginnings of a new 'continental' era to the coaching and development of players at Liverpool was about to take hold.

The New Future

Following the eventual uncertainties and traumas under the troubled Dalglish, and the harsher failures under Graeme Souness, by the end of the Roy Evans era at Liverpool, and despite his own difficulties in securing any of the major trophies for the club, many of the core strengths of the Liverpool club were still clear and intact. Evans, in fact, had produced a team which at certain moments was very close to title success. Attendances at Liverpool were still strong, the club's fan base more than loyal and secure. The stadium at Anfield was being modernized, though it was also clear that its size and facilities could yet restrict the club's preferred future as a top European club for the next century. Developments on the 'business' side of the club were also accelerating, with new deals in place with media partners which would later release large capital sums for new player investment. The club was, finally, planning for a future in what was likely to be a new European elite of top football clubs.

Liverpool FC's capacity among English football clubs in the late 1990s to be able to draw on a *national* and even an active *international* following was surpassed only by the corporate giant which was nearby Manchester United. The club's new Youth Academy was also nationally acclaimed and was continuing to produce able first-team candidates. However, between 1997 and 1998 wages and salary costs at Liverpool had climbed, with no proportionate noticeable improvement in playing performance. By 1998/99 Liverpool was paying 80 per cent of turnover in salaries and wages, reflecting both the residual 'narrowness' of the club's commercial activities and the wage inflation both inside the club and in the game more generally (Deloitte and Touche, 2000). In fact, the club's turnover in 1998 was by now comfortably less than *half* that of Manchester United. Liverpool FC had, critically, yet to play in the new extended version of the European Cup, the new international stage for top European football talent, and a TV-driven competition now securing vital extra revenue for its competing clubs. In an age of increasing reflexivity and mobility for footballers, top foreign players – and many domestic ones, too – were increasingly choosing their English clubs on the basis of *current* European credentials and lifestyle choices, and not in terms of past footballing glories. In the 1990s, neither post-industrial Merseyside, nor Liverpool FC, seemed especially attractive options to Europe's football crème. In short, many of the distinct capabilities referred to by Szymanski and Kuypers, and which the Liverpool club had nurtured, perhaps not always consciously, in the 1970s and 1980s, were simply no longer quite as relevant in this new 'globalized', more capital-intensive and more technically proficient and 'scientific' period of the sport's development. Liverpool FC then took a new direction to try to reassert the club's position in this new era. We pick up the story of Gérard Houllier's introduction at Liverpool, and what it also said about wider developments in the British game, in the next chapter.

References

Adams, T. (1998) *Addicted*, London: Collins Willow.

Armstrong, G. and Giulianotti, R. (1999) *Football Cultures and Identities*, London: MacMillan.

Bowler, D. (1996) *Shanks: The Authorised Biography of Bill Shankly*, London: Orion.

Bromberger, C. (1993) 'Allez L'OM, Forza Juve; the passion for football in Marseilles and Turin', in S. Redhead (ed.) *The Passion and the Fashion*, Aldershot: Avebury.

Brown, A. (ed.) (1998) *Fanatics! Race, Power, Nationality and Fandom in European Football*, London: Routledge

Cornwall, P. (1999) 'The making of Saint Michael', in M. Perryman (ed.) *The Ingerland Factor*, London: Mainstream.

Dalglish, K. (1996) *Dalglish: My Autobiography*, London: Hodder & Stoughton.

Deloitte and Touche (2000) *Annual Review of Football Finance*, Manchester: Deloitte and Touche.

Gibson, J. (1999) 'Stakes rise in battle of the box', *Guardian*, 14 July.

Gilmore, S. (2000) 'Out of the frying pan: new theories of Football Management', unpublished PhD, University of Portsmouth.

Giulianotti, R. (1999) *Football: a Sociology of the Global Game*, Cambridge: Polity.

Hansen, A (1999) *A Matter of Opinion*, London: Partridge.

Hill, D. (1989) *Out of His Skin: The John Barnes Phenomenon*, London: Faber & Faber.

Hopkins, S. and Williams, J. (1999) 'The departure of Roy Evans from Liverpool', *When Saturday Comes*, No. 143, January.

Keith, J. (1999) *Bob Paisley: Manager of the Millennium*, London: Robson.

Kelly, S. (1999) *The Boot Room Boys*, London: Collins Willow.

King, A. (1998) *The End of the Terraces*, London: Leicester University Press.

Lacey, D. (1998) 'French technocrat left to nail the door shut on Liverpool's bootroom', *Guardian*, 12 November.

Lambert, C. (1995) *The Boss*, London: Vista.

Morrow, S. (1999) *The New Business of Football*, Basingstoke: MacMillan.

Parkinson, M. (1985) *Liverpool on the Brink*, Hermitage, Berks: Policy Journals.

Rowe, D. (1999) *Sport, Culture and the Media*, Milton Keynes: Open University Press.

Rush, I. (1986) *Rush*, London: Grafton.

—— (1989) *Ian Rush: My Italian Diary*, London: Arthur Barker.

—— (1996) *Ian Rush; an Autobiography*, London: Ebury.

Sik, G. (1996) *I think I'll Manage*, London: Headline.

Souness, G. (1999) *Souness: The Management Years*, London: André Deutsch

Szymanski, S. and Kuypers, T. (1999) *Winners and Losers: the Business Strategy of Football*, London: Viking.

Walter, T. (1991) 'The mourning after Hillsborough', *Sociological Review*, **39**(3): 599–626.

Wagg, S. (1984) *The Football World*, Brighton: Harvester

Williams, J. (1986) 'White riots: the English football fan abroad', in A. Tomlinson and G. Whannel (eds) *Off the Ball*, London: Pluto.

—— (1996) 'Sir John Hall and the New Geordie Nation', in S. Gerhmann (ed.), *Football and Regional Identity*, Munich: LIT.

—— (1999a) 'Hillsborough: ten short years', *When Saturday Comes*, No. 147, May.

—— (1999b) *Is it all Over: Can Football Survive the Premier League?*, Reading: South Street Press.

—— (2000) 'Ian Rush', in P. Stead and H. Richards (eds) *For Club and Country: Welsh Football Greats*, Cardiff: University of Wales Press.

Young, P. (1968) *A History of British Football*, London: Stanley Paul.

−8−

Gérard Houllier and the New Liverpool 'Imaginary'

Stephen Hopkins and John Williams

Introduction

In the nearly five years Roy Evans spent as manager of Liverpool (1994–98), much of the traditional football culture and the economics of the English game were in the process of being radically transformed (King, 1998). This was occurring at the level of business and finance (Deloitte and Touche, 1999; Morrow, 1999) but on the playing side in terms of managing and coaching, football was also globalizing and facing new demands in terms of professionalism (Williams, 1999). A new generation of imported foreign coaches, players and managers were in the vanguard of these shifts. Often treated with undisguised media disdain initially, the success generated by Arsène Wenger (at Arsenal) and Gianluca Vialli (at Chelsea) had the effect of convincing many English fans that their clubs were not only in safe 'foreign' keeping, but that this technocratic innovation brought by foreign coaches was by now long overdue.

These sentiments have been powerfully reinforced, of course, by the poor performances of the England national side in the 1998 World Cup and, especially, at Euro 2000. Wenger and Vialli had also been especially successful in recruiting talented foreign stars to their increasingly wealthy and powerful clubs – if not always managing to hold on to them in the new post-Bosman era. In this era, it is the larger football clubs and leagues which are in the ascendant – which can mean problems for national teams (King, 1998; Williams, 1999). According to Wenger: 'Foreign players are a threat in rich countries like Italy and England because young [home grown] players have no real chance to play. But in France, for example, it is good because the exodus gives young people a chance' (quoted in Fynn and Guest, 1998: 91).

This chapter seeks to illustrate where Liverpool FC might fit into this 'transitional' phase in the development of English football, by examining the principles and early practice of Gérard Houllier as manager of the club. We centre this analysis around a lengthy interview which we conducted (see pp. 184–193). However, while much of what Houllier says could be read as a 'manifesto for change', it also quickly becomes clear that things are rather more complex than this.

Houllier's passion for elements of the traditional English game in general and for Liverpool FC in particular, not to mention his more generalized Anglophilia, stand out. English football reporters covering Euro 2000, which Houllier watched as a technical expert on behalf of UEFA, were amused to hear this Frenchman not only defending some of the qualities of the English game (while commentators in England were ready to condemn it in *all* its aspects), but also identifying himself as an England *supporter*, experiencing the real pain of the defeats against Portugal and Romania, and the short-lived high after a poor German team were beaten in Charleroi.

This is no convenient cover for Houllier's real feelings. In the interview that follows, Houllier openly confesses himself to being bored when he had to sit through highly skilled but cagey, slow-moving Italian league matches as the French national coach. The high pace of the English game excites him. It is also clear that, right from the beginning of his association with Liverpool as a city, in 1969, here is a man and a football manager who is no mere technocrat. Houllier certainly does not view the sport (or the Liverpool club) as in any way divorced from its social and economic surroundings. Quite the opposite. In fact, he sees no contradiction between a highly disciplined, carefully planned, and well-organized administration of the club – something easily associated with technocratic foreign coaches – and a passionate, empathetic desire to connect with the 'spirit' or 'heart' at the core of the club's identity.

There are several key themes that Houllier concentrates upon in the interview, and they resonate loudly in some of the recent debates concerning the direction being followed more generally by the footballing elite in England. For instance, he addresses the question of increasing player mobility, and the large numbers of foreign players now working in England; he also raises the interrelated issues of traditional English styles of play, and the general culture associated with the game in this country. At a more parochial level, he also demonstrates he has an understanding of what we have called, taking from Raymond Williams, the 'structure of feeling' in Liverpool about the sport. He knows something, for example, about why the Liverpool club has, and has had, such a critical place in the life of the city, and the special role the particular approach to playing the game in Liverpool holds in what he calls the 'imaginary' of the Liverpool people.

Preparing for Liverpool

Let us say something, briefly, about Houllier's links with Liverpool, and how he ended up as the club's first overseas manager and a potentially key figure in the wider English game. Houllier was a long-time admirer of the club, who had decided to come to the city in 1969 (aged 22) in order to work on his Masters dissertation – on poverty in the city. He lived briefly in Liverpool, teaching at Alsop school in the north of the city, playing local league football, and supporting Liverpool as a visiting 'Kopite'. His first game at Anfield, in the company of current first-team coach Patrice Berguès, saw Liverpool beat Dundalk 10–0 in the European Inter Cities Fairs' (now UEFA) Cup. He struck up a friendship with Liverpool Secretary Peter Robinson, which cemented Houllier's admiration for the club and the values it espoused on and off the field. A sporadic visitor to Anfield in subsequent years, in 1986 Houllier (by now the coach of Paris Saint-Germain) brought along another friend and football coach, Arsène Wenger, to share his appreciation of the English game (George, 2000).

Houllier's own ambitions to be a professional player had been dashed early on by his father's insistence that he should learn to teach. However, his father was the director of a small amateur club, and passed on his passion for the game to Gérard. Houllier made his way in the sport in France as a young, innovative coach with a reputation for meticulous attention to detail and a determination to apply a more 'scientific' approach to player preparation and strategies for play. After beginning as player-coach at Le Touquet in 1973, aged only 26, the young Houllier spent a couple of years as youth coach at Arras, before he took over at modest Noeux-Les-Mines. Between 1976 and 1982, Houllier guided this obscure team from the fifth to the second division of the French League. Recruited by another club from the old coal-mining region of the Nord-Pas de Calais, Houllier then took Lens into the French first division and to a UEFA Cup place, before leading Paris Saint-Germain to their first French League title in 1986.

Overtures from England, in the shape at least of Peter Robinson's recommendation to Spurs' then chairman Irving Scholar, came to nothing. Later on, after Kenny Dalglish stood down as Liverpool manager in 1991, Houllier was apparently considered for the vacant post, and the FA also thought about him as their inaugural technical director. However serious these possibilities were, the appointment of a foreign coach/manager in English football during the late 1980s/early 1990s would have been an imaginative, though not entirely unprecedented step, but also one that would undoubtedly have been greeted with hostility in many quarters. Indeed, it may be true to speculate that particularly *at Liverpool*, where the principle of 'boot room' succession still dominated, such a move would have been looked at askance by many of the club's devotees.

By 1988, Houllier had been appointed assistant to French national team coach Michel Platini, eventually taking over the top job in 1992. His 16-month spell as coach of France ended when the national team failed to qualify for World Cup 1994 after a last-minute home defeat to Bulgaria. As national technical director, Houllier then concentrated on youth development in France, contributing via this route to the emergence of the 1998 World Cup and Euro 2000 winning

French squads. Houllier was by now widely respected in UEFA and FIFA circles because of his central role in the dramatic transformation of the moribund French game.

Houllier came to the wider attention of the footballing elite in England when he captivated an FA national coaching conference in Birmingham in May 1997, with his use of video clips and coaching drills to illustrate the power of forward passing on counter-attack – 'the rattlesnake effect', as he described it to a rapt audience of English coaches (Ridley, 1997). The importance of the initial pass forward was a theme he would return to many times later at Anfield. At the same coaching conference, the FA pledged to follow for the English game the lead on youth development Houllier had established so successfully in France. Howard Wilkinson's 1998 *Charter for Quality*, which later established youth academies at all the major professional clubs in England, owes much to the transformations in France which were engineered under Houllier's astute direction.

A second theme that Houllier develops in our interview is the need for football technique and skills to be closely integrated with the evolution of players' all-round education and culture. This 'holistic' view of sportsmen is really quite alien to English football, where the culture is expected to produce young players who require direction, discipline and supervision almost all of the time. Thus, English footballers are little prepared to be good decision-makers on the field. In strictly playing terms, Houllier stresses the need for players who can demonstrate *flexibility* during matches, who have the intelligence to see the broad contours of a game, and to adapt according to different challenges that will be posed by tactically astute opponents. Supporting this argument, Houllier points to the fact that *substitutes* won the Euro 2000 final for France and the 1999 European Cup for Manchester United, and therefore, 'In the modern game now, you need a strong bench with flexibility, players who can create new problems for the opposition' (Ridley, 2000; George, 2000).

The English Failing: Players and Player Culture

During his two close seasons at Liverpool, Houllier has signed eleven new players, transforming the side within eighteen months. The rapid movement of players through top clubs has become more generally a new feature of the sport's late-modern development (Giulianotti, 1999; Williams, 1999). Clearly, Houllier also believed that the squad he inherited at Liverpool lacked sufficient depth to compete with the best in England and Europe, but he has also admitted that he was surprised by the scale of the rebuilding that he judged to be necessary (Ridley, 2000). He has preached the virtues of constructing a solid defensive foundation, around a 'square base' composed of central defenders and two central midfielders. Liverpool fans who had become used to inconsistency and costly individual and collective lapses in concentration during the 1990s, were pleasantly surprised to find Houllier's team with the tightest defence in the FA Premier League in 1999/2000, conceding only thirty goals.

On the flanks, he has sought out capable defenders, but of greater significance here is the premium Houllier places upon the attacking abilities of wide players, even when, nominally, they occupy primarily defensive roles. The expectation that seasoned German internationals Marcus Babbel and Christian Ziege (significantly, in place of *local* youth-team products) will provide this kind of flexibility remains to be definitively tested. Nonetheless, what is clear is that they represent a close approximation to Houllier's vision of responsible, mature, intelligent, and astute footballers who can also cope with the physical demands of the English game. Houllier has stressed, repeatedly, the sheer athletic endeavour required from footballers in this era, and it remains the case that the high tempo of English league football (in comparison with that of the Italian, French or Spanish leagues) means that this requirement necessitates a much more professional approach to the physical and mental preparation of players.

Thus, Houllier recognized the need for a root-and-branch revision of the prevailing player culture. This was partly a question of player discipline and professionalism during a specific period at Liverpool, which had reached a low ebb during the previous decade (see Chapter Seven), but it also had wider ramifications for ingrained aspects of English football's 'code of masculinity'. This pitted well-worn stereotypes of 'laddish' English behaviour and mentalities that had been the professional footballer's stock in trade over several generations (Wagg, 1984; Williams and Taylor, 1994), against a new emphasis upon the all-round education and personality of the modern elite player.

The *Guardian* journalist Richard Williams, writing after Euro 2000 and another close season when English footballers had rarely been out of the limelight, argued that young footballers' cultural experience was narrowly confined to 'What they see or hear or read in the over-heated and hyper-sexualised mass media, in the tabloid exposes and prying docu-soaps . . .' (R. Williams, 2000). In the same article, John Cartwright, director of Crystal Palace's academy for young players, and one-time technical director at the FA's coaching school at Lilleshall, is quite brutal in his assessment of the problematic, heavily masculinst values of many young English footballers:

If you even try to speak properly, people think you must be a fool. We've developed a thug culture. Football follows the culture of the country, and sometimes vice versa. We've played thug football and we've produced a thug relationship between the player and the spectator . . . There have been gradual improvements. Coaches and players have come in from abroad and they've shown a different attitude to preparation. But we still go out there with a gung-ho attitude. If you can't think it out, fight it out.

Even well before the frantic inquest into England's national malaise during the summer of 2000, Henry Winter, one of the most thoughtful of current English football journalists, was bemoaning Kevin Keegan's insistence that 'We need to revert to more traditional qualities, like getting into them . . . I want intensity and aggression to become trademarks of my England side'. As Winter noted, 'Some of Keegan's players need to control their aggression, not unleash it.' The national team manager insisted that the 'tempo' and the 'intensity' of the English game could still bring success in international football, something that Houllier might agree with – but only up to a point. However, as Winter puts it, other necessities of the modern international game must also feature, namely, 'composure', 'shape' and 'possession'. For Winter – and almost certainly for Houllier too – 'Keegan's idea of tempo involves sustained velocity when the best teams . . . race through the gears, keeping the ball well and then counter-attacking on espying a defensive chink' (Winter, 1999).

Houllier argues forcefully that respect for teammates and opponents, communication and inter-personal skills (crucial in an era of media saturation coverage of sport), and commitment to embrace a 'learning culture' where change is not necessarily viewed as threatening – these are the sort of values and skills that will mark out successful football clubs in the future. Again, these points have a wider relevance. In terms of communication, for example, it has been pointed out that 'At Euro 2000 many of Keegan's players were sullen and uncommunicative. With a couple of honourable exceptions, what thoughts they may have had about what was unfolding in Holland and Belgium remained locked inside minds that have been closed to the joys of thinking and talking publicly about the subtle complexities of the game.' (Hayward, 2000).

If a certain suspicion of the voracious British media – especially the tabloids – is to be expected from English players, there is no doubt that this refusal or inability to reflect and theorize about the game is also a potent indicator of the paucity of the cultural resources that the bulk of English footballers can currently draw upon. This deep 'anti-intellectual strain' in English football (present, too, among many administrators, managers, coaches and supporters) clearly reflects a more generalized cultural problem, but after Euro 2000, there were some signs that insularity and chauvinism could be challenged more forcefully now than perhaps at any previous time in the recent development of the game in England. Speculation even extended to either appointing a foreign coach to manage England, or, given Keegan's evident deficiencies, asking Houllier or Wenger to 'help out' with the preparation of the English team (Powell, 2000). Interestingly, the advocates of this idea were not immediately laughed out of court, but Houllier himself, perhaps mindful of one failed 'joint experiment' at club level, immediately quashed the idea.

It is by no means clear that this struggle over the professional ethos and identity of footballers in this country will be easily resolved, for there are powerful currents that stand out against this perceived dilution of 'traditional' strengths of the English game. Houllier seems to understand the complexity of this issue and, critically, argues that this type of cultural transformation need not stifle spontaneity or belittle the spirit of collectivity and teamwork that, for example, the drinking culture in English football was supposed to embody. Indeed, he often uses aspects of the vocabulary and imagery of this old culture ('When each of my players wears the Liverpool shirt, I expect him to die for it'), but sees no contradiction in marrying this attitude with meticulous professionalism, and a much more rigorous and serious approach to planning for success.

When Houllier took charge at Liverpool he, predictably, took firm steps to tackle drinking: 'There used to be a time when, as soon as the young go through to the first team, they have to start drinking to show they are men . . . That's finished; if they do that, they last two years.' He also made the specific comparison with Arsenal's new regime: 'Arsene Wenger started by changing the attitude of players as regards their training, their diet and their behaviour off the pitch. We've done that here, with a good response. I don't think we have a booze problem. Previously, perhaps, but not now' (George, 2000).

Managing at Liverpool and the 'new' English game

On his arrival at Liverpool, as we have seen, as well as being internationally acclaimed Houllier also had the added attractions to the Anfield hierarchy of being a knowledgeable respecter of the club's traditions and, following the alleged excesses of the Evans regime, a reputed disciplinarian. He had turned down other British clubs, effectively to job-share at Anfield. Lacking the heavy egotistical baggage of some of his English equivalents, he also even seemed genuinely moved by his new appointment, and he appeared convinced that joint decision-making was perfectly possible at a top English football club, even one which was now frantically rebuilding in full media glare. 'Gérard must be in heaven', commented Alain Tirloy, a friend of Houllier who had also played under him at Lens in the early 1980s. 'He's always been completely mad about Liverpool' (Brodkin and Henley, 1998).

Predictably, however, the new managerial partnership did not last long. Press mutterings about the lack of a single 'decision-maker' at the football helm at Anfield added to the pressures on the new pairing; but it was poor performances and results which claimed Evans in the end. The Liverpool team which lost at home to Spurs in a League Cup tie in November 1998, a result which finally led to Evans's resignation, capitulated feebly. It was, like many of Evans's talented teams of the time, simply overpowered. This experience confirmed Houllier's insistence that physical strength and athletic ability were now absolutely vital as prerequisites for a successful team. Equally, passing for the sake of passing, and maintaining possession (often in their own half) with no clear attacking purpose, had become problems in the Evans' years, and Houllier made no apology for his conviction that Liverpool needed to revert to 'passing and movement', particularly movement *forwards*.

Houllier recognizes that this can easily be construed as a call for the introduction of 'long-ball' football and, particularly at Liverpool, this would not only be met with resistance from many players, but also from many of the supporters. He argues that he is not suggesting that Liverpool should take lessons from Wimbledon (the arch-exponents of 'route one' play), but that the Liverpool emphasis upon passing had become something of a fetish in recent years, producing an exaggerated 'purity'. As a result, home matches against lesser opponents ended up all too often in draws rather than victories. He also brought in new players who could improve Liverpool's *physical* presence (the central defenders Stéphane Henchoz and Sami Hyypia and the midfielder Dietmar Hamann are good examples). There were also to be important attempts to change Liverpool's off-pitch preparation.

At his valedictory press conference Roy Evans, tellingly, remarked that the players at the club had been 'his best friends'. Typically, too, when approached by the press for a comment about the 'new way' ahead for the Liverpool club, Gérard Houllier commented that 'Out of decency', and because he had 'so much respect for Roy Evans and what he was for this club', journalists should ring him again after an appropriate period of 'mourning' (Ridley, 1998). A *Guardian* editorial at the time (13 November 1998), significantly, and probably correctly, 'read' the departure of Evans from Liverpool and his replacement by Houllier in rather broader terms. This was not just a seminal moment in the recent history of Liverpool FC; it was also an important social marker for aspects of the wider transformation of 'new' football in England:

The fate of Roy Evans at Liverpool is a sad one. He has been a loyal servant of a great club, and his going puts paid to its proud Shankly tradition of longevity in the dug-out; the 'double header' with Gerard Houllier has been personally humiliating. The Liverpool board has given the impression it believes foreign managers make magic. Ruud Gullit's far-from-immediate impact at St. James Park, let alone Liverpool's structural problems, ought to dispel that. But in the longer run the arrival of these French coaches must be deemed good news. They bring with them – witness Arsene Wenger – standards of education and culture hitherto unknown in club management, and above all they import sports professionalism antithetical to the drunken amateurism still evident in certain quarters . . . French managers, like Italian, Dutch and German are trained, examined and middle class. And that, like it or not, is football's future.

Following Evans' departure, Liverpool's immediate and long term future now depended substantially on whether Houllier – certainly an urbane, cultured and educated Frenchman of the sort described above, a man with a highly professional approach to his job, but one who actually also liked the 'difficult' areas of the city and the young players they produced – could successfully *manage*, as well as coach, in the English FA Premier League. It would also depend upon whether the Liverpool club, under Houllier and Chief Executive Rick Parry, *together*, could properly negotiate its move into the football age which was likely to be dominated by the so-called 'G14' grouping of European super clubs. Here, the balancing of the playing side of the club's activities, with the necessary *commercial* and *structural* development needed in order to keep pace into the new millennium with the sprawling economics of the Manchester Uniteds, Barcelonas and Milans – and perhaps the River Plates and Flamencos, too – would be crucial.

Houllier's first full season in charge of the club in 1999/2000 was dogged by injuries, suspensions and not a little ill luck. Club form was inconsistent, but improvements had clearly been made in key areas, especially in defence. His determination to recruit younger players, and to do so heavily from abroad, startled some Liverpool supporters, and the media made much of this arriving 'foreign legion'. His reasoning for this *continental* spending spree was that the technical quality of available players in Britain was simply too low, and their price too high for the money he had available to spend. There was also the rampant inflation of the English transfer market to take into account (Morrow, 1999). Other clubs were also investing heavily abroad, with the number of foreign players (who were full internationals) in the Premiership reaching 130 by 1999/2000 (*Rothmans Football Yearbook*, 2000). Nevertheless, the central core of the Liverpool team which began the 1999/2000 season was not only very young and inexperienced; it was also resolutely English, and it actually hailed from Merseyside. In some matches at the start of the new campaign, as many as six or seven players in the Liverpool line-up were actually young 'scousers'; not even the Shankly era could produce figures to match these. When Liverpool thrashed Southampton 7–1 at Anfield in January 1999, all of the scorers were local graduates from the club's youth team.

Houllier's transfer coffers were boosted by a large part of a controversial £22 million cash injection into the club from the Granada media and leisure group in 1999. This new financing was also a sign, of course, of the new commercial diversification of the administrative approach of the club under the direction of the increasingly influential Rick Parry. By the summer of 2000, reports suggested that the club was analysing the possibility of building an entirely new ground, only a matter of several hundred yards away from Anfield, on Stanley Park, with a projected capacity of 70,000 (Parry, 2000). Parry claims that Manchester United make £1 million more than Liverpool for every home match staged. He also knows that stadium capacity, income and the size of one's international fan base will be crucial factors in the event of the establishment of some future European League, which may well be organized by the top clubs themselves (see, King, 1998).

Houllier's maxim is that in the 'global' age, fans of the club will care little about the nationality of the players in the side if they can soon begin a new period of sustained success. This was an approach, of course, which had also stood the club in good stead back in the 1890s when 'honest' John McKenna was ransacking Scotland for players for the first great Liverpool side of the early 1900s. It was there again in the 1970s and 1980s when the team was successfully stocked with Scots and Irish players. Was the famous first 'team of the Macs' at Anfield really any less startling a century ago than was the recruitment of Smicer, Camara, Hyypia and the rest in the newly 'globalized' sport of 1999?

The FA Premier League now offers highly attractive salaries and an international stage for some of the world's top players, even if the hype about the quality of football played in England was still rather forced and overblown. The new 'scientism' of this continental drift extolled the virtues of greater club 'professionalism'; a more holistic view of player development and education; the need for rigorous control of player diets; a place in the game for top-class medical back up; and careful psychological, as well as physical, player preparation for matches (Williams, 1999). This new direction seemed, finally, to herald the beginning of the end of the 'muddy boots/chalky fingers' more informal traditions of the English approach to football coaching, which had been exemplified, in many ways, by the cosy mystique and information gathering of the Anfield boot room (Wagg, 1984). It also ruled out of court the associated ideas that player bonding in the club bar, and a strong dose of British 'team spirit', were still sufficient to overcome most of the tactical and playing challenges now posed in the British game and in Europe.

Early signs

Houllier's strong insistence on 'professionalism' in his staff was, then, very clear; senior players who were deemed to be 'negative' influences at Anfield were soon on their way out of the club. Ironically, the explosive and departing ex-England captain Paul Ince cited 'lack of respect' from Houllier towards senior players as a central weakness in the new Anfield regime. As the 1999/2000 season progressed, with a 25-match run in the League where Liverpool lost only twice, it appeared as though this very young team (often Hamann, at 26, was the oldest player in the side) was definitely responding well to the new regime. But for a terrible run of results in April and May, when Liverpool failed to score in their last five League games, a place in the European Champions' League would certainly have been secured. Chief Executive Rick Parry argued that 'If you leave aside the way it finished and judge the season as a whole, it was ahead of schedule' (Parry, 2000). Other close observers in the city were not quite so charitable.

Houllier is clearly both a technocrat and a humanist; a man who has an organic vision for the club and one which is designed to span the next decade, rather than a few months. He has signed young, ambitious players who are willing to make a personal investment in the new Liverpool project. In the interview he talks of the importance of the players' collective involvement in a football 'adventure'. He is also fully aware of how far, and why, the Liverpool club has now fallen behind the 'new' football innovators – and how long it might yet take the club to catch them up. Houllier also shows, in what follows, an engaging vulnerability, a realism about the immediate future, something which is not always matched by the club's keenest followers. As he points out, the wider difficulties of managing players on and off the field today bear little relation to the sorts of work performed so magnificently by Shankly, Paisley and Fagan in the club's recent past.

Houllier has warned that it may take five years for Liverpool FC to even begin to close in on its previous heights. By May 2000, Liverpool had clawed their way from the lower levels of the League table into a top four position and a European qualification spot – the minimum now demanded by most of the club's fans. Whether Houllier is actually allowed the time needed to see through his putative 'revolution' for the Anfield club – especially in an era when the demand for football success, urged on as it is by a rapacious English popular press, is measured in weeks, not years – remains, as they say, to be seen.

Can he carry the Liverpool fans with him, this modest, 'owlish' Frenchman? Will he have a wider role to play in the transformation of the English game? Will he also carry, especially, those supporters who have seen such great things from the Liverpool club in their living memory, and who still value the strongly local links of Liverpool FC? Can the club, in the wider sense, restructure itself in a way which matches up to the new futures for football in Europe, where, according to Houllier in our interview, a new European (or World?) League looms on the near horizon? Despite the club's preparations in case of a European breakaway, Rick Parry argued recently that he had never been a supporter of the proposition. Still, 'it's actually a huge dilemma that we may be faced with one day . . . If, for example, we were offered a place and all the big guys are going, do we take it or do we stay true to our principles?' (Parry, 2000). Most supporters – and Parry, himself – already knew the answer to this question.

One early hint of what might be in store for Houllier from club supporters came from a Liverpool visit to Leeds United in August 1999. Among a lively away contingent at Elland Road, a group of 'scouse' fans unfurled a new banner for the season. It read: '*Cosmopolitisme Vaincra*' ('Cosmopolitanism will triumph'). A year on, an uncertain start to season 2000/2001 had some Liverpool supporters calling for his head. It was already clear that, both on and off the field, Houllier's reign at Anfield, and his time in England, would be at the very least an interesting ride.

The Gérard Houllier Interview

The interview which follows was conducted by John Williams and Cathy Long and it took place over two days: on 21 September 1999 before a Liverpool home League Cup tie v Hull City, and on 24 November after a Liverpool training session. John Williams transcribed and re-assembled the written account. The meetings took place in Houllier's compact office at the Liverpool training ground, Melwood.

Can you recall when you were first aware of Liverpool – of the city and of the club?

When I was a student in France. There were two clubs here, Everton and Liverpool. If you play football, if you're a football fan, and if you are involved in foreign languages you know the clubs in England, I think. That was one of the reasons I came here the first time, because when I picked on Liverpool – to come and teach here – I knew it was a football town. I was already 'Liverpool-minded', not Everton.

Why?

I don't know; I always liked Liverpool. You are just brought up with it. Everton were the better team then. But even before coming here to the city I knew it was Liverpool for me. I remember, as [one of] the teaching staff, one of the first questions the boys would ask you is not where you are coming from, it's: 'Are you Liverpool or Everton?' – and you better have made your mind up first!

What kind of image did people in France have of the city of Liverpool when you were growing up

You mean thirty years ago? Well, a big port, you know, a big harbour, and not much more than that. I would say the image now is darker. They will think that Liverpool is a dull city and it is difficult to live here, because of the tradition of strikes and everything that happened here in the past 20 years maybe. In my university years when I decided to come and teach here for one year [1969–1970], I had to write a thesis for a final degree. I wrote a thesis about growing up in a deprived area of the city for the MA at Lille. It was an English MA, but I chose to write on social issues. So I worked here and I was linked to a youth club, and all sorts of things went on there. I won't tell you what sort of situations I got involved in! So the Liverpool 8 district I know well!

I picked Liverpool because of the football and because of Liverpool, the city. At that time I was Liverpool-orientated, but I knew there were two clubs so I said, well, maybe when I cannot go to [watch at] one club, then I'll go to the other. But, as soon as you arrive here you know that's finished. Because if you are committed to one club you're not committed to the other one . . . What struck me here is that you can have within the same family people supporting Everton and also Liverpool. I couldn't believe that! That's impossible on the continent. It's odd but interesting – funny.

Tell us about your time as a fan.
I went to see games – it was in the Kop. I went every time I could go. But sometimes I was playing myself so I couldn't go. But it was quite nice, I enjoyed it. I played for the Old Boys of the school I was working at [Alsop]. I enjoyed local football. It was a good atmosphere. The Kop was very unusual. You wouldn't find that in France or anywhere else 30 years ago – maybe in Marseilles, maybe. The noise, the singing, the moving. It was swaying all the time; you could hardly see half of the game! It was quite an atmosphere. When I came back and saw games like St Etienne, for instance [European Cup, 1977]. Or even when I saw cup finals where Liverpool were involved. Then you could feel there was a very strong link between the fans and the club. And, of course, that became even more acute to me with some of the games we played at Anfield this year. A couple of games we were down two–nil and we won three–two or four–two and it was a great atmosphere.

Was it something about the English game, the way football is played here, which was attractive to you, especially?
At that time the English game had a reputation to be direct football. Some guys would say it was 'kick and rush'. But Liverpool had a tradition of better football at that time; playing the ball round the floor, and so on. They were supposed to be successful because they were more continental in their approach to the game and had more skills. You know, the mid-1980s is the beginnings of television starting to show football in Europe and I would say so, Liverpool did have more of a continental style. It's true that I always think that at some stage the football you play must some way, somehow, please and entertain your fans. And, if it entertains them it must appeal to their emotional, or to their subconscious, things. I think there are some values here [in Liverpool] which are very important.

First, the effort. Here, you can miss a pass, I mean if you miss a pass but you run 20 yards and do a tackle they [the crowd] applaud you. That means something. Provided the players show effort, they show a resilience and tenacity in their effort, that's very important. I don't know about football in London, but if you miss a pass in Chelsea maybe it's different than if you miss a pass here. I think even in my first professional club in France, Lens, which is a bit like Liverpool – it's a mining area, it went through difficult periods because of the mines collapsing, and so on – they like that effort, too, first and foremost, no matter the talent, they like that.

The second thing is that you know the Liverpool club has a tradition of passing football. Whether it is linked to the fact that the passing is a language between people – it's a bond between people, it's a link between people when you play football. Everybody involved in the passing, everybody working for the same aim, and so on. Has this got something to do with it? It must, probably, appeal to the 'imaginary' of the people [in Liverpool], that's what I think. All I know is that having been a technical director I notice that the football you play in some towns, even in France, is not the same and it couldn't be the same. And it has got something to do with the way of living, the culture, the history; it's funny.

Is there something about the working-class industrial traditions of towns like Liverpool and Lens which attracts you?

I've always liked the town, Liverpool. I know the town has not a good reputation abroad. I know that some people would come through various districts of the city and would say, 'Well, this is absolutely ugly', or 'This is dirty', and it's funny because I surprise myself because I say, 'Well, I like it!'. Don't ask me why, but I like it. I like the people and their sense of humour, this is important, this is a part of it. This is part of the game here. I think the people here like to have a good time. They like to have a laugh. Have you noticed, when there is something funny in a game, they always laugh? There was a game – I think against Watford – and there was a lot of tension and we were playing poorly and they, Watford, were one–nil [up]. And something happened. And they [the fans in the Kop] were all laughing!

What do the people here want from the team?

I know, for sure, that the people here like to take pride in what's on the field. They take pride in the people, the players, who've got the shirt. Talking in the city and everywhere, it's the first thing the fans want. When you talk about the link, the bond between the fans and the club, first of all they like to be really, really proud of the club and the team. And then there is no matter of national identity. They don't matter if it is Song or Riedle, or whether it's Fowler. It is totally out of order if you think they prefer the local lads. The fans want the team to be successful, to play well.

But, here, you cannot reach places or win trophies without a certain way of doing it. Because of the tradition, because of the culture of the football that was on the field here for years and years, with the good teams, with Keegan and Dalglish and all those players, it was different from the other football of other clubs. Here, you have got to play a certain type of football. I knew that when I came as a supporter, but even more as a manager in France and as a technical director I would watch Liverpool and the way they would play. I don't think you could play the Wimbledon type of football here. Suppose I would come here and say: 'Well, this is the quickest way to get from box to box, let's do that'. Well, it wouldn't work. And that's not just because of the players. Football is more than just eleven players; it's an environment, it's a context and they [the fans] have had so much of the good football practice in the successful years that you could not break away from that.

Even now I am trying to break away from the passing: well, not from the passing, because I like the passing. But I want to pass forwards, God, yeah. They [the players] like to pass the ball. Two years ago Liverpool made more passes than any other team, they were the best passing team in the Premiership. But to me that doesn't mean anything. You can be the best passing team and win nothing. You have to verticalize, and to go deeper with passes. The passing, like a bond, was more, 'Let's keep our hands like that' [a sideways clasp], but I think we have to be more provocative than that, and go forward.

These fans have been to matches for 20 or 35 years. They have been to many games. They know the type of football that was developed here. They've kept that in mind. They know more when the team is playing well. You cannot win without a bit of 'the manner' here. You can't win without entertaining here. It's my philosophy, but I think it's even more here [among the fans]. They like winning, but they like winning in the way they want to win. It's got to be a good, entertaining and fascinating way of playing it. That's important. We can win one–nil and play crap and they would not like that.

Is the English game too focused on action, not enough on thinking?

The English game is changing now. I mean you cannot say that Manchester United is playing a 'typical' English game. The football in Italy and France is very, very skilful, sometimes the level of skill is very high. It's very tactical, but the pace is not as high as here. Here, you never have a free half-a-second. The physical demand of the game here is much higher than anywhere else. When you go to Italian football it's a different sport. I was the French national coach so I had to go and see my players playing everywhere, including Italy. Sometimes I got absolutely bored, because there was nothing! Suddenly, five minutes of good football and then a slump again. But here, in England, if you go and see Stockport playing Tranmere you get a lot of excitement, and this is a good thing about it. An English Champions League team, they can have problems against Watford, or Wimbledon, because it's difficult to play games of that intensity all the time.

Here, football is different. But, personally, I think the English football is also changing. Tactically it is getting richer. You have different systems, different approaches, more discipline now. The skill level is not bad at all. Don't be misled; it is because the pace of the game is so high here that players make mistakes. I mean, Michael Owen, if he played in a French team he will probably never miss a control of the ball.

How do you get this sort of change?

There are experienced players at the club. I say, 'Why don't you just sit there and pass the ball when you are ahead? Just pass the ball, and move, and pass, and move. What's going to happen is that you are going to tire them out.' But my players wanted to keep the pace of the game at the same level!

I think there is a crowd influence in this. The crowd plays a part because they want that. They like that, and they always want 100 per cent effort. They don't understand that, sometimes, you just need to keep the ball. They think we are taking risks when we do that. In Italy you would not see this crowd impatience. This is a habit of always playing 'pacy' football. To me, the best football means that you master the rhythm.

Is it a special problem of teaching English players to change?

They think, if they are not giving 100 per cent, maybe they are feeling guilty of not doing their job. Abroad, the youth development of players implies a professional youth development. A sociologist is a professional job, you have to go to university, to be trained. The same thing to be a professional player at the age of 20; you need five years of hard work as a professional, youth trainee. And if you don't do that now you can't be a professional at a club like this. Those days of coming to the club at 20 to be a professional footballer, that's finished now. The Academy system means that now, you have to be aware that to be a professional player and to respond to between 50 and 70 games a season, between 15 and 20 years old you must learn your trade. And you learn your trade through physical strengthening, the technical, the tactical and the mental processes. I hope the Academy system will bring here what it brought in France and in other countries: that you can feed good habits of professionalism into players at 15 and 16 years of age. That's what Lippi [Juventus coach until 1998] told me. He said the good thing about buying a French player is that he has a good education, good attitude, very professional, very focused and tactically fully aware. He knows all the systems; he can play in that, play in this. In about ten years, of course, that will be the same here. Provided the youth coaches change as well.

Is it difficult to make these sorts of changes in Liverpool?

It is always difficult to change in a city which has a long history and a tradition behind it. You will always have people who say, 'Well, in the past we had 12 players, we played 70 games, and it went alright.' 'In the past we had no physio, and we didn't need a physio.' Those same people now use a mobile phone at the moment, so they have changed! It's always more difficult when there is a great tradition of success. The past weighs heavy here.

I think the club is very strong, very powerful. One of its main roots is the fans, the supporters, because they feed that strength at the club. The players on the park will feel that strength from the back. They know how important it is; when we travel we see a full stand of Reds. But the loyalty to the club in the Bosman era is to me extremely limited. One of the appeals of the club is its tradition and its name. The other one is the fact we have a young team at the moment – which is interesting. I would say that all the players except one we have taken into the side this season are young players, between the ages of 23 and 26. So you can think about passion and everything. I prefer to think we have a good bunch of players here, whatever the nationality. They just bloody want to win something together. And its got to be for them and for the fans, but it's got to be for them [the players], first. To me the passion comes from the inner competitiveness of the players. Do they have the drive, do they have this thing? Some local lads are top class; Carragher is a model of commitment, passion, everything on and off the pitch and in training.

How did you 'sell' the club to new players in this period?

We have been extremely fair to all of them. We've said, 'This is where we are and this is what we want to do.' This is our target, to get back into the top three. It will take time because our team is relatively young and inexperienced. We've got the quality, we just need to build that success on the way together. But we'll be a professional club. You forget about the booze, forget about parties. You're part of the deal; you don't want to do it, if you don't feel for it, then get away.

You see, there are definite routes. You can have the Chelsea route. We were offered Deschamps [French captain]. He is over 31 and is experienced, and is a very good player, could have been a top-class player for a couple of years. But we preferred Hamann [German international], who is 26 and who needs to build up his trophies with us. Deschamps has already won European Cups, the World Cup. It's a different route. We have taken the route of faith and belief in what we do. Everyone is talking about the city resurging, about Liverpool coming back. I think our team is about the same. The players we've signed are young, they want to succeed, they are committed to the club, they enjoy being here: let's go.

Managing a club in England must be very different from being a technical director in France.
I was talking to Arsène [Wenger] about this. When I was a manager and then I became national team manager and then national technical director, as a technical director, even given the huge amount of work I had to do, I could still keep in touch with reading *Le Monde* every day, reading papers, books, and so on. But when you are a club manager it is very focused. All that goes. Not being involved in a club I missed what we in France call 'the powder', the gun and fire. I needed to go out into the trench again! It was a very strange move I did. Liverpool was important in that, but they pinched me in a way. I would have gone to another club anyway. When you have just passed your 50 and you say, 'Oo-la-la, listen: you're the top position in France, good salary, good respect from everybody in UEFA and FIFA, life could not be better'. I said, if I don't go into the fire now I will never go back.

Did anything surprise *you when you came to Liverpool?*
The approach to the professional side of the job was totally different from what I expected it to be, in terms of preparation, application and concentration. I don't think some players felt the relationship between the training and the game was important. They didn't understand the connection. Players thought training was something to pass the time between matches. For instance, the game requires a maximum concentration, but that means they must focus during training. The players enjoyed the good side of the job. This job is not just about being focused for an hour and a half. Keegan said, the way you train, you carry it over into games. That is changed here now. It is not perfect, but it has changed.

Do you ever think fans care too much for a club like this one?
I prefer that they care too much than that they don't care! It's important to have a heart and a passion. The Heysel disaster and the tragedy at Sheffield

probably links in even more the fans and the players. I think the players at that time were very affected. And there is the memorial and a service each year for Hillsborough. When you suffer together, you are drawn together. Even if you wanted to forget you can't, and that helps to make the club. No player has ever told me that he has not been moved at the [Hillsborough] service held in April.

What is it about football, itself, which makes it so appealing to you?
My father was a player, then a team manager, and then a team director. I was immersed in football. I think people like football because of the dramatic intensity of the game. I mean, you are never sure to be winning or losing. It's not like basketball or handball, where there are many goals. In volleyball you can see right at the start who is going to win. In football here you can never say who is going to win. I think the people like football because your breath is being taken all the time. There's always a drama somewhere. The new stadiums now mean that people are sitting very close. There's like a communion with the players. In France it is not like that. In France the players are 'on the stage'. Here they're not on a stage; the players are here and the fans are there with them. Like life, you have good times and bad times in matches. The rhythm of a game could be like the rhythm of your life.

Why have Liverpool fallen behind other clubs do you think?
The physical demands of the modern game, especially in Europe, that has gone so high. They are athletes of football now, that's what they are. That makes the entertaining side of the game. The combination of skills and the physical thing makes the game entertaining. The pace, the challenge, the movement. In that case it has gone very high in some leagues in Europe. Here, it's physical, it's tough, but sometimes it's not the same. One difference here is the European gap of five years. Until 1985, Liverpool were top. When you play with someone and they beat you, you have to respond. It's not complacency here [in Liverpool]. It was just, 'We were winning and it worked. We were just doing five-a-side and it worked'. Like in life, if you don't question and try to update your methods, you will be left behind. The passion of this game is that it is traditional, it is orthodox, but at the same time you have to be adventurous; you do this, but sometime you have to do something which is more forward thinking. That's how you progress. Here, it was: 'This is the way we play, this is the way we train, this is the way we travel'.

At the moment we haven't changed everything. There are a couple of sectors I still want to work on. Some of my worries are about the youth and the way we deal with them. You have to do better all the time. We missed that European experience because between 1985 and 1990 Europe has changed, I can tell you. And the second thing is that here [in England] the clubs have changed. Arsenal, Tottenham, Leeds, Chelsea, Manchester, they have all changed. Would you know that other clubs have cameras everywhere analysing the play? Here, there was no change at all like that.

Was it difficult to change the coaching at the club?
The tradition of the boot room meant nothing had changed here. Changing the coaching was easy. We still do a lot of work with the ball. The only players who did not want to change, we got rid of. We knew that, because they preferred not to do anything. The good thing about working here is that there is a lot, a lot, of tremendous assets to the English players. The frame of mind, the attitude, the enthusiasm. They like the game. They've got a big heart, they put everything into it. I would say that I prefer to be a coach for the English players than working with young players in France. It's easier maybe on some aspects of the game with the French, but from the human point of view it is much more exciting here. Because I knew the type of environment the young players used to live in, and what it would mean for them to be there in the team, nobody wants to help them more than I do. It might be easier to work with other players from a technical point of view. But I enjoy the human things about working with the players here, especially, in some ways, with the players who come from the city itself.

Do you think the way clubs in England play makes it harder for English players to play in international football?
That's a very good point and I had a discussion on that one day with [Michel] Platini and he thought the English play too quickly and make technical errors. When they play at international level and they have to master a different rhythm, a different pace to the game, they can't do it: because they are used to playing flat out all the time. I believe in skill. The game will go with skill, I believe that. In ten years time you won't be able to tell if a player is right- or left-footed. In ten years time you will have to be able to do that to succeed. Skilful players solve problems on the field.

How has management in football changed over the past 20 years?
When a player knows he has two years on his contract, now with Bosman, he can just sit. The manager, ten years ago, was extremely powerful. Now you have counter-forces from everywhere. Because the profile of the player has changed, the profile of the manager has changed, too. The power of the players means a new way of managing. Twenty years ago a manager could tell players to do this, and do that. Now that's finished. Now you manage different nationalities, different players. They're more aware of their interests

and their careers, through their agents. They're multi-millionaire, multi-national. At the same time, passion, commitment, teamwork, this is still what you need from them. This is something which gives players something to work for. There is some kind of pride to belong to Liverpool, there's no doubt about that. Here, it is different from other clubs because of the great traditions of Liverpool. But the job of the manager is still to create an environment in which players can produce their best. The job is more human now than it used to be twenty years ago, because it was easy twenty years ago. You *told* players what to do then. Now it's finished; today you have to explain. The most important word with top players now is 'Why?' 'Why do we do this, why do we do that?' This is a very important move in the mind of the players.

Players are human. They need confidence. They need a positive feedback; they need targets; and they need a strong sense of belonging. The manager must create a kind of 'human adventure'. There must be an atmosphere of work at the club, but it must also be relaxed. You need jokes, sometimes. You have to put the players in the best condition to find the motivation to play. Players like to be treated the same way. But you must have a slightly different approach to each of them. Players expect from their manager three qualities: you must be an expert in football – a top man in that. But you must also be able to communicate the message. You must also have a strong personality. If they get on top of you, you have had it. The third thing is that you must have a plan, a logic or a strategy. You must know where you are going and how to get there. A group reduces the amount of the initiative of the individual. You need to try to keep that. You must keep enterprise and initiative as well as having a strong spirit and a strong team.

What do you think will be the future direction of the game?
I think we are bound to have a European League. It is inevitable. They have resisted with the new version of the Champions League, but in five years we will have a new league. The power of players also means a new way of managing. All players say they love their club, and to be fair, most of them do. But we can also admit that the attraction to English football has something to do with the attraction to the English pound. They have a short career and they have to make the most of it. I am angry at the media at the moment because they lack respect for managers. The players have the attention of the media, they have the money; they can be very powerful if the manager has not a strong personality.

Players here can sign the biggest contract in the world, but as soon as they pass the gate [into Melwood] everybody is worth the same rate, they have no privileges and they do the work. Some players, though, they sign the contract, they take the money, they wave to the crowd, and they give ten minutes of football at the end of the game to show that they are 'committed'. The rest of the time they are invisible. They may fool some of the fans, but not me.

References

Brodkin, J. and Henley, J. (1998), 'Houllier'll never walk alone', *Guardian*, 14 August.

Deloitte and Touche (1999) *Annual Review of Football Finance*, Manchester: Deloitte and Touche.

Fynn, A. and Guest, L. (1998) *For Love or Money: The Business of Winning*, London: Boxtree.

George, R. (2000), 'What makes this man tick?', Liverpool Season 2000/01: Official Matchday Magazine, *The Big Kick-off*.

Giulianotti, R. (1999) *Football: A Sociology of the Global Game*, Cambridge: Polity.

Hayward, P. (2000), 'Islanders marooned as adventurers disappear over the horizon', *Daily Telegraph*, 4 July.

King, A. (1998) *The End of the Terraces*, London: Leicester University Press.

Morrow, S. (1999) *The New Business of Football*, Basingstoke: Macmillan.

Parry, R. (2000), 'The Road Ahead', Liverpool Season 2000/01: Official Matchday Magazine, *The Big Kick-off*.

Powell, J. (2000), 'Just say non to the foreigners', *Daily Mail*, 28 June.

Ridley, I. (1997) 'Houllier hails the revolution', *Independent on Sunday*, 18 May.

—— (1998) 'Houllier must do it the hard way', *Observer*, 15 November.

—— (2000), 'Houllier first among equals', *Observer*, 13 August.

Rothmans Football Yearbook, 2000–2001 (2000).

Wagg, S. (1984), *The Football World*, Brighton: Harvester.

Williams, J. (1999), *Is it all over? Can football survive the Premier League?* Reading: South Street Press.

Williams, J. and Taylor, R. (1994) 'Boys keep swinging: masculinity and football culture in England', in T. Newburn and B Stanko (eds) *Just boys doing Business?*, London: Routledge.

Williams, R. (2000), 'Wild things', *Guardian*, 12 August.

Winter, H. (1999), 'England cannot force themselves on Europe', *Daily Telegraph*, 12 October.

9

Sitting Pretty? Women and Football in Liverpool

Liz Crolley and *Cathy Long*

Introduction

> Shankly was a great motivator but Paisley was the brains behind the team. You have to
> be tactically aware as well as being able to inspire. Evans was great at getting the team
> to pass the ball, but now Houllier's getting the shape of the team right as well.

The above is an excerpt from a conversation overheard between two Liverpool
football fans. It is the kind of exchange that goes on in public spaces all over the
city. The fact that those involved were two middle-aged women in a hairdressing
salon in Liverpool should surprise only those who don't know the city well. In
some areas of the UK it is perhaps still seen as unusual for women to be 'involved'
in football. In Liverpool, however, and although attending matches is still strongly
dominated by men, football is a major part of living in the city – for almost
everyone.

Men and women of all ages participate in the game in some way, whether as
players, avid supporters or casual fans. Children are inculcated into supporter
traditions at an early age, especially because it is easy to 'lose' potential recruits
to the opposing side of the sport's blue and red divide on Merseyside (Edge, 1999).
Those who take little or no interest in the game are in a distinct minority and are
likely to suffer the sort of cultural exclusion which is catastrophic for male identities
and sometimes damaging for those of local females.

Our aim here is to outline some 'typical' experiences of female football fans in
Liverpool, to open a wider debate about the role of women in football and to
discuss the contention that football is now more 'female-friendly' or has become
more 'feminized' in England and in Liverpool (Coddington, 1997). This is done
by using interviews with female Liverpool football fans as well as by drawing on
personal experiences and other sources. Like any investigation into football culture
in Liverpool, a backdrop of essentially working-class values and traditions in the
city, including very traditionally defined gender roles, needs to be borne strongly
in mind. Our evidence, however, casts doubts over the adequacy of these narrowly-
defined roles within the football context.

Since the mid-1980s, a wealth of literature has been written which focuses on women's role in sport. Interest in this subject matter has often been triggered by an interest, especially perhaps, among 'feminist' academics based in the USA. While it is not our specific aim to contribute to the feminist debates over the wider role of sport in society, it is important that we bear in mind some of the conclusions of this recent body of research. This will also help better to contextualize the evidence of our own oral testimonies. Some of the key themes of recent sports theorists which are relevant to our study include:

- the role of sport in creating and defining a sense of masculinity. 'From the ancient Olympiad to the present, sport has been a primary site for defining, cultivating and displaying Western ideals of masculinity' (Sabo and Curry Johnson, 1998: 202). Traditionally-considered masculine characteristics of physical prowess, strength and courage are still positively associated with football, both by players and by fans and by both by females and males.
- the role of sport in reinforcing male hegemony. 'Sport in the twentieth century has given men an arena to create and reinforce an ideology of male superiority' (Duncan and Messner, 1998: 170). By making characteristics which involve the expression of physical prowess or strength more or less synonymous with masculinity, male superiority becomes self-fulfilling.
- the marginalization and alienation of women via sport. 'By excluding women from this arena . . . sport provides opportunities for men to assert their dominance at a time when male hegemony is continually challenged and opposed in everyday life' (ibid.). We will also see evidence that, despite the recent changes in football culture and the process of 'feminization' that will be discussed later, women can still be marginalized and alienated at times, sometimes deliberately, but more frequently inadvertently.
- the trivialization of women's role in sport (especially via the popular media) and the formulae of exclusion. In our data some women complain that they are not considered to be as committed as fans as were their male counterparts. Women's football is not taken seriously by most commentators, certainly not in England, and there still persists strong elements of the masculinist legacy of the notion that football is still 'a man's game'. Media coverage of women's role in sport is often reduced to 'the humorous sexualisation of women' (ibid.: 182) in which women's participation in sport is either ridiculed or patronized.
- questions raised over sexuality and gender. 'Sport experiences masculinise girls and women' (Kane and Jefferson Lenskyi, 1998: 188). Females involved in sport, as fans, but especially as players, may well have their sexuality questioned. In our own sample, several females felt that following Liverpool FC required them, somehow, to become 'honorary males'. But again, we realize that football culture is evolving in such a way that, nowadays, many females can – and do –

go to football in 'feminine' garb – a skirt, make-up, or even carrying a handbag – and that this can be socially acceptable in the football context. Equally, we see evidence of infinitely complex notions of masculinity; the 'out-of town' fan (from outside the city) in particular casting new nuances onto formerly accepted concepts.

All the above issues, which routinely arise in theorizing on women and sport, are relevant to our own small study and they provide a useful starting point from which to examine the current situation and developments which appear to be taking place in changes in the 'new' gender order of English football.

Playing and Watching

Women's general role in football in England is slowly being redefined as they are increasingly visible both on and off the field (Lopez, 1997). After a slow start on Merseyside, there is now, for example, a Liverpool FC 'Ladies' team, and the women's game in England, though some way behind its equivalents in Scandinavia, Germany, the USA and China, is slowly beginning to make an impact on the footballing world (Williams and Woodhouse, 1999). However, marginalization of women's football continues in England as the game still struggles to attract sponsorship and TV coverage and it receives only modest funding support from the Football Association. As Hargeaves (1994) points out, female sport remains very much a subsidiary of (male) sport, and its role is trivialized.

Liverpool Ladies, despite their recent progress, still play their home matches in the Premier Division of the National Women's League at the local police playing field and there is little or no marketing or promotion of their games; even finding out the kick-off times of fixtures of top women's matches can be an ordeal. It is in schools that there has been a recent boom in female participation. More young girls now play football at school, an important development not just for the growth of football but for the fitness, personal development and identity of girls. Traditionally, of course, when boys leave school, many of them continue to have a kick-about with their friends at a local park or nearby field. Local junior clubs also cater extensively for boys' football. Girls, on the other hand, are still encouraged to associate physical team sport with a challenge to conventional femininity, thereby raising 'difficult' questions about sexuality and gender identities. Girls are also more likely to have been inculcated into netball and hockey as team sports; these sports involve considerably more organization, and more specialized kinds of facilities and equipment. So, relatively few girls continue to play team sports after their education, especially as peer-group pressure, too, presses for young girls to be conventionally competitive in seeking out the company of boys. Increasing numbers of girls also now opt for aerobics classes or gym sessions as a way of socializing and keeping fit, though these options are likely to be more limited – and regarded as less appropriate – in a strongly working-class city such as Liverpool. In contrast, of course, football can be played almost anywhere.

Perhaps unsurprisingly, in the age of 'new' football in England, it is in the media that women have begun to play a more obviously conspicuous role in football. Although many of the women now employed to front football programmes on television, such as Sky Sports's Clare Tomlinson and ITV's Gabi Yorath, may be conventionally attractive, but they also 'know' their football (Williams and Woodhouse, 1999). Yorath's father was an ex-player; Tomlinson was a committed season ticket holder at Spurs. Women have also now become established as part of the sports teams on radio and in some sections of the sporting press (e.g. Eleanor Oldroyd at BBC Radio Five Live, Amy Lawrence at the *Observer*; Alyson Rudd at the *Times*), though few women actually write or comment on the women's game. Women's football remains largely excluded from mainstream media (again marginalizing this arm of the sport). But it is also in the administration of the men's professional game that perhaps progress made by women has been less significant. Marginalizing female players seems somehow more explicable – if still depressing – than the exclusion of females from key administrative positions, where strength and technique are no longer factors. No female holds a senior role at Liverpool Football Club, for example. None has ever held such a position. It is hard to avoid the conclusion that this is a product of institutionalized exclusion, rather than accident or coincidence.

Even a visit to Liverpool FC's official club shop today can be something of an alienating experience for female supporters of the club. This is ironic, of course, given that 'shopping' is supposed to be a strong female identifier. In an age when football club superstores sell pretty much everything from wallpaper to school shirts, and when females make up around one in eight of all fans – and many more of those who actually shop in the club store – there are still few women's items on sale. As for female involvement as football fans, rather than just as consumers of football products, it is our aim here to provide some insight and reflection.

Football Feminization?

Despite these strides made in recent times, football in the UK is still perceived as being a sport played by men, and male dominance in the sport remains pretty much unquestioned. However, in recent years there has been much talk of the alleged 'feminization' of football (Coddington, 1997). This, usually, refers to a perceived change in the climate and atmosphere within football grounds rather than to any real modification in the power structures within football clubs or in the game in general. It implies some sort of change in football culture for the supporters. 'Feminization' is taken to suggest either an increase in the number of female fans in football grounds or that the presence of females is increasingly significant in softening the behaviour of football crowds, or both. Giulianotti (1999: xi) claims in his eloquent sociological study of football as a global sport that: 'Though football reflects the wider distribution of gender-related power in most societies, the game is also undergoing varying degrees of feminization among players, spectators and officials.' We are interested in this notion of 'feminization': we also need to know more about how to 'read' female perceptions of various aspects of this 'new' football culture today.

First, it is useful to refer to the often reported rise in the number of female football fans (Williams, 1997). While some research suggests small rises in the number of female fans at top clubs, lack of data prior to the 1980s means that there is simply no conclusive evidence to prove that significantly more females attend football today than did so in the past (Waddington, et al., 1996). Oral records and historical accounts suggest that, contrary to much speculation, it was not uncommon for females, actively, to follow their favourite football teams in the 1940s and 1950s. During the course of our own research we have come across innumerable cases in Liverpool of women, now over the age of 50, who went to football in their youth, gave it up when they had a young family and were forced to let other commitments take priority, but have recently gone back to attending matches at Liverpool FC. **Margaret**, now in her sixties, is one of these fans:

> I used to go to the match with my sister, Milly, when I was a teenager. We had a great time and were looked after by all the men as if we were their daughters. Then we both had to stop going when we got married and couldn't afford to go any more. It was only when I went back to work, when the children were a bit older, that we both started going to football again.

Notwithstanding the fact that some women have, clearly, always been attracted to football as fans (Mason, 1980; Fishwick, 1989), and that many women were present at matches prior to the recent so-called 'revolutionary' changes in the game, it would not be surprising to find recent increased female participation in football support. After all, female involvement in almost all public leisure activities has probably increased over the last two decades. But a number of more specific questions about the game also come to mind here. Has football really become as 'female friendly' as we are led to believe? Has football really been 'feminized' – and what exactly does this mean? Or, has football resisted changes which are perhaps taking place at a faster pace in other spheres of society? What is it that makes football unattractive to some females and yet so compulsively attractive to others? Has football ever been really 'unfriendly' towards females?

The oral testimonies of older female fans suggest that the 'feel' of the standing Liverpool Kop in the early 1990s, for example, was actually little different from that of being present on the Kop and other football terraces in the 1950s, although a few of our interviewees did suggest that the Kop of old 'respected women more' or that the men were 'more polite towards women' than it later became. Shifts in expectations between generations are important here, of course. Older women probably expect, and expected, men to behave differently – to be more 'chivalrous' towards women – than do the younger female products of the so-called post-feminism era. Most younger female supporters today probably aspire to equal, rather than special, treatment by men at football, as in all things.

There is some evidence that the promotion in the 1980s of the ideologies of the 'family' for football was a deliberate attempt by the then Thatcher government to 'soften' the rough image of football's support during the latter half of that decade by promoting more female support for the sport when hooliganism had hit something of a peak (Giulianotti, 1994). Government Ministers might have hoped that attracting a higher proportion of women to football crowds might have a potentially 'civilizing' effect on rowdy male spectators, thus curbing their sometimes violent and aggressive behaviour. This policy, which saw the introduction and expansion of special areas, often designated as 'family stands', enjoyed some success, arguably, in encouraging more women and children to enter football grounds. Family areas were advertised as 'safe' spaces. Any 'feminization' effect here, however, would surely be limited to these designated areas; it would have relatively little impact on the goal-end terraces, where hooligan problems were actually perceived to exist (Dunning et al., 1988).

It is questionable whether more female fans actually took their place *alongside* those male fans who, it was hoped, were going to be 'feminized' or 'cleansed' of the more traditional, overtly masculine and violent image of football fans at that time. More effective, here, was probably the discourse of 'the family' which was widely used in Liverpool and elsewhere in the early 1990s to discuss the aftermath of the Hillsborough tragedy in 1989 (Brunt, 1989; see also Chapter Five). Here, football fans were reported as victims, not as violent perpetrators, and the stories which unfolded about Hillsborough victims, male and female, located them within conventional codas about family life. Probably for the first time in more than two decades, English football fans were widely discussed in the media outside the conventional masculinist and hooligan frame – instead, 'ordinary' supporters turned out to be 'like us': they were fathers, sons, daughters and aunts. Thus, the role of female fans in the sport was acknowledged, albeit in the most tragic of circumstances. What followed Hillsborough was certainly a less 'closed' and less masculinist popular view of the culture. But is it really the case that it was specifically more women attending football which diluted the 'masculinist' atmosphere of matches? Or, were more women simply attracted to football at a time when other factors – new stadia, seats, marketing, decline of hooliganism, etc – were already reshaping aspects of the culture in this general direction? It is worth examining, in this context, the reasons why women begin to follow football clubs in the first place.

Why Do Women Like Football?

Sport socialization research (that is, research into how social forces shape involvement in sport) has most frequently been explored via social-learning theorists. In most studies into sport socialization research, the family, peer-groups members, teachers and role models are identified as the primary agents of sports socialization (Higginson, 1985). During early childhood, results of research show that the family and peer group are clearly more influential than the school in shaping the behaviour of both girls and boys under the age of twelve. Then, the balance of influences shifts. Among the girls, the family declines in importance, the peer group increases in importance, and sometimes teachers do too. Unsurprisingly, those girls who receive positive reinforcement for interest in a sport are more likely to remain involved than those who receive negative messages (Greendorfer, 1987).

Our research concurs with much of this sport socialization theory. Females who became hooked on football in early childhood quoted parents, then peer group, as significant influences, whereas those who developed an interest in football during adolescence more often quote peers alone as the prime influence. Few mentioned school, however, as being a major agency in developing their interest in football or in a club such as Liverpool. But those who liked football enjoyed playing sports at school. Girls who received positive reinforcement for their interest in football were usually those who either socialised with male peers a lot, or who had brothers who were interested in sport. Hence, it is easy to see how the link between girls liking football and girls being 'tomboys' can be made.

Research suggests that most female interest in football clubs is sparked in much the same ways as is male interest (Williams, 1997). The experiences of the two authors, for example, in terms of football background and the 'football family', differ significantly, but in neither case was gender a central issue. For many children growing up in Merseyside in the 1970s, it was largely understood that you supported your *local* team, and so it was rare for anyone in Liverpool to support a team other than Liverpool or Everton. We all knew exactly who supported Liverpool and who followed Everton in much the same way that children in the city who don't go to church still 'know' whether they are Catholic or Protestant.

Quality of football was not a determining factor here. At the age of five (or whatever) there was no such thing as 'quality' to take account of, though performances were judged on results. To play badly and win was a confusing contradiction. Even by the time we grasped a fuller understanding of the workings of the Football League table, we were already hooked – as a blue or a red. Media hype for football then was nothing like on the scale we enjoy/suffer today. BBC's

Match of the Day, the sole exponent of football on the television in the early 1970s, was on so late at night that by the time many children were old enough to be allowed to watch it, football allegiances had already probably been established. TV was not a factor. Parental influence usually encourages an interest initially, but other factors – school, friends – play their part. **Julie** claims that 'I got hooked because I actually went to matches from a young age. Here, the spirit of terrace culture played its part. I just loved the atmosphere.' **Pam** believes that although the gender issues seemed irrelevant at the time, being a female football fan actually made you that bit extra-special. It provided for a distinct and attractive additional status:

> As a young fan, being a girl was irrelevant to my interest in football. It seemed so natural for me to love football, until it became obvious that everyone else found it odd. Then I became something of an oddity – a girl who knew her football – something special, something to be talked about. I was different – even more reason for me to stick with football! I wasn't afraid of terrace culture. On the contrary, it could be very female friendly.

Parents could be highly influential, of course, in a child's choice of football team. That isn't to say that Evertonian parents inevitably spawned Evertonian children, or vice versa. Children either followed their parents' lead, or else wilfully rejected their pressures. Children might also, artfully, oppose the football choice of an older sibling or, in a 'divided' football family in Liverpool, follow either a mother or a father's lead. Parents – especially male parents – also worked harder on *boys* as potential active recruits to the match. Many fewer girls were regarded as youngsters who may eventually be taken to football by a male parent. Nevertheless, the influence of parents was rarely irrelevant, in this context: unless, of course, these were parents who, perversely, lived in the city but were not interested in football at all!

In the 1970s and 1980s, most girls in Liverpool rarely played football in school. Except for occasional rumblings of discontent, we largely accepted the fact that football was a 'boys' sport' and that we were destined to play netball and hockey. Putting fifteen or sixteen girls onto a hockey pitch for the first time could have been chaotic, of course. No one had seen or played the sport before. But, somehow, we all knew where to stand: we just took up the familiar positions of our *football* heroes.

Although female fans did have football heroes at that time, they were never strictly role models. We always knew we would never follow in our favourite player's footsteps and we never dreamed of lifting the FA Cup at Wembley, as many of the boys did. Today, this sort of role-modelling is a little more appropriate for young girls; the women's FA Cup Final is even televised, today, as long as you can grope towards the right satellite TV station and search out the timing in the press. One is more likely to lift the WFA Cup at Millwall or Oxford, however, than at Wembley Stadium. It is not quite the same. Although opportunities for girls to play football are increasing (Liverpool Football Club now runs coaching sessions for girls as well as for boys), those females who take playing football seriously are still in a distinct minority. Young girls in the city are well aware that girls' football is still tolerated rather than supported locally, and they also know well it does not lead to high-profile, professional football; there is no career option here for female players. In three years' time the new professional league for women in England may offer other options (Williams and Woodhouse, 1999). There is some evidence to suggest that the stigma of playing contact sport seriously is also still strong for females, despite recent changes. Most younger female fans we interviewed are not, or were never, interested in playing football themselves. Perhaps kids at school now see things differently?

Actually going to a football match for young girls is a very special experience. They are both immune to some of the demands made of football 'lads', and often cosseted by male sections of the crowd. **Jane** comments:

> The match atmosphere attracted us in the same way as it would attract lads, but we were different. There were never any pressures on us to be 'macho', to 'act like men', to grow up before we wanted to, or to join in the fighting in Stanley Park and along Utting Avenue after the game. We could even go along to watch with immunity. Female fans enjoyed a freedom to appreciate football culture and on top of it all the men made us feel special, looked after us, protected us from swaying crowds and generally spoiled us. We became part of a big family, our football family.

This notion of the 'football family' has probably always existed at Liverpool and elsewhere. Perhaps in the past there weren't quite as many females in the 'family' as there are today, but the idea of football being a 'family' experience, in this wider sense – not in the sense used by marketing men at football clubs – is not a new one. Most people at Anfield enjoy the company of the 'football family', a series of connections in a complex but largely informal network of relationships. Links here are made and acknowledged unobtrusively but with certainty; a nod at 'away' matches, a simple 'Hiya' or 'Alright' at home. To be included on the Kop, in this way, or as a loyal traveller, is to belong, to have a place.

For a number of years, **Cathy** went to the match with two other girls. The introduction of seating on the Kop coincided with her two friends moving away. Maybe it's because she's not with 'the girls' anymore; maybe it's because the terrace has gone: but her football experience is different now: 'I still miss the closeness we had and the other people we stood with on the Kop. Some people said seating would encourage more women to the game, but we liked the atmosphere on the terraces just as much as the men did.'

Liz's experience of the Kop has been very different from **Cathy**'s. Her football 'family' has always seen males and females mixed together. The ratio has varied over the years, but women have always been in the minority. Far from feeling alienated or excluded from the terrace culture, the overwhelming experience, for her, like that of so many girls and women we interviewed, has been one of welcome inclusion; although women can be treated differently at times, even by the 'family'.

The feelings conjured up by girls and women describing their experiences on the Kop so often contradict the rather negative images frequently portrayed by the media and the sports critics of the macho, aggressive and violent football crowd. Yet, should it really surprise us that most male fans can actually be so accepting – and even protective – of female fans? Are there characteristics of the football fan that the media and fans alike choose to ignore? There is this particular side to football culture – which often involves looking more closely at the terrace work of older male fans, especially – that makes Skinner and Baddiel's laddish portrayal of the generic football fan in TV's *Fantasy Football* (see Carrington, 1999; Crolley, 1999), or the Brimson brothers' nostalgic portrayal of 'lads' football (Brimson and Brimson, 1997) appear highly over-simplistic and even insultingly unidimensional.

There have always been elements of football culture that appear decidedly 'unmasculine'. Fans of both sexes vent their emotions at the match. They talk openly, male and female, of 'loving' their team and certain players: 'We love you Liverpool', 'She Loves You', 'I can't help falling in love with you', and so many more songs and chants at the match are really, well, quite . . . feminine. Giulianotti (1999: 156) hints at a more complex notion of masculinity in the sport when he argues that 'football cultures have always embraced diverse expressions of masculinity – and appreciated its expression in different forms'. Although in this context he refers more specifically to the style of *play*, his comment can easily be transposed to refer to terrace culture, too. Far from reflecting a narrow drama, made up of overtly macho elements, the bonding experience in football is far more complex. Indeed, some of the most touching, the most emotional and moving moments we both experience take place in the football context. Where else, one might ask, do even grizzled men get to hug each other – and sometimes us – unabashed?

King Kenny

An illustration of how male football fans can reveal characteristics which hint at a more complex expression of footballing masculinity than that to which we are accustomed emerges, for example, in the relationship between fans and the team or manager, which can be astoundingly intense. It can go beyond mere admiration or even adoration and is more complex than simple hero-worshipping. The fact that it is the same men who so often claim not to be able to verbalize their emotions that make public proclamations for the men who shape their football teams should not be trivialized!

Bill Shankly became a father-figure to many Liverpool supporters drawn from an earlier generation. His hero status is assured and his departure from the club in 1974 shocked the city (Taylor and Ward, 1993; see also Chapter Three). More recently, it was for a short time Kenny Dalglish's *status* at Liverpool FC that epitomizes how fans, male and female alike, can have feelings for a club servant that go way beyond that of the conventional fan/player (or fan/manager) relationship. When Dalglish suddenly left Liverpool Football Club in 1991, it was, for many Liverpool fans, as though he had walked out on them after years of a seemingly happy relationship or 'marriage'. Some felt betrayed. Others went into a temporary state of shock. Committed fans of the time can probably remember where they were when the news broke. Dalglish had been such an important part of the lives of Liverpool fans in a critical and successful phase of the club's history, but also in one deeply scarred by tragedy. He had 'stuck by us' and helped us through the hard times post-Heysel and Hillsborough. Maybe female fans, especially, felt this more deeply than men. And then he was gone. We could try to explain this by telling ourselves he was troubled and that there was nothing we could have done to keep him: that he just couldn't handle this sort of intense relationship anymore.

Then, Kenny joined Blackburn Rovers, and so soon after leaving Liverpool. As one distraught fan put it, 'It was like finding out he'd run off with your sister.' Many fans, female and male, still have mixed feelings about Kenny's success at Blackburn Rovers and his troubles at Celtic. It's too painful for many. There is still an incredible pride among Liverpool supporters with respect to Dalglish – witness their mischievous chanting of his name at Newcastle United after he had been sacked by that club. Some Liverpool fans probably harbour secret desires that, one day, he will come back; others find the pain of the break-up has made them, surprisingly, bitter. Some are more forgiving than others. In short, the emotions felt here are deeply felt and in some cases remarkably similar in nature and range to those experienced by many individuals who go through personal or domestic trials. Is all this simply 'displaced' emotion? Are these apparently 'sensitive' male fans – dockers, factory workers, office staff alike – the same macho hooligans we were told needed a 'feminizing' influence in the mid-1980s?

Perhaps terrace culture has never really been quite as 'masculinized' as we have been led to believe. It is certainly not homogeneous. Or perhaps there exists a 'covert', hidden masculinity at football, which involves a more emotional side to the character of men that is kept 'contained' within the private sanctuary of the football ground. After all, in the crowd one is not really 'accountable' for what one does and how one acts. It is these collective feelings and expressions of intimacy, as much as being able to let off steam together at the match, which form a central feature of the bonding process which takes place within the football ground. We talk often about the violence, little about these male emotions expressed at football.

Our own experiences suggest that the concept of masculinity within the football context is rather more complex than is usually recognized. It is not appropriate to adopt, uncritically, a social-scientific role theory. Role theory simplifies the complexities of gender (Stacey and Thorne, 1985) by relying on the notions of a single 'male sex role' and a single 'female sex role'. This consequently perpetuates mythical conceptions, almost stereotypes, of masculinity and femininity and does not allow for the development of relational processes through which notions of masculinity (and femininity) can be constructed, contested and redefined. Our view is that a binary vision of masculinity and femininity is inadequate. Many theorists tend to divide fans into 'male' and 'female' and treat (cultural) gender synonymously with (biological) sex, in binary terms which might no longer be appropriate in today's society. We suggest that we can no longer segregate fans into 'masculine' or 'feminine' categories. We should recognize, instead, the evolving complexities of gender identities.

Sexism in 'The Family'

Before the introduction of seats at football, the collective feeling of shared identity, among both males and females on the Kop, was strong. The Kop could be a forbidding place for those with the 'wrong' accent or lacking the necessary intuitive insights into the sport; it was never a true melting-pot of the social classes and diverse social groups. Black Liverpudlians, especially, felt the culture much less welcoming (see Hill, 1989) and fans from outside the city; 'posh' supporters or 'day trippers' may have found the Kop more suspicious, less inclusive.

Nevertheless, 'football families' across the Kop consist of groups of people from highly diverse social backgrounds. Maybe now, as the standing Kop as we knew it has gone, we view the past in a more favourable, nostalgic, light. For its last few years we had been talking about how the standing Kop just 'wasn't the same as it used to be', that the atmosphere had faded, that it had lost its strong sense of passion and identity. Yet compared to the 'new' seated Kop, it still had a strong feeling of togetherness, of mutual suffering yet support, something like being part of a 'class' or work struggle. The shared experiences of the 'red side' of the community could be found there. Seen in this context it is perhaps no surprise that women want to be part of this community, perhaps especially as their exclusion from such experiences in other aspects of the city life – in work, and in formal politics – has often seemed so acute in Liverpool (Parkinson, 1985).

We need to beware of the danger of warmed-up nostalgia, as it is clear that for some girls and women experiences of football culture have involved unpleasant encounters, albeit sporadically. Many of the female fans we interviewed recounted tales of how they had been singled out on the terraces and treated in a disagreeable manner. Most also claimed that there had been moments in their football-following careers when they had been made to feel uncomfortable because of their sex. It was generally agreed, too, that since the Kop became seated these moments had become less frequent. In a seated environment there are fewer opportunities for men physically to intimidate women; the standing Kop offered an anonymity for abuses. The seats better identify and expose male culprits.

Helen, however, says she has the misfortune currently to sit on the Kop in front of what she calls a genuine misogynist; a man who actually still thinks it's cool to be aggressively sexist. Hence, she has been subjected to his taunts and snide comments such as 'Get back to your kitchen where you belong!', 'You slag!', 'You bitch!', 'Women shouldn't be allowed out except to go shopping!' and so on. Men around her seem to think this fan is an irritating idiot and several times his status as 'a moaner' about the *team* has almost got him into serious trouble with other supporters. But none say a word when he launches into his specifically sexist abuse. The truth is, no one really takes this part of his match-day persona seriously. He's just being 'a lad'. Sexism is not stigmatized in the same way that, say, racism is at football these days. Anti-racist campaigns in football have raised the profile and awareness of the issue to such an extent that, although far from eradicating the problem altogether, today the bigots are stigmatized and quietened. No one bats an eyelid, however, at sexism. 'If women can't take it, they shouldn't be here', seems to be the response. There is also an assumption that to address overt sexism at football would effectively sanitize the culture; that somehow only 'middle-class' (and therefore unwanted) women fans could possibly object to being abused in this way.

The repercussions can be more sinister. At Arsenal away a couple of seasons ago, an incident took place on the steps at the end of the game. A 'scouse' lad in his late twenties was 'groping' a very young girl; when she protested, he began calling her a 'slag' for even being at a football match. Several hundred men were around at the time, and dozens were in the close vicinity. Yet no one stepped in to defend the young girl. No one else got involved. The notion that football is always a 'safe' space for females is, clearly, by no means watertight. In this specific context, sex divides and empowers/subjugates, even as common football club support ostensibly unites.

Almost any female who goes to football as a younger fan probably has experiences of this kind to recall. Sexism can range from an inappropriate glance to a vicious verbal attack or even a physical assault. Sexism at its most extreme can be aggressive, threatening and intimidating. Most female fans probably consider it a price you inevitably pay for entering this 'male' world. Such incidents are infrequent and, generally, football-going for women is still a positive experience. Arguably, female fans suffer this sort of prejudice because our sex makes us more immediately visible and different, in much the same way as some fans deride obvious 'out-of-town' followers at Anfield. Male attempts to undermine opposing players using sexist innuendo – the attacks on the Beckhams, David and Victoria, for example – are similarly inappropriate and are unlikely to be taken up by female fans interested in gender issues.

However, evidence drawn from interviews of young female fans at Liverpool suggests that relatively few fans have recent experiences of overtly aggressive sexism to recount. There are fewer reports of collective sexist chants or wolf-whistles around football grounds today than there were a decade ago. On the whole, female fans' tales of football are upbeat and the 'gender issue' is rarely perceived as a significant problem. Yet anecdotes of more subtle examples of sexism are still commonplace. Female supporters feel resented by some men. Female fans sometimes complain that they are seen as fickle, as not true fans, people who are ignorant of footballing matters, or who only go to football because they 'fancy' the players.

The more subtle illustrations of sexism that take place today involve instances when (male) fans belittle women's views or refuse to accept that we have valid opinions (trivializing female support). When **Cathy** started a new job in Manchester in a male-dominated office in the early 1990s, she was the only member of staff who went to matches, but was effectively excluded from office conversations about football. In similar vein, even in Liverpool as she began another new job in the mid-1990s, her new boss accused the men in the office of being 'unfriendly' to the 'new girl' by talking endlessly about the game.

Some male fans seem to find it troubling or confusing that many females go to football for the same reasons as males. Maybe they misunderstand the nature of the footballing experience? There is much talk of it being a fundamental experience of 'male bonding'. Perhaps it is better described as an experience, simply, of 'bonding'. It happens that for most men they are bonding with other men; but even where this is not the case the presence of women does not always change the male experience. It is often said to **Liz**, for example, by the men in her own football 'community', that the experience of attending for them now – with **Liz** involved – is actually much the same as it had been previously in all-male groups.

Recent Transformations

Recent transformations in football culture have probably made the game more attractive – or at least less unattractive – to some women. Improved facilities in football grounds are usually mentioned as being an attraction to women – yet no *real* fan, male or female, could be put off following their team because of a dirty toilet or a cold, stale pie. Nevertheless, fortunately, the days are long gone – if not forgotten – when women 'away' fans needed a police escort right across the pitch to the home end at some grounds if a half-time toilet visit was required. Invariably, the public return to the 'away' end would be accompanied by 'We know where you've been' ringing around the ground.

The changed image of football is likely to appeal to certain females, just as it is likely to appeal to certain males: the game is no longer perceived as being a hotbed of hooliganism and violence, for example. Most fans of both sexes are glad of that. The role of women in society has changed too: we are no longer excluded from social life or from work outside the home and we increasingly participate in leisure activities. Women who were already interested in football now feel more able to attend matches, and are not afraid to admit to an interest in the game. The new perception of football as a more 'cross-class' and 'cross-gender' leisure option has also meant that women generally don't feel as alienated from the game: it is now more acceptable for women to talk about football and to actively support in a way that was seen, narrowly, as 'unfeminine' only a few years ago.

Perhaps some 'traditional' male fans have resented the encouragement of football support among females? Perhaps they feel threatened? Their territory is being 'invaded' and the last bastion of maleness/masculinity is being eroded, when other male roles are also under attack (see Brimson and Brimson, 1997, for an example). Sport, and football in particular, is no longer quite as active in perpetuating male superiority as it has done throughout most of the nineteenth and twentieth centuries. Perhaps, as football culture has evolved over the last decade, the more 'traditional' fans – males and females *together* – are trying to resist some of these changes. They have, at the top level at least, witnessed subtle changes in the type of people who attend football, an increase in prices, an unwanted 'feminization'/'de-masculinization' of the sport, and they resist by deriding all those they see as representing this shift under one label: 'newcomers'.

At Liverpool FC, it is often the 'out-of-town' fan, rather than the female fan, who is at the receiving end of most of the derision from traditional ('scouse') fans. Nevertheless, the gender card is relevant here, too, as 'out-of-towners' are often indirectly derided for not expressing their 'masculinity' in the same way as 'scousers' do. Their dress code is totally different; many of them wear colours, scarves, for example. They might even carry a merchandise bag. They dare to stray from the classic mega-short hair 'style' which is regarded as compulsory for 'proper' 'scouse' lads these days. They arrive at the ground too early before a match (see also King, 1998, on 'lads' and 'consumer' fans). They are argued to be contributing to a cultural transformation which involves, as one of its processes, the redefining of masculine values at football.

Many of these 'outsider' fans (although at Anfield perhaps fewer than at other clubs) are also 'new fans', another reason for locals why they should be abused and not be taken too seriously. All these features contribute to their exclusion from 'lad' status (though not that many 'out-of-towners' want to be a 'lad'). They are immediately identifiable and their motivation for supporting Liverpool is, for their doubters, questionable. This isn't to say that all 'out-of-towners' are resented. But many are unmistakably *different* and they do not have, or exhibit, the same local masculine identities or codes of their dominant 'scouse' equivalents. Several female 'out-of-town' fans we interviewed claim to share the same *multiple* feelings of exclusion as local female fans. **Julie,** for example, a season-ticket holder who moved from Cumbria to Liverpool in the late 1980s, recalls standing on the Kop and simply not singing. 'My sister and I were afraid of people hearing our accents. As women we were welcome, but we didn't want people to know that we were from out of town.' 'Out of town' men feel alienated at times because they are 'not allowed' to become part of the 'scouse' Liverpool-supporting community. They feel they are *tolerated* by the locals rather than welcomed as one of the community, and they are certainly made to feel different. One female fan, **Jackie,** actually pointed out that for 'out-of-town' men:

> It's like being a women; you are present, and kind of accepted, but without being one of the lads. Deep down, most 'scousers' believe they are the true fans and that we are hangers-on and aren't really committed. Some think we shouldn't even be allowed tickets until the 'scousers' have been allocated theirs.

In short, 'out-of-towners' can also be held responsible for aspects of the 'feminization', or rather the 'demasculinization' or 'detraditionalization', of football. Women and 'out-of-towners' are still very much the 'other' at football, on occasions.

Mind yer Language

One of the myths of modern-day football, perpetrated in club marketing departments and elsewhere, is the idea that women as a group are more sensitive to swearing in public places than are men. Consequently, so this homogenizing argument goes, men at football must curb their language when women are present. For most women at football this is a rather irritating debate. That women can be so essentialized on this issue and so misunderstood for so long is baffling. True, there are well-documented differences in speech styles between men and women (see for example Johnson and Meinhof, 1997), but it is extremely simplistic to suggest that all women object to swearing. Have men really never heard women swear? Do they think we grow up in a city like Liverpool without being exposed to swearing? Or do they, perhaps, have a preferred image of how women *should* behave, and amend their views accordingly? When we hear a man say 'Watch your language, there's a lady present', some women – and men – will empathize and think he's well-meaning, if somewhat old-fashioned. To swear and then apologize to women for doing so is, however, a way of excluding women (again marginalizing and alienating). It tells us that men feel they have to behave differently simply because we are present.

To generalize in this way, and to brand all women as 'puritans' who are offended by swearing, is insulting and ignores the truth. It is quite simply a myth, perpetuated by men who make assumptions based on prejudice or essentialist or patronizing views of women. However, it is more likely that where differences do exist between men and women it is in the use and acceptance of extreme sexist language. This is hardly surprising really. In a recent (unpublished) survey of swearing at football matches carried out by a group of undergraduate students in the Department of Languages at the Manchester Metropolitan University, the results demonstrated, overwhelmingly, that male and female supporters shared the same attitudes to language at football and most were actually ambivalent towards swearing at the match. Indeed, some fans (of both sexes) expressed disappointment that some grounds were reportedly clamping down on swearing and punishing offenders. Swearing at football is widely seen by fans as a way of venting frustration and emotions in a non-violent manner; it is therefore not unhealthy to swear.

However, when individuals were asked which words or concepts they found offensive, or which they actually employed themselves, marked differences between the sexes became more apparent. Overwhelmingly, the differences in opinion and experience lay in the use of those terms which referred to parts of women's bodies or which were offensive to women as a sex in some way. Some of these terms could not even be classed as swearing. Females found them highly gendered and offensive, and simply didn't use them. Many men used them 'naturally' and had often not given much thought about their overtly sexist nature. To call a player 'You woman!' or 'You tart!' when he is performing badly is not among the most aggressive of insults, and few stewards would act to eject a fan for using such an expression. Yet a 'gentle' insult based, for example, on 'race' could, and occasionally does, quite rightly, lead to some punitive response.

Attempts to make football more female-friendly have been sporadic and poorly targeted. Research seems to suggest that women who like football but don't go to football matches are put off by high prices and the fact that they still carry the burden of family responsibilities which occupies their time (Williams and Perkins, 1999). One of these issues has been addressed by some clubs who have offered (controversially) significant price discounts for women, and some clubs (not Liverpool FC) now have child-minding facilities, such as crèches. Women do not, we would suggest, tend to be discouraged from attending football by abusive or aggressive language but, like some men, they do feel intimidated by the threat of violence. Neither do women relish being singled out as being different from the rest of fans. Few clubs, then, address all these issues and although significant changes were experienced over the last decade of the twentieth century in particular, football still seems to be lagging behind in terms of equality of opportunity and greater acceptance of females into the sports environment.

Most women fans we talked to are not especially interested in attracting more women to football. We do not lack company. Women who do not like football presumably have no desire to become more involved anyway. Those female fans who are already connected to football are often hooked precisely because of the way the game is (or was, when they first became fans), hence they are not keen to change its nature. As has been noted in pertinent observations by Williams and Woodhouse (1991: 105) female fans themselves rarely see gender identity in football as a bone of contention and prefer to play down or even deny accusations that football appeals to the macho side of men and is unwelcoming or threatening to women. We fear that making football more 'female friendly' as a matter of policy might well contribute to the game losing some of its appeal, at least part of which includes being hugged and slobbered over by sweaty, scruffy men who have lost themselves momentarily and gone berserk as we score. Part of us, as committed female fans, seems to want the status quo to be maintained and for football to remain a mainly male domain, but one into which those 'privileged' few women can peek – and even become a part of – thereby awarding us with a special status denied to other females. **Joy** says:

> It's selfish, but true. Going to football gives us an insight into the male world. It's at least partly the aura of masculinity that makes it special. And we have something in common with 'the lads', without having the oppressive pressures of having to be one of them and being forced to behave in a way in which we'd really rather not.

Ch-ch-ch-ch-changes

We are always being told these days that football is 'fashionable' and more accessible to women than ever before. But have things really changed that much? The football authorities are certainly keen to encourage more women to attend matches, strongly believing that better facilities and a more family-oriented promotion of the game will do the trick. If more people of any age or either sex feel more welcome at football matches, then this is a positive step. But is this approach the most appropriate one? Simply to suggest to women that they should like football more, either because it is fashionable and glamorous or because it appeals more to families, is somewhat patronizing. It is also misguided. Actually, male fans are more likely to attend football with children than are female fans today (Williams, 1997).

Women's football in England is still an extremely poor relation of the men's game, as we have seen, and considerably more investment is needed there. Sexism remains institutionalized in professional football at generally, higher administrative levels and in terms of the wider organization of the sport. Perhaps attention might better be directed there, too, rather than strongly at existing football fan cultures in Liverpool and elsewhere, where 'negotiated' change is already taking place.

References

Brimson, E. and Brimson, D. (1997) *Capital Punishment*, London: Headline.

Brunt (1989) 'Raising one voice', *Marxism Today,* September 1989.

Bullock, B. (1999) *Reflected Glory*, Dudley: Brewin Books.

Carrington, B. (1999) 'Too many St. George's crosses to bear', in M. Perryman (ed.) *The Ingerland Factor: Home truths from Abroad*, London and Edinburgh: Mainstream.

Coddington, A. (1997) *One of the Lads: Women Who Follow Football*, London: HarperCollins.

Crolley, L. (1999) 'Lads will be Lads', in M. Perryman (ed.) *The Ingerland Factor: Home Truths from Abroad*, Edinburgh and London: Mainstream.

Dunning, E., Murphy, P. and Williams, J. (1988) *The Roots of Football Hooliganism*, London: Routledge.

Duncan, M. and Messner, M. (1998) 'The media image of sport and gender' in L. Wenner (ed.) *MediaSport*, London: Routledge.

Edge. A (1999) *Faith of Our Fathers*, Edinburgh and London: Mainstream.

Fishwick, N. (1989) *English Football and Society, 1910–1950*, Manchester: Manchester University Press.

Giulianotti, R. (1994) 'Social identity and public order' in R. Giulianotti, N. Bonney and M. Hepworth (eds) *Football Violence and Social Identity*, London: Routledge.

—— (1999) *Football: a Sociology of the Global Game*, Cambridge: Polity Press.

Greendorfe, S. (1987) 'Gender bias in theoretical perspectives: the case of female socialization into sport', in *Psychology of Women Quarterly*, 11.

Hargreaves, J. (1994) *Sporting Females: Critical Issues in the History and Sociology of Women's Sports*, London: Routledge.

Higginson, D. (1985) 'The influence of socializing agents in the female sport-participation process', *Adolescence*, 20.

Hill, D. (1989) *Out of His Skin: the John Barnes Phenomenon*, London: Faber & Faber.

Johnson, S. and Meinhof, U. (1997) *Language and Masculinity*, Oxford: Blackwell.

Kane, M. and Jefferson Lenskyi, H (1998) 'Media treatment of female athletes', in L. Wenner (ed.) *MediaSport,* London: Routledge.

King, A. (1998) *The End of the Terraces?*, London: Leicester University Press.

Lopez, S. (1997) *Women on the Ball: A Guide to Women's Football*, London: Scarlet Press.

Mason, T. (1980) *Association Football and English Society, 1863–1915*, Brighton: Harvester.

Parkinson, M. (1985) *Liverpool on the Brink*, Hermitage, Berks: Policy Journals.

Rudd, A. (1998) *Astroturf Blonde*, London: Headline.

Sabo, D. and Curry Johnson, S. (1998) 'Prometheus unbound: constructions of masculinity in sports media', in L. Wenner (ed.) *MediaSport*, London: Routledge.

Scraton, S. (1986) 'Images of femininity and the teaching of girls' physical education', in J. Evans (ed.) *Physical Education, Sport and Schooling*, London: Falmer Press.

Stacey, J. and Thorne, B. (1985) 'The missing feminist revolution in sociology', in *Social Problems*, **32**(4).

Taylor, R. and Ward, A. with Williams, J. (1993*) Three Sides of the Mersey: an Oral History of Everton, Liverpool and Tranmere Rovers*, London: Robson.

Waddington, I., Dunning, E., Murphy, P. (1996) 'Surveying the social composition of football crowds', *Leisure Studies*, No. 15.

Watt, T. (1993) *The End: 80 Years of Life on Arsenal's North Bank*, Edinburgh and London: Mainstream.

Williams, J. (1987) 'Young people's images of attending football matches: an analysis of essays by Liverpool schoolchildren', Sir Norman Chester Centre for Football Research, Leicester: University of Leicester.

—— (1997) *FA Premier League National Fan Survey 1996/97*, Sir Norman Chester Centre for Football Research, Leicester: University of Leicester.

Williams, J. and Perkins, S. (1999) 'Ticket prices, merchandising and the new business of football', Report to the Football Task Force, SNCCFR, Leicester.

Williams, J. and Woodhouse, D. (1999) *Offside? the Position of Women and Football in Britain*, Reading: South Street Press.

Williams, J. and Woodhouse, J. (1991) 'Can Play, Will Play? Women and Football in Britain', in J. Williams and S. Wagg (eds) *British Football and Social Change*, Leicester : Leicester University Press.

10

Liverpool FC in the Global Football Age
Rick Parry

The Shankly Legacy

In football it is easy to focus on tradition in the wrong way. There is an inclination to remember only what was good (which in Liverpool FC's case was extremely good) and a tradition of success creates a weight of expectation that is difficult to bear. This creates a damaging reluctance to change – in the hope that the magic formula will eventually bring everything right again. The outcome is likely to be losing ground on competitors.

But viewed in the right way, tradition is very important and a great strength. It is essential to identify the values, the principles, the essence of what a club such as Liverpool is all about, because these provide a stable framework in an increasingly unstable football world. This is not to be confused, of course, with doing things the *same* way – but it does mean that you always ensure that what you do fits within the established framework.

To me, the traditions that matter at Anfield started with the arrival of Bill Shankly in 1959; we must be talking, in this context, about the twenty-five years of unparalleled on-the-pitch football success. Distilling what every Liverpool supporter instinctively feels about that period into words is a challenge, but not one to be shirked. So what did Shankly bring to the club. He brought winning football played with a certain style – in what Stephen Hopkins in Chapter Four and others elsewhere have described as 'the Liverpool way'. Nothing can be more important than this. Shankly also forged a special bond with the supporters of the club and the people in the city because he understood them and he treated them with openness, honesty and respect. He had huge enthusiasm for the game, which rubbed off on everyone around him. Players and supporters had self-belief and pride, they had passion. There was no place for losers, no place for anyone prepared to give less than one hundred per cent. No individual was bigger than the Club (see Chapter Three for more on Shankly).

The real secret of Liverpool's success at that time was the ability to spot players who were winners; players who would add something to the team. There were always plenty of good players at other clubs, of course – but Liverpool FC repeatedly identified that something special, that extra dimension that made players winners. Look at the number of games that were won in the last few minutes by Shankly's teams and those at Liverpool which followed. This was all down to character and determination, allied to self-belief. It had little to do with coincidence or with luck.

Off the pitch the club also had a reputation for doing things the right way. Nothing flash, nothing pretentious. Envied by others but always respected, never despised. Always planning ahead, never resting on recent glories. Simply put, what matters for this football club, moving forwards, is to win trophies and stay close to its supporters. Easy to say – a little more difficult to do. But, guiding values should be simple so that they are understood and remembered by everyone.

The Origins of the FA Premier League

In what follows I will say nothing about the Heysel and Hillsborough disasters and their consequences. Of course, they have been a central part of shaping the recent history of Liverpool FC, but that issue is covered at length in Chapter Five. Given a whole book, it might be possible to give a comprehensive account of the recent modernization of the game. Given a single chapter, it is necessary to be highly selective and to focus on those elements that have the most direct bearing on the immediate future of Liverpool Football Club. The 1990s saw enormous changes in the game. They have been well documented by the burgeoning army of commentators, analysts and experts that is a by-product of the growing interest in football. But it may be helpful to give a perspective from someone fortunate enough to have been very close to many of the key events.

The origins of recent changes in football in England can probably be traced back to the fact that tensions within the old Football League had escalated during the latter half of the 1980s. Big clubs were uncomfortable with a complex voting structure on policy which tended to favour the clubs in the lower divisions; they constantly cried that the tail was wagging the dog. There were also complaints that a Football League Management Committee comprising club chairmen carried in-built conflicts of interest. Finally, it was argued that the formula for sharing television and sponsorship income resulted not from any kind of objective analysis of what was 'fair', but instead from a series of high-profile rows and horse-trades which had been going on across the previous five years. At best, it represented no more than an uneasy truce.

But it was the Taylor Report on Hillsborough in 1990 that proved to be the catalyst for change and prompted the then 'Big Five' clubs (Liverpool, Everton, Manchester United, Arsenal and Tottenham Hotspur) to take action. These clubs approached the Football Association in late 1990, to seek its support for the foundation of a new breakaway league. It was estimated that £250 million would be required to transform top football stadia in England into all-seated arenas. At the time this seemed (and was) a huge sum of money, and the top clubs felt there was too little direction from the Football League as to exactly from *which* source the money for stadium redevelopment was to come. At the same time, relations between the FA and the League were at a particularly low ebb; the FA was upset about 'power-sharing' proposals which had been promoted by the League as part of the general debate after Hillsborough about 'leadership' in football. Given these circumstances, the governing body was especially receptive to the approach of these five powerful clubs. Hence the FA Premier League was born.

It transpired, however, that it wasn't just the 'Big Five' clubs that wanted a new beginning; many of the other First Division clubs were unhappy too. They were unhappy with the Football League management structure, but they also had a deep mistrust of the 'Big Five' themselves, and they wanted the opportunity to create a new structure, one which had much more transparency. The constitution of the FA Premier League was, therefore, designed to be simple and fair. All decisions were to be made on a one club/one vote basis (with a two-thirds majority to prevent too many damaging mood swings); there were to be no committees; and there was to be an independent Board comprising a Chairman and a Chief Executive. Perhaps most important of all, a formula for the sharing of TV income, which balanced membership, popularity and performance, was devised. To paraphrase the Chairman of one middle-ranking club in the new league: the new structure didn't produce equal *shares* – but it did provide equal *opportunities* for all clubs.

Television and 'New' Football

This constitution worked and after some hairy moments in the first twelve months, there was a unity and sense of purpose among clubs that was quite rare in football. Perhaps inevitably it was the TV deals that grabbed the major headlines and it is instructive to sketch out, briefly, aspects of the history of football on television.

First of all, it is worth noting that there was no live televised League football in England at all until 1983. Then, ITV and the BBC paid £2.6 million per season between them to share the broadcasting of ten games. During the passage of the Broadcasting Bill in 1995, it was amusing to read the misty-eyed reminiscences of politicians and journalists who talked about the grainy black and white images of the great games of the 1960s that were now 'denied' to the public at large with the advent of satellite television. The truth, of course, is that these images of 'live' football on TV never really existed.

In 1985 the League had had the temerity to demand more money from the TV companies, famously pointing out that the broadcasters needed football more than football needed the broadcasters. As a result of the dispute which followed, there was no football on television at all that season until Christmas, when the League backed down and accepted a short-term TV deal – with *no* fee increase. In 1988 British Satellite Broadcasting (BSB) appeared on the scene, breaking the BBC/ITV duopoly and usefully establishing the principle that when it comes to dealing with broadcasters, two's a cartel but three's competition. After a bout of 'public' negotiating that did little for the image of football or broadcasters, it was the terrestrial ITV which emerged with a four-year agreement to screen eighteen live matches each season for an annual fee, starting at £11 million. A new word entered the football lexicon at this time – 'exclusivity'; ITV paid a significant premium to keep football *away* from the other broadcasters. But this was at the broadcasters' instigation, and it was not a concept that the League itself had devised.

It was this deal that gave rise to most of the mistrust that then existed between clubs; the perception was that some clubs who had taken part in the negotiations were subsequently favoured by ITV. The facts are that over the four years of the contract the 'Big Five' clubs received 65 per cent of all the TV coverage, and in every season of the deal at least six First Division clubs received no TV coverage at all. In turn, this led to an imbalance in the value of sponsorship and advertising contracts at clubs. If you were on TV all the time, sponsors were not difficult to attract.

Hence, the strongly held views among the majority of clubs that with the advent of the FA Premier League, the clubs themselves should no longer be involved in any TV negotiations and that any new TV deal should be subject to the stipulation that *every* club should be covered 'live' at least once each season. Liverpool FC, incidentally, were at the forefront of the push for independent, transparent negotiation along precisely these lines.

The deal that was struck with BSkyB and the BBC in 1992 was worth £214 million over five years (this compared with ITV's losing bid of £165 million). Taking a long-term view, it was crucial from the FA Premier League's point of view that BSkyB grew in strength, otherwise there was a danger of the old cartel reforming. Thus, an element of satellite coverage of top football was important. But the FA Premier League would happily have seen this satellite deal sit alongside terrestrial coverage. ITV, on the other hand, wanted to secure *exclusive* rights in order to stop BSkyB, a dangerous new competitor, growing. The terrestrial channel made it plain that they would bid on an all-or-nothing basis; there would be no sharing of TV rights for them.

Understanding the FA Premier League's genuine concerns about the potential absence of any terrestrial coverage (essential to promote the game to a wider audience), BSkyB forged a new partnership with the BBC. As a result, BBC's *Match of the Day* made a welcome return to the screens after a four-year break and, for the first time ever, offered a comprehensive round-up showing every goal scored in top matches. Another of the attractions of BSkyB was its real commitment to ensure the sort of fair spread of 'live' TV coverage that was so important to the clubs. In fact, in each of the five years of the contract, every club received at least *three* live televised appearances. In addition, BSkyB readily agreed to broadcast a minimum of twenty hours' support programming every week, something no terrestrial broadcaster could offer. Despite early misgivings on the part of some clubs, an excellent working relationship between the new League and the broadcaster developed.

In 1996, the deal with BSkyB and the BBC was renewed for a further four years, on exactly the same basis as before – except that the total fees from the deal rose to £743 million. This time there was competition from two potential pay-TV consortia, each of which included one of the leading ITV companies. Annual rights' fees had risen by a factor of 70 in a little over 10 years, which is impressive growth by any analysis. The reason? In 1983 there was no competition; in 1992 a pay-TV broadcaster did just enough to outbid an advertising-funded broadcaster which was pushed to its limit. By 1996 there was competition between pay-TV broadcasters. Arguably the League had realized the true value of 'live' football TV rights for the first time. Competition in 1996 was driven, of course, by the eagerly anticipated arrival of *digital* transmission.

The nature of the early TV deals was shaped by limitations on *distribution* – initially, there were only two channels and they couldn't even find time in the schedules for a game every week. The multiplicity of digital channels provides almost limitless capacity – there is no reason, in theory, why every match can't be shown live and, as BSkyB have shown, there is scope for an à la carte service, with viewers selecting their own camera angles and commentary tracks. As technologies converge, links to the Internet provide enormous scope for immediate access to statistics and to archive material, interaction and home shopping.

One estimate has argued that the number of digital homes in Europe will grow from three million in 1998 to 53 million in 2005, figures which suggest that enthusiasm from broadcasters for live sport, and in particular for football, is scarcely going to wane. The challenge for football now is to make the most effective use of this exciting, but potentially bewildering, new landscape. Perhaps ironically, given the furore over the first BSkyB deal in 1992, the FA Premier League took a cautious view in 1996. 'If it ain't broke, don't fix it' was the approach, as the urge to rush headlong into all-embracing pay-per-view deals was firmly resisted. Meanwhile, in Italy, in Spain and in France armchair season tickets and impulse pay-per-view football coverage are already established.

The Bosman Effect

In both 1992 and 1996 the BSkyB/BBC deals took the FA Premier League to the top of the European rankings in terms of TV income. This has an increasing relevance thanks to the landmark 'Bosman' ruling in the European Court of Justice in 1995. For several years, a relatively unknown Belgian footballer of average ability, Jean Marc Bosman, had been challenging the football establishment over what he considered to be unfair restrictions at the end of players' contracts. Failing to get satisfaction from the Belgian FA or UEFA, Bosman resorted to law and won an emphatic victory.

In summary, the Court held that it was illegal for there to be any restrictions on the number of players from other EU member states in a team (thus outlawing UEFA's so-called 'three foreigner' rule) and, further, that clubs could no longer demand any transfer fee when a player moved clubs from one EU member state to another at the end of his contract. Had Bosman been playing in England it is likely the problem would never have arisen. The worst excesses of the retain and transfer system here were abolished in 1963, as a result of the challenge brought to them by George Eastham. But the English system was never placed before the European Court and there was no suggestion that modifications that took on board the better elements of our system might now suffice. Nor was proper consideration given to the argument that transfer fees were actually a 'good' thing because they simply recirculate money *within* the game and benefit the majority of players with smaller clubs.

The inevitable, and immediate, impact of the judgment was to increase the movement of players between EU member states and change, forever, the basis on which clubs recruit players. In an effort to retain a degree of stability in England, the FA Premier League went into immediate dialogue with the Professional Footballers Association (PFA) with a view to modernizing the domestic transfer system, but not abandoning it. With a fair dose of goodwill and common sense on both sides it was agreed that there would still be a limit on the number of *non-EU* players that clubs could field in any match (essentially three). It was also agreed that players would only be free to move from one English club to another at the end of contract without a transfer fee once they had reached the age of 24. This provided protection for clubs that develop young players, while at the same time allowing players their first 'free' move before they reach their peak.

From the point of view of clubs, the big shift is that the reward for investing in the development of the players will be four or five years' first-team service rather than a guaranteed pay day, via a transfer fee. This certainly requires smarter thinking and forward planning, but it is by no means the disaster that many predicted. Those clubs that are genuine developers of, rather than traders in, players will be fine.

The European 'Super League' Debate

The changes in the TV landscape – the battle for supremacy amongst the pay TV moguls leading the digital revolution and the constant speculation over pan-European alliances – and also the impact of the Bosman judgment, led to new proposals for a European Super League in 1998. There had been regular talk of such a development for at least a decade and a variety of half-baked plans emerged from time to time. The difference with this particular scheme, conceived and backed by Italian sports rights agency *Media Partners*, was that it had been properly researched and was well thought-through. Attention to detail was impressive, as were the potential rewards.

In brief, the idea was that thirty-two clubs would take part every season. There would be two leagues of sixteen clubs, followed by a knockout phase. The controversial aspects of the scheme were that it would be co-ordinated by a private body, *Media Partners,* rather than by UEFA, and that sixteen founder clubs were to be selected on the basis of historical status rather than current performance. These founder clubs would have guaranteed membership for at least six seasons, being joined each season by sixteen teams that qualified on merit. It was estimated that founder clubs would each earn upwards of £20 million every season from TV income and sponsorship – more than twice as much as the most successful FA Premier League clubs receive, for example, from the BSkyB and BBC contracts.

Liverpool was invited to join the proposed 'super league', but the Liverpool board felt distinctly uneasy about the concept of permanent membership and about its likely impact on the game as a whole, and on the FA Premier League in particular. The club took the position that the matter should be debated by the League as a whole and not by individual clubs; predictably, when *Media Partners* addressed an FA Premier League meeting, the *overall* reaction was very negative.

Elsewhere in Europe, interest in the new concept was stronger. The Spanish footballing giants – Barcelona, Real Madrid – burdened with massive debt, have a voracious appetite for additional revenue. And it is easy to see the dilemma for a club such as Ajax in Holland. Losing its best young players to Spain and Italy as a result of the Bosman ruling, and with modest domestic TV revenues that give no scope to compete in the European market, how on earth does this club, with its great European traditions, maintain its place among Europe's football elite? As it turned out, UEFA responded to the challenge of this new competitor by introducing their own new format for the Champions League. As a result, support for *Media Partners* waned. More guaranteed games and more TV revenue for the major clubs in 1999/2000 was the outcome, and everyone, for now, was happy.

But at what cost? Clubs reaching the final of the Champions League will have to play at least seventeen games, which is an absurd burden. And it is now a fact that in terms of the distribution of TV and sponsorship income, the gulf between the top three clubs in the FA Premier League and the rest is greater than that between the bottom of the FA Premier League and the top of the Nationwide League. There is an argument now that the worst place to finish in the FA Premier League will not be in the lower reaches, but *fourth* – with Champions League wage levels but *without* the necessary revenue to cover them!

Whether we have seen the end of *Media Partners* and their idea of a European Super League remains to be seen. There are uneasy echoes here in Europe of the situation in England in the late 1980s when breakaway threats were met with a succession of offers to increase the First Division's share of the television cake. This delayed, but did not in the end prevent, change. Irrespective of the format of European competition, the distribution of income suggests that over the next five years the emergence of twelve to sixteen 'super clubs' will de facto take place. In marketing parlance, these will be global 'brands' with effective commercial operations spreading worldwide.

A graphic example of this came with the announcement in autumn 1999 that BSkyB were to buy Manchester United. From day one of their links with the FA Premier League, BSkyB had demonstrated a refreshing determination to boost the strength of the League as a whole. This was reflected in the broad spread of their TV coverage and in a desire at BSkyB to rise above club politics. Against this background, the decision to buy the League's biggest and most successful club seemed extraordinary. An analysis of the number of News Corporation companies holding the rights to FA Premier League matches in overseas territories provides some pointers to the logic; increasing promotion of the Manchester United brand worldwide would in turn boost the popularity of growing TV stations. Of course, speculation also linked the purchase of United to European Super League talks, but there is no evidence of a direct connection. However, for those of us striving to bring success back to Liverpool FC, the news of the BSkyB takeover bid for United certainly served to focus minds. To an extent, the focus shifted when the Monopolies and Mergers Commission, rather unexpectedly it must be said, ruled against the bid. Nevertheless, the lid to Pandora's box had been lifted, if not yet completely removed.

Off to Court

While the Manchester United story hogged the domestic headlines there were further developments in Europe which will have repercussions for us, at Liverpool FC. Again they relate to digital television and the growth of European super powers. In Italy and Spain clubs have started to sell rights individually rather than through their domestic league. Bizarrely, Real Madrid and Barcelona have already sold their rights for the period 2003–2008, reportedly for sums in excess of £50 million per annum. Top Italian clubs are making £30 million per season from TV. On one level, we might fear for the implications for domestic leagues of these sorts of developments. Who will be able to compete with the TV 'super rich'? On another, we might say it's no wonder we lost Steve McManaman and on *that* salary.

Thus far in England we have all resolutely supported the principle of collective selling of TV rights on the basis that it is so obviously good for the game.

Obviously? Well, not so obviously to the Director General of Fair Trading. In 1996, the FA Premier League's rule book and the contracts with BSkyB and the BBC were referred to the Restrictive Practices Court on the basis that they contained restrictions which potentially inhibit competition. Uniquely, in this forum, the onus is on the defendant to prove that, on balance, any such restrictions are necessary and not against the public interest. You are, therefore, guilty until proven innocent.

The attack was on two fronts. First of all, the TV contracts were challenged on the basis that exclusivity is anti-competitive. Bearing in mind that exclusivity only emerged in the 1980s at the behest of ITV and was the factor that broke the cosy cartel of TV companies, there is more than a tinge of irony here. More fundamentally, it was argued that by selling rights collectively the FA Premier League operates as a cartel. And cartels are bad.

This always seemed to be an extraordinary analysis which demonstrated simply that the Office of Fair Trading completely misunderstood the way in which sports operate. Very elementary economic theory suggests that there are two key features of a classic cartel. First of all, the cartel comprises producers of a homogeneous product, such as cement, gas or oil. Secondly, the cartel will restrict competition because the members agree to fix prices or to limit supply. Indeed the OFT argued that the FA Premier League restricted the supply of 'live' matches on BSkyB to sixty matches, simply to force the price up.

It is clear that neither of these features actually applies to the FA Premier League. If a cement makers' cartel is disbanded, the members continue to produce cement. The cartel *itself* does not co-operatively produce a distinctive product. But the FA Premier League *does* produce a product that is quite separate and cannot be readily subdivided – it produces the FA Premier League Championship. Every club contributes in equal measure, and every match has a bearing on the outcome of the Championship. The interest in any given game will depend, in part at least, on the relative position of the two teams and on the effect the result might have on other teams. The story of the Championship unfolds, gloriously, across the whole season.

It is a simple matter of fact that the restriction of the number of 'live' TV games to sixty is driven, purely, by football considerations, but even if that is not accepted (and the OFT didn't accept it) then, surely, economic argument falls at the very first hurdle. Why does a cartel restrict supply? It does so because every demand curve tells us that as output rises, the price drops at the point at which the cost of producing extra units exceeds the price at which they can be sold. In other words, a loss is made on each extra unit produced and so there is no incentive to produce more. But hold on. There are 380 Premier League matches, irrespective of any interest at all from TV companies. The 'cost' to the FA Premier League of producing an extra game for television, for increasing coverage from, say, sixty to sixty-one games, is obviously nil. And yet it is clear, by reference to evidence and the application of common sense, that BSkyB would have paid more money for seventy games than for sixty. So, if the FA Premier League simply wanted to *maximize* TV revenues it would actually make more games available.

Is this argument flawed or over-simplistic? Evidently the Restrictive Practices Court didn't think so. And yet it took three years of effort, the compilation of thousands of documents and in excess of £20 million spent on legal fees to get to this point. If this isn't frustrating enough, the resounding victory won by the FA Premier League and the broadcasters has a hollow core. First of all, this is because this was the last case to be brought under the Restrictive Trade Practices Act. The new Competition Act gives greater power to the Director General and applies a whole new set of tests. And, within weeks of the judgment, the European Commission announced that *it* was going to examine the rules and the contracts all over again. Bearing in mind the Commission's quest for harmonization, and the recent developments in Spain and Italy, this examination must be taken seriously.

Liverpool FC's position is still to support the *collective* selling of TV rights because it is good for the FA Premier League as a whole and for the game in general. It brings a fairness of distribution that cannot be replicated. But while a central package will undoubtedly still be a feature, it is almost certain that there will be increasing *individual* selling of club rights. Archive rights will revert to clubs, leading to regional magazine programmes or, perhaps, club channels. And there will be pressure for games not included in the central package to be sold individually through armchair season tickets, or pay-per-view. The truth is that whatever it is that clubs and supporters want, the competition authorities want to see more 'live' football on television.

New Directions for Liverpool FC

It was against this background of constant change, and mindful of the fact that the *rate* of change is undoubtedly quickening, that the Board at Liverpool decided to take stock in early 1999. Instinctively wary of public flotation, and determined to remain a *football* club at heart, it was nevertheless clear that standing still was no longer an option. The guiding principle that matters most at the club is to win trophies. If there is to be a group of 'super clubs', then Liverpool FC has to be one of them. If this means being as successful *off* the pitch as the others, then let's get on with it. But let's be smart; let's try to find a way of doing it without losing the soul of the club.

If this means being in a position to exploit the new television opportunities effectively then let's do it first. And let's be the best at it. Let's *anticipate* the trends rather than follow them. The first priority has to be to get into the Champions

League, quickly; if we can't get into the top three soon there is a danger we'll be left behind. To bring about a rapid restructuring of the team the club needed capital; it could simply not be done from internal resources. But capital alone was not enough. To support a rapidly rising cost base it was essential to find ways of driving turnover up.

A conscious decision was, therefore, taken to find a 'strategic partner'. This would have to be a partner that would invest capital, but one which would also bring the skills and resources needed to help the club exploit the worldwide commercial opportunities it was now presented with, not least those from television. This would also have to be a partner that would allow those running the football club to concentrate, without interference, on football.

It was expected in the wake of the BSkyB/Manchester United talks that there would be widespread changes in the ownership structure of clubs in England. If Liverpool FC took an early, pro-active approach it should have the pick of the potential suitors, and also the *time* to make a properly considered choice, rather than joining the stampede of 'me-too' deals that would inevitably follow. So it was that in July 1999 Liverpool FC announced that the *Granada* group had acquired a 9.9 per cent stake in the club. *Granada* has all the right credentials – in TV terms it is a strong regional player, it has a key voice on the ITV network and, through it's half-share of On-Digital, it is firmly in the digital race. But its skills go well beyond television and they provide an almost perfect fit for the opportunities now presented to a successful football club.

Crucially, too, *Granada* is a company with its roots, firmly, in the North West of England. Many of its customers are Liverpool supporters and, having covered so many of the success stories in the glory years, it understands the importance of a winning team.

In keeping with our focus on building a winning team, all of *Granada's* investment went into the club rather than to existing shareholders and, with the exception of £2 million invested in the Academy, the proceeds of the deal were devoted wholly to team-building. This is a partnership that should see us well set to face the challenges and opportunities of the new Millennium.

What are the immediate priorities? We need a bigger stadium; to compete with Europe's best we need at least 55,000 seats. We want to stay at Anfield because it is our home. But, significant expansion will require an imaginative partnership to be forged with the City Council and the local community in Liverpool 4. Successful football clubs are demonstrably good for cities. They generate huge publicity on an international scale – why else would our under-19 team have been an integral part of Liverpool's visit to Shanghai to formalize the twinning agreement between the cities in 1999? And professional football clubs do have a direct economic impact. A recent report by the Football Research Unit at the University of Liverpool concluded that 3,000 full-time and 1,400 part-time jobs on Merseyside are dependent on the presence of the two football clubs and that 750,000 visitors come to the city every year *because* of football.

But beyond this, there is every reason to believe that expansion can be a focus for the *regeneration* of the Anfield area. Successful regeneration brings rebirth rather than rebuilding: which means that people come first. The trend in the USA for the construction of functional, multi-purpose edge-of-town stadia, with vast plains of car parks, is starting to reverse. Baseball teams are moving back to purpose-built retro-look urban stadia.

Why is this? It's because the car parks sit empty for vast periods, rendering areas devoid of life and activity. And it is also because spectators travel *through* the surrounding neighbourhoods rather than *to* them. Take away the car parks, and stadia disgorge large number of people *into* a neighbourhood. They will congregate in pubs, before and after games, and spend money in local shops. Such stadia bring vitality to areas and local businesses benefit, too.

Of course such interaction also brings problems which have to be handled sensitively – litter, noise and on-street parking being the obvious ones. But given the will, there are solutions to these understandable concerns. The club has to be mindful of the needs of its neighbours and it has to work *with* the local community. There are many things that can be done – for example directing employment opportunities to local people, encouraging the use of local suppliers, and actively involving people in sporting and educational initiatives. The club must be prepared to turn its face *outwards*.

The desire to stay at Anfield should also be seen as a clear signal that the need to maintain – and, indeed, strengthen – the bond with the local supporters is recognized. Indeed this bond is crucial. And it is wholly *consistent* with the development of the Liverpool FC brand on an international scale. The brand *is* the successful club that cares about its roots. That is exactly what people around the world want to be a part of. And successful commercial development will centre on finding ways of enabling local people to feel a sense of belonging. From this flows a need for better communication. Which, in part, means providing information more effectively, but it also means being better at listening; it has to be a two-way process.

The future is already upon us. At Liverpool we aim to be ahead of the game. We need to continue to develop the club's new Academy at Kirkby. The investment of over £10 million is a clear statement of the club's recognition that, in the post-Bosman era, the development of young players is more important than ever. In economic terms, wage levels simply reflect supply and demand. If outstanding players are in short supply it makes sense to produce more. And if players are free to leave in their mid-twenties this has to be a continuous process. Perhaps more importantly, the longer young players are with us, the more we have the opportunity to influence their attitudes and approach to the game as well as their technical ability; we can ensure that they understand the Liverpool philosophy. It is no coincidence that given the opportunity to choose the postal address of the Academy we instinctively and immediately went for 'The Liverpool Way'.

Afterword: Hillsborough – Flowers and Wasted Words

Colin Moneypenny

In April 1989 Merseyside mourned massively and magnificently for the victims of the Hillsborough Disaster. At least for a couple of weeks the emotional restraint and the masks of respectability we all wear for 'normal life' were set aside just a little. The shock of sudden and needless death on a sunny afternoon on such a scale and involving so many young people united the community in a way not seen before. Public tears merged with private grief throughout that dreadful funereal period.

If the religious ceremonies at both Liverpool Cathedrals served their formal purpose and the funerals fulfilled some of the private needs of individual bereaved families, it was at Anfield that the wider community was able to focus its grief immediately after the disaster. For a time the 'them and us', which had in some way created the conditions for what had happened, was swept away as Liverpool Football Club opened its doors to the public and the bereaved.

Players who, even by 1989, had in many cases begun to live in very different worlds from those who followed their professional fortunes were made available to meet the bereaved, to visit survivors and to attend the far too many funerals. Yet despite the immense efforts of the footballers and in particular their manager, Kenny Dalglish and his wife Marina, it was clear, not least to them, that they were hardly trained to counsel people in such immense trauma.

How sad that, with the exception of local boys such as Steve McMahon and John Aldridge, for some players and officials, as Alan Hansen admits in his autobiography, it was only death on such a large scale which brought it home to them how much the football club meant to its supporters. The pain of the region was symbolized, visually, to the watching world by the spontaneous laying of flowers at Anfield. Within a week this simple gesture of love and loss had escalated as tributes were sent from all corners of Britain and indeed the world. The inspiring carpet of flowers that covered the 'sacred' turf as a result was kept fresh by the ocean of tears that accompanied them.

In the twentieth-century history of Liverpool FC, the photographs of the Anfield pitch in 1989 bedecked with the united colours of nature will surely be images which radiate in historical resonance at least as much as those of the working docks and boats, the May Blitz, the Beatles at the Cavern, or, indeed, the Toxteth riots of 1981.

Many of the flowers sent to Anfield were accompanied by words of love and often extremely moving verse. There's something about the closeness of death, particularly on a large scale and particularly when the young are involved which can make ordinary people, who normally would shun anything to do with poetry, discover the Wilfred Owen inside them. It's almost as if the intense expression of grief can move beyond even the most technologically advanced mortal communication.

The poetry was just one part of the torrent of words, including articles, letters, memoriums and a million traumatized private conversations which poured out after the disaster in a collective attempt to heal the emotional scars and to try to make some sense of the senseless. The agony of having to write such words however was compounded for many by the knowledge of so many wasted words in the previous few years which should have prevented the tragedy and thus made the 'if onlys' unnecessary.

Liverpool Football Club, through its then Secretary, Peter Robinson, had issued warnings to the relevant football authorities about the intended arrangements prior not only to Hillsborough but also the equally awful disaster at the Heysel Stadium in Brussels four years earlier. The warnings, then, about the blatant stupidity of creating a so-called 'neutral' Z section in the midst of the Liverpool 'end' fell on deaf ears, even though the advice given was simple and sensible and would almost certainly have prevented the thirty-nine deaths which occurred on that evening in 1985.

Not to have played such an important match in a crumbling wreck of a stadium would, of course, have been an even simpler way to have avoided the net effects of the mayhem which was created by some elements of both sets of supporters that evening. My overwhelming memory of Heysel is of meeting some Liverpool fans in the centre of Brussels who vividly described, some seven hours *before* the Disaster, the deathtrap conditions which their cursory examination of the stadium had revealed that morning. The question remains unanswered as to why UEFA had sanctioned the playing of the top game in European football at a ground that building surveyors in England would have refused to license for probably any public event whatsoever.

A Belgian journalist once remarked to me that having visited Merseyside, he thought that Liverpool fans only want to talk about Hillsborough – never Heysel. I told him that, obviously, for many of us the hurt of Hillsborough was closer to home, but there were many examples of the huge distress and soul-searching caused locally by the 1985 tragedy. One example is that the week after Heysel, the Football Supporters Association was formed by two Liverpool fans, distraught like so many of us, by such needless loss of life at football.

Their view was that if a group of ordinary Liverpool fans had got together with a group of ordinary Juventus fans prior to the European Cup Final to make the arrangements for that occasion, then they would have made a much better job of it than the highly paid officials of UEFA. Certainly, some Liverpool fans behaved despicably at Heysel, but it is equally the case that the club and its entire fan base took more of the responsibility and the opprobrium generated worldwide than they were really due. This meant that the wider lessons about crowd safety became lost in the headlong rush into condemnation and hooligan hysteria which was eventually to bequeath a terrible legacy.

Despite the fledgling beginnings of a supporter movement through the FSA and the fanzines, the hysteria about hooliganism, fuelled at every instance by the national press, refused to go away. The stone-age approach to the control of football crowds, and particularly those on the standing terraces – perceived as the home of the wildest of the hooligan 'beasts' – paid scant if any attention to safety. It was a mindset carved not out of imagination or intelligence but from a brutal assessment that all standing football fans should be treated as potential criminals.

It was not surprising that against such a backdrop the words of those who cautioned about the inherent dangers of fencing and the militaristic approach to policing were paid scant attention by those with the decision-making powers. For them, safety was a distant consideration obscured by an absolute obsession with 'security' and specifically the sanctity of the professional football pitch.

And so as the disaster in the Leppings Lane unfolded the futility of words when faced with the power of a manufactured perception became chillingly apparent. 'Get us out of here', was screamed in terror. There was nothing here that was vague, equivocal or ambiguous, no double meanings or irony, no nuances or clever repartee, no spin-doctoring to create a softer image or researched wordplay to sell a product. These were soundbites of pure terror and primal screaming born of the original reason for the development of language, the need to communicate an idea or a feeling simply, honestly and speedily.

The message being sent to those a few feet away in safety was that there are people dying here, please do something about it. For the few vital minutes when it could have made a difference, the message received by policemen who were saturated both with years of hooligan hysteria and orders for the day, reflected exactly that same barren and inelastic way of thinking.

The war of the words has continued pretty much unabated ever since the disaster. From the start, the eulogies for the dead were mixed in equal measure with the anger of the living. Recrimination and apportioning blame will follow any disaster that is not an 'act of God', and even many that are. Getting answers to the human failures is essential for the bereaved and survivors whose wish is always to find out exactly what happened and why. In addition, they cherish the idea that their loss will create a future benefit and so they wish to ensure that 'it doesn't happen again'.

Hillsborough, though, has always had another 'victim-blaming' dimension to it that was likely to make the pain worse than it otherwise would have been. No one blames the victims of a train or air disaster but the bereaved and survivors of Hillsborough have always had to combat the quite scandalous allegations, utterly disproven by Lord Justice Taylor, that a drunken, ticketless, rampaging mob were the true cause of the tragedy.

This web of deceit born out of the marriage of leaden stereotypes about football supporters and people from Liverpool and topped with a double helping of 'Heysel' has been so vicious, wide-reaching and persistent that it is impossible to count-enance that it has been anything but orchestrated and deliberate. This disinformation has been a permanent backdrop to a campaign for justice – to unlock the 'what happened, and why' – that has stretched interminably from the generic Inquest verdict to the private prosecutions of the two most senior policemen on duty on the day. It does not take much to heed the often used words of Trevor Hicks, to the effect that Hillsborough has been two disasters – the one on the day and the huge miscarriage of justice that has followed ever since.

As well as inflicting more pain on individuals who are already severely traumatized, the campaign of vilification has ranged from the sinister to the bizarre. Bernard Ingham's obsessive but fact-free blaming of Liverpool fans stems from his visit to Sheffield with the Prime Minister the day after the disaster, but he refuses to say from whom he inherited his second-hand opinion. More laughably, Brian Clough's attempts to defend himself after boosting publicity for his autobiography by treading the same path became a farcical descent into abusive stereotypes about 'scousers' which forever destroyed any residual affection for him on Merseyside.

All in all, the press coverage of Hillsborough nationally has been largely disgraceful and has extended far beyond the *Sun* newspaper which at least lost many sales after their sickening *'The Truth'* story provoked a very successful local boycott on Merseyside. Many, many other newspapers, journalists, columnists and broadcasters unfortunately escaped the fury reserved for the *Sun* as they also deserved to be boycotted for the disgraceful comments they have made both about the disaster and in Liverpool since 1989. Of course, the trash has, from time to time, been punctuated and factually corrected by quality journalists such as Brian Reade and James Lawton, but the whole process generally has been one of lies and myths feeding on each other in gratuitous displays of mutually supporting ignorance.

Notwithstanding the immensely important contribution over many years of Liverpool City Council's Hillsborough Working Party, the local authorities of the region and the supporters of Liverpool FC, citizens generally perhaps should ask themselves if their response over the years to this cover-up has been robust enough. The Mersey Partnership these days rightly talks up the positive aspects of the region, but not enough was done to counter the Hillsborough-led stock of negativity which was constantly thrown the way of people in the city after 15 April 1989. More importantly, there is no doubt that this process has weakened the lessons which should have been learned and did increase the probability – as the later Guatemala stadium disaster so tragically showed – that something eerily similar could, and would, happen again.

More positively, Hillsborough, again perhaps only for a short time, shook away the enmity, sometimes bordering on hatred, which can affect relations between fans of rival clubs. Ninety-nine per cent of English football supporters recognized that this was a tragedy which could have happened to them and so their almost universal kindness in the aftermath was accepted with comradely gratitude.

The fact that players from a number of football clubs, including Everton, Tranmere Rovers and Manchester United, attended funerals was similarly appreciated while the salutes from fans further afield and notably the incredibly poignant rendition of 'You'll Never Walk Alone' in Milan, were moving in the extreme. However, in recognizing how so much grief was expressed by, for example, the symbolic tying together of football scarves, it also has to be said that this was a human tragedy which like Heysel (1985), Bradford (1985), Ibrox (1971) and Bolton (1946) transcended all the meaningless rivalries which give football its only meaning.

The ninety-six people who died were mainly, but far from exclusively, from the Greater Liverpool commuter area. Their link in life, as in death, was a passion for Liverpool Football Club, but they were all warm and complex individuals with many more things away from football which they didn't have in common and many differing reasons for living. For all of their love for Liverpool FC and for all of the thoughtless cliches even now still tossed out by dim-witted journalists and footballers, they surely would not have chosen to die for their club. The specific and communal loss across Merseyside should be seen in these human terms and not in football colours. Paying specific tribute to Evertonians is pointless as some Blues will have suffered more personally than many Reds, while some who were most grievously affected will have had no great love for the sport at all.

When the football restarted again in Liverpool, as it did fittingly with a 'derby' match at Goodison Park, it was in a spirit of intense goodwill and fraternity. Of course it was unlikely that that spirit could be maintained forever. Yet, at a time when it is routine in some circles to argue for the degeneration of the relationship between Reds and Blues on Merseyside it is warming to note that on derby day any commemoration of Hillsborough or associated cries for 'Justice' immediately, if briefly, restore the unity of 1989. Hopefully, without the recourse to quoting our beloved Bill Shankly, I hope that future generations of fans on Merseyside will know that, great game that it is, football in the end isn't really *that* important.

Index

Printed in the United Kingdom
by Lightning Source UK Ltd.
123678UK00001B/521/A